100 Wonderful Women

100 stories of women's service in the British Army since 1917

Compiled and edited by

Tanya-Jayne Park

First published in Great Britain by

The Women's Royal Army Corps Association, 2019

Copyright © WRAC Association

Edited & compiled by Tanya-Jayne Park

ISBN – 978-1-9162319-0-0

Cover design by Dave Brogden – www.deadbunneh.com

Publishing assistance by Tiger Ink Ltd – www.tigerink.co.uk

Printed in the UK

Foreword

It is such an honour to write the foreword to such a meaningful, thought provoking and excellent collection of 100 wonderful women's personal histories. Each and every account tells the story of profound dedication, self-sacrifice and service to the country. By bringing their personal stories together in the way captured here, brings to life the history of women that have served in the Army since 1917 – a history that I am personally very proud of.

As I reflect on the experiences of my sisters before me, I recognise just how fortunate I am. I serve now as the Army's Director of Personnel – the first female to serve as a member of the Army Board. Before promotion to major general I commanded at every level - including for the first time an operational brigade, held at readiness to provide command support to national and NATO corps level headquarters. I have served and led men and women over the last 27 years, in three operational theatres, at home and overseas, within the Field Army, at our strategic headquarters and the Ministry of Defence. I am very proud of my service, but I know I could not have achieved all I have, had it not been for the wonderful women reported here and those not - I have benefitted from following in their footsteps.

Whilst my experiences have been so very different, I smile at some of the similarities. I highlight two, but there are many. **Dame Helen Gwynne-Vaughan** battled to introduce appropriate Terms of Service for women in the Women's Army Auxiliary Corps in 1919. As the Army has recently opened combat roles to women I, as the Personnel Director, continue to lead on equality of opportunity and experience for our serving men and women. **Jane Knight** served as the first Signal Master in Italy in 1944, and became an honorary member of the Royal Signals Association. I commissioned into the Royal Corps of Signals, have commanded Royal Signals units, and hope that in the future I too will do my bit as a member of the Association.

Whilst I highlight two, I commend all the women's stories to you. They are inspiring and remarkable women, pioneering the way for servicewomen, for their contribution to the Army as a progressive and inclusive institution, and for their service to the country. I salute them all.

Major General Sharon Nesmith
See images in centre pages

The WRAC Association's Centenary

1919 - 2019

This book is published by the WRAC Association to mark its centenary year in 2019. When the First World War ended the women, who served in the WAAC & QMAAC, banded together and formed the 'Old Comrades Association' in 1919. This then became the ATS & Old Comrades Association during the Second World War and later became the WRAC Association in 1949.

Today the WRAC Association is a vibrant veteran's charity, providing support to all women who've served. We have over three thousand members, a network of over 50 branches around the UK and overseas. Our Benevolence Funds helps those women who need financial help, in 2018 awarding grants totalling over £200,000 to qualifying female veterans.

More information about the WRAC Association, how to join and the work it does can be found at www.wracassociation.org

Supporting women who served

A Brief History of Women in the British Army

Women have served alongside men in nursing roles since at least the Crimean War (1854-56) but it wasn't until 1917 that women served alongside men, in non-nursing roles, as part of the British Army.

WAAC & QMAAC

The Women's Army Auxiliary Corps (WAAC), known as Queen Mary's Army Auxiliary Corps (QMAAC) from 9 April 1918, the women's corps of the British Army was established in February 1917 and disbanded on 27 September 1921. More than 57,000 women served between January 1917 and November 1918.

ATS

The Auxiliary Territorial Service (ATS) was formed on 9th September 1938, more than 190,000 women served in the ATS before it became the Women's Royal Army Corps on the 1st February 1949. It was originally a volunteer force until December 1941 when Parliament passed the National Service Act, which called up unmarried women between 20 and 30 years old to join one of the auxiliary services.

WRAC

The Women's Royal Army Corps (WRAC) was the corps to which all women in the British Army belonged from 1949 to 1992. The corps was formed on 1st February 1949. For the first time women in the Army became subject to all sections of the Army Act. The Corps Charter stated that it was 'to provide replacements for officers and men in such employment as may be specified by the Army Council from time to time'. By 1992 women were serving in over 40 different trades in 20 different Arms and Corps.

Present Day

When the WRAC was disbanded in 1992 women were integrated into the rest of the Army, many of them becoming part of the Adjutant General's Corps (AGC). At this time women were still restricted to support positions, though over time the scope of the roles available grew to include non-combat frontline roles. In 2016 all roles including combat roles became open to female soldiers.

Contents

Editor's Note:

The stories which follow have come from various sources Including from first-hand accounts, some written especially for this book, whilst many have been taken from articles that have appeared in the WRAC Association Journal - Lioness.

The editor wishes to thank all of those whose stories have appeared in this book.

The following contributors also have books available which may be of interest to readers of this book.

Dr Samantha Philo-Gill - Her book "*The Women's Army Auxiliary Corps in France, 1917-1921: Women Urgently Wanted*" is available from booksellers.

Dr Barbara Walsh – Her upcoming book "*Irish Servicewomen in the Great War: From Western Front to Roaring Twenties*" is to be published by Pen and Sword in 2020. www.barbarawalsh.com

Charlotte Webb MBE – Her book *"Secret Postings: Bletchley Park to the Pentagon"* is available from booksellers.

Dame Helen Gwynne-Vaughan

Helen Gwynne-Vaughan (née Fraser) was born on 21 January 1879 in London. She graduated in 1904 from King's College London with a BSc in botany. In 1907 she was awarded a Doctor of Science degree. By 1909, she was the head of the Department of Botany at Birkbeck College, University of London. In 1911, she married David Gwynne-Vaughan but in 1915 she was widowed.

In February 1917, Mona Chalmers Watson was appointed as the Chief Controller of the soon to be inaugurated Women's Army Auxiliary Corps (WAAC). She did not want to serve in France due to family commitments and was granted permission to seek a Deputy to work overseas. Mona's cousin, Dr Louisa Garret Anderson, introduced her to Helen with whom she had established the University of London Suffrage Society before the war.

On 11 February 1917, Helen and Mona met for the first time. Helen was thrilled at the meeting and in her autobiography, Service with the Army, she wrote that the plans for the women's corps were 'like the realization of a dream'.

Helen was interviewed on 13 February 1917 by Sir Nevil Macready (Adjutant General at the War Office) for the post of Controller in France. She was well suited to the role as she was a woman of social standing, a professional working woman and had worked with young working-class women, as well as being the daughter of an army family. At the interview, Helen asked to be sent to France even if she was not appointed Mona's deputy and she believed that this was one of the reasons why she was subsequently appointed Chief Controller (Overseas) six days later. On 25 February 1917, Helen left for France on an initial visit to review accommodation options.

As the first Chief Controller of the WAAC overseas, not only did she design and implement the Corps in France but did this in the context of significant opposition from society and many in the Army. She had to negotiate and find solutions to the issues of socialising between the women and soldiers, pay, discipline and uniform. At all times she pushed for equality between the women and the soldiers, as well as suitable accommodation and medical care. This was new territory and her decisions had a significant impact.

She was a strong and respected leader who made herself available to women under her command at all grades. The WAAC in France was a success and enabled men to be freed up to serve at the frontline.

In January 1918, Helen was appointed Commander of the Most Excellent Order of the British Empire (CBE). She was listed in the Military Section and was therefore the first woman to wear the insignia of a Military Commander of the Order of the British Empire.

On 01 September 1918, Helen was ordered to return to the War Office. She was informed that she had been appointed Commandant of the Women's Royal Air Force (WRAF). She served in the WRAF until December 1919.

After the war, Helen returned to Birkbeck as the head of the Department of Botany. In 1919, she was appointed Dame Commander of the Order of the British Empire (DBE) and in 1921 was appointed Professor of Botany.

Between the wars she ensured that she remained in contact with the younger generation and worked with the Government to ensure that women could be quickly mobilised to assist in the Army in a future war or emergency. In 1936, Helen was one of the ex-service women on the committee of the Emergency Service, set up to train women as officers if the need for a women's unit in a national emergency were to arise. The Emergency Service was superseded by the formation of the Auxiliary Territorial Service (ATS) on 09 September 1938 but it was not officially closed down until March 1939. Helen, representing the Emergency Service, was a member of the Advisory Council that designed the ATS.

On 03 July 1939, Helen was appointed Director ATS. She was sixty years old. In the first year, she dealt with many of the same issues as she had with the WAAC: status; discipline; pay; rank badges; medical care; accommodation (including in France); and the mixing of men and women. It was not until April 1941 that the ATS was awarded full military status. As a result, pay was revised, women officers were commissioned and were permitted to wear officers' badges of crown and star.

Helen held a commission for only a month as she retired shortly after the announcement. She had worked tirelessly to establish a place for women in the Army, as well as significantly contributing to the safety and security of the nation.

She returned to her former role at Birkbeck until her retirement in 1944. She then concerned herself with the welfare of veterans. Until 1962, she worked full-time as honorary secretary of the London Branch of the Soldiers, Sailors and Air Force Association (SSAFA).

In March 1967, the WRAC Association held a reunion dinner to commemorate fifty years since the WAAC had embarked for France. Helen, aged eighty-eight, addressed the one hundred or so members in attendance. She passed away in her sleep five months later on 26 August 1967 at Sussexdown, an RAF Convalescent Home.

Written by Dr Samantha Philo-Gill
See images in centre pages

Mabel Dymond Peel

Mabel Dymond Peel was born in 1879 in Lancashire. She studied languages at the University of Manchester. In February 1914, she was appointed as assistant mistress at Bridlington High School for Girls.

In September 1917, the Intelligence Department of the War Office began the recruitment of women into the Intelligence Corps. They required fluent German speakers who could decode intercepted communications. The officer in charge knew Mabel and wrote to her asking her to join.

The women were recruited into the Women's Army Auxiliary Corps in order for them to be accommodated in France. Mabel enrolled at Devonshire House, London and on 24 September 1917 reported to WAAC HQ at the Connaught Club, London. On 28 September 1917, she and five other women left for St. Omer, France. She wrote 'We had a good send-off... as we had attained a certain amount of dignity and prestige from the fact that we were going out to do some mysterious work, the nature of which we knew no more than anyone else.'

The women worked in an office near the cathedral. Mabel explained how, on the first day, the women felt overwhelmed by their new role:

"I think none of us will ever forget that first morning at the office, when we sat there, with sheets of paper in front of us on which were arranged in the form of sentences, meaningless groups of letters... We were to try and solve them. Never having seen a code message in our lives before, you can imagine the despair that filled our hearts."

Within a month, the women settled into the work. They were nicknamed the 'Hush WAACs' and worked long hours, including on Sundays and had one half day off a week when they stopped work at 1600. After May 1918, they were permitted to have one day off a month. The women slept in a separate part of the camp and had their own staff.

Their camp was subjected to bombing raids. Mabel wrote of how raids would often catch them on their way to work:

"We used to take shelter anywhere, sometimes in indescribably dirty cellars... sometimes we took no notice of the raid, but kept on our way passing the townsfolk scurrying to shelter, who in their turn, were I think heartened by our seeming indifference."

In April 1918, with the advance of the Germans, the Hush WAACs were moved to Le Touquet where they lived in the Villa Joyeuse until the Armistice. Mabel asked to be discharged as soon as the war was over. She returned to England in December 1918, the last Hush WAAC to leave France.

In 1921, she published an account of her time in the WAAC, albeit sanitised, titled The Story of the Hush-Waacs. She wrote:

"It seems however a pity that some record should not be kept of the work and life of the first women ever admitted into the Intelligence Office at G.H.Q. in 1917, precincts sacred up till that time to the other sex."

In 1925, she went to live in Rouen and helped to establish a branch of the British Legion there. She latterly returned to England and worked as a language teacher.

She died on 25 January 1938 near Welwyn Garden City, Hertfordshire. Her death was announced on the front page of the Welwyn Times. The article referred to her then lesser known war time experiences and that tribute had been paid to her at a service at All Saints Church in Rouen by the Honorary President of the Rouen branch of the Legion.

Mabel's World War One medals and journal, as well as documents and photographs, are held at the Military Intelligence Museum in Bedfordshire.

Written by Dr Samantha Philo-Gill

Ethel Parker

There are 531 names etched onto Canterbury's memorial to those who died in the Great War. Despite the Buttermarket memorial being clearly dedicated to 'the men of Canterbury' who gave their lives, only 530 of those listed are men, Ethel Frances Mary Parker is the lone female somberly recorded there.

Born in Islington in 1898, the eldest of eight, she and her siblings moved to Bridge near Canterbury when their father took a job as a miner in the area.

After enlisting in the QMAAC Ethel was sent to Abbeville, France in April 2018, where according to her service records, she was serving as a waitress to the officers stationed there, taking the place of a man who could then be released to the frontline.

Only a few weeks after arriving in France, on the night of May 30th the trench in which Ethel and other QMAAC women were taking cover, took a direct hit from a bomb, which killed Ethel and 8 other women.

All were buried the next day in Abbeville Cemetery with full military honours. She was later posthumously awarded British & Victory Medals.

Besides Ethel the following QMAAC women were also killed that night Blaikley, Mary; Campbell, Beatrice; Caswell, Margaret; Connor, Catherine; Grant, Jeanie; Moores, Annie; Thomasson, Alice; and Watson, Jeanie.

Written by the editor for this book.

Margaret Annabella Campbell Gibson

Margaret Annabella Campbell Gibson was born on 12 July 1877 in Mauritius. Before the war, she worked as a warden in a hostel for working ladies. In July 1917, she was a forty year old widow when she joined the Women's Army Auxiliary Corps. She worked as a unit administrator in WAAC Camp 2 in Abbeville and was very popular with the women under her command.

In May 1918, leaflets were dropped by the Germans on Abbeville warning that the town was going to be bombed but the WAAC remained. On the night of 21 to 22 May 1918, Abbeville came under significant bombardment. WAAC Camp 2 had been hit by an aerial torpedo and four huts out of seventeen survived. The WAAC area controller visited the camp and issued clothing to members as uniforms and belongings had been blown across the camp, as well as trapped in the high branches of the trees.

No women were killed but several received minor injuries as a result of the partial collapse of a trench in which they were sheltering. Margaret received the Military Medal (MM) for her gallantry and devotion to duty during the raid. Her citation reads:

For conspicuous gallantry and devotion to duty during an enemy air-raid when in charge of a QMAAC camp which was completely demolished by enemy bombs, one of which fell within a few feet of the trench in which the women were sheltering. During the raid, Unit Administrator Gibson showed a splendid example. Her courage and energy sustained the women under the most trying circumstances and undoubtedly prevented serious loss of life.

She was the first member of the Corps to receive the MM. Women in the WAAC were not able to be awarded the Military Cross as they did not hold commissions.

Margaret did not survive the war. She died, aged 41, of dysentery on 17 September 1918 at No. 16 General Hospital, Le Tréport, France. She is buried in Mont Huon Cemetery in Le Tréport.

Written by Dr Samantha Philo-Gill

Dr Phoebe Chapple

Phoebe Chapple was born on 31 March 1879 in Adelaide, South Australia to English parents. In 1904, she graduated as a Doctor of Medicine from the University of Adelaide.

During World War One, Phoebe wanted to undertake war service but was frustrated by the fact that women doctors were not employed by the Australian Army. In February 1917, she travelled to England at her own expense and joined the Royal Army Medical Corps (RAMC) as a house surgeon at Cambridge Military Hospital in Aldershot.

Mona Chalmers Watson (Chief Controller) and Helen Gwynne-Vaughan (Chief Controller Overseas) of the Women's Army Auxiliary Corps wanted female doctors working with the RAMC to be formed into a section with responsibility for the WAAC. The War Office agreed to their proposals and the RAMC formed an Auxiliary Section which was responsible for the medical services of the WAAC under Army Council Instruction 1676 on 12 November 1917. The section was staffed by women and came under the control of the Director General, Army Medical Services. Similarly, to the WAAC, the female doctors had civilian status and therefore no formal rank. They wore a similar uniform to the WAACs, including WAAC rank (or grade) badges on their shoulder straps but wore RAMC collar and hat badges.

Phoebe was the second female doctor in the new section to travel to France. She arrived in November 1917.

On the night of 29 to 30 May 1918, three aerial torpedoes were dropped on WAAC Camp 1 in Abbeville. One of the torpedoes made a direct hit on a covered trench in which women were sheltering. Eight WAACs died at the scene and one was taken to No 2 Stationary Hospital but died of her injuries. They were the first women in the British military to die on active service. Six women were injured. Dr Phoebe Chapple was at Camp 1 at the time of the raid and was able to assist with treatment.

Phoebe was one of three WAACs to receive the Military Medal (MM) for their actions on 30 May 1918. The citation reads:

For gallantry and devotion to duty during an enemy air raid. While the raid was in progress Dr Chapple attended to the needs of the wounded regardless of her own safety.

She was the first female doctor and the first Australian woman to receive the MM.

In September 1919, Phoebe returned to Australia where she continued to work at the Adelaide Hospital. She specialised in obstetrics and gynaecology. She died on 24 March 1967 and was given a military funeral. She was unmarried, had no children and bequeathed a bursary in her name to the University of Adelaide.

Written by Dr Samantha Philo-Gill

Elizabeth Johnston

Elizabeth Johnston was born on 26 December 1890 and grew up in Anstruther, Scotland. She had a natural aptitude for art and writing but worked as a Post Office clerk and then as a telegraphist for the Western Union Cable Company in Glasgow. When the Women's Army Auxiliary Corps began recruiting, Elizabeth did not want to join as a telegraphist but rather a motor driver in France. She acquired the necessary qualifications, as well as learning French at evening class. But due to her parents' concern regarding the potential dangers inherent in such a job, she opted to be a telephonist instead.

Before she left for France, she wrote 'Of course, I have counted the cost, and if death should come to me out there, why then, THEN I SHALL KNOW THE GREAT SECRET.'

Elizabeth worked as a telephonist at an exchange in Rouen. The signallers, which included telephonists, wore a blue and white armband and were sometimes referred to as the blue and white angels. The men that they replaced carried out signalling work further up the line.

It was a pressurised environment in which accuracy was required and the highly skilled WAACs worked in shifts to operate the exchanges on a twenty-four-hour basis. The women were also required to deal with a significant amount of sensitive information and signed a statement that they would not divulge outside of the office any information relating to their work. Many of the telephonists were required to speak French, which Elizabeth did, so that they could communicate with the French telephone exchanges.

She enjoyed the camaraderie of the WAAC, writing: *"We are so happy in our hut. Everybody borrows and lends; we swop continually, the whole secret is "bonne camaraderie." Whoever is in first makes the beds for the others and fills the hot water bags, then gets into her own bed and sits up waiting for the late workers."*

While in France she wrote letters and diaries, as well as articles on the WAAC which were published in her local newspaper back home in Scotland. One of these articles was about the Armistice, in which she wrote: *"We decided to leave the town, and await the news on the hill-top; we knew what the signal was to be, and how the signing of the Armistice was to be proclaimed. When we reached the summit of the hill, we came on a party of German prisoners burying a dead comrade. How significant it seemed!"*

At the beginning of December 1918, Elizabeth fell ill with influenza. She wrote home from hospital but to save her parents from worry, did not reference any deaths from influenza until she had been discharged from No 8 Stationary Hospital and returned to Camp 4 at Quevilly.

On Christmas Day 1918, Elizabeth died aged 27, after falling from the tower of St Ouen Church, Rouen. She had come off of a night shift and rather than go to the Cathedral service, she evidently changed her plans and visited the church. The reason for her fall was never determined, but it was believed that she had a dizzy spell while sitting on a low balustrade encircling the gallery. Her unconscious body was found by an English soldier and two American soldiers on the roof of a chapel beneath the tower. Aid was administered at the scene but she passed away on arrival at No 8 Stationary Hospital where she had previously been admitted with influenza.

Elizabeth was buried at St Severs Cemetery in Rouen with military honours. She had once mentioned that she would like the St Andrew's flag laid on her coffin and this wish was fulfilled. A few months before her death, she had written home of her visit to the cemetery with a friend, telling them how it was maintained so beautifully by WAAC gardeners.

Elizabeth's letters and diaries were edited by her friend Agnes Anderson into a biography entitled *"Johnnie" of QMAAC*. Her name is recorded on Anstruther's war memorial and she is the only woman to be listed there.

Written by Dr Samantha Philo-Gill

Beatrice Ethel Lithiby

Beatrice Ethel Lithiby, known as Bel, was born on 04 December 1889 in Richmond, Surrey. She studied art at the Royal Academy Schools. During World War One she served for eighteen months as unit administrator in the Women's Army Auxiliary Corps.

In January 1919, Beatrice wrote to WAAC Controller-in-Chief Florence Leach that she was keen to perpetuate the memory of the Corps through a pictorial record. That same month, Florence Leach had received a letter from the Women's Work Sub-Committee (WWSC) at the Imperial War Museum (IWM) stating their intention to send out an official war artist to France.

In February 1919, the WWSC met with Beatrice Lithiby and wrote to Florence Leach that 'this would be an excellent way of procuring an artist who thoroughly understands the work of the QMAAC.' After reviewing a sample of Beatrice Lithiby's work, particularly a watercolour of WAACs working in a kitchen, they agreed that she should be employed to record the work of the WAAC in France. There was an initial disagreement between the War Office and IWM as to which should fund her time in France, but this was resolved by Florence Leach and aided by Beatrice Lithiby's agreement to be paid £120 a year by the War Office rather than £175. The IWM did provide funding for her materials.

In May 1919, Beatrice travelled to France and stayed for six months. While she was there, her father travelled back and forth to visit her. He took her finished paintings to Lady Priscilla

Norman, the Chair of the WWSC. He carried them with him, however, on his return visits to France because, by showing them to the officials at subsequent locations, she was able to generate greater interest in her work and secure better facilities. The sixteen watercolours finally obtained by the WWSC, included WAACs engaged in work, for example as telephonists and mechanics. There were also a number that showed the interior of the Nissen huts in which the women lived, as well as a Young Women's Christian Association (YWCA) hut. When in France, Beatrice was advised by the IWM that they would no longer be able to pay for her artwork and she agreed to donate them to the museum.

Beatrice was awarded the MBE for her service in the WAAC. After demobilisation, she continued to play an active role amongst ex-WAACs. In 1923, she was asked to produce a membership card on vellum to be presented to Queen Mary on the occasion of her joining the ex-Service Women's Club. She led sixty members of the QMAAC Old Comrades Association in the 1934 Armistice Parade in London.

Between the wars, she worked as a painter and designer, specialising in stained glass and church furnishings. She was elected as a member of the Royal Society of Artists.

Beatrice Lithiby served as a Senior Commander (temporary Chief Commander) in the Auxiliary Territorial Service (ATS) during the Second World War, for which she was awarded the OBE.

Beatrice never married. She was to be engaged to Frank Skinner who was a fellow student at the Royal Academy Schools. Frank died in July 1916 at the Somme, France. Beatrice was a committed Christian and was an Exterior Sister of the Community of St. Mary the Virgin. She died on 25 July 1966 in Wantage, Berkshire.

Written by Dr Samantha Philo-Gill

Two former WAAC Signallers

In her forthcoming book on the Irishwomen who served with colleagues from England, Scotland and Wales in the Great War, 1917-1919, entitled *Irish Servicewomen in the Great War : From Western Front to Roaring Twenties,* to be published by Pen and Sword in 2020, Barbara Walsh has described how the 1920s ushered in radical life changes for the many Irish-born former members of the WAAC. Their experiences often ran in parallel with their English army colleagues who made the same decision to seek new, and often challenging lifestyles at that time. For example, the outcome of a move to Australia for Martha Hanna, a young woman from a farming family in Poyntzpass, five miles north of Newry in Co. Armagh was to take a similar course to that of English-born Winifred Dennett, from the town of Sandown on the Isle of Wight, who had likewise moved 'down-under' when dispersed from the WAAC/ QMAAC.

Both girls had been former employees of the Post Office who had served as rank and file WAAC attached to the Royal engineers on the Western Front in the "L" Signal Units which controlled the army's security sensitive Lines of Communication. Working 24/7 rosters side by side with their male army colleagues, these six hundred or so members of the Corps - known informally as the 'Signallers'- were technically skilled and well experienced telegraphist and telephonists – all volunteers – who had been individually selected by the General Post Office to provide crucially needed telecommunication support in France. It had been demanding and often dangerous work.

When the call for help went out in 1917, both Martha and Winifred had brothers who saw action in the war and one can understand their keenness to offer any assistance they could to ensure a swift ending to the slaughter. When she enrolled, Martha Hanna's younger brother, Willie, had already been wounded by shrapnel at the battle of the Somme, 1916. Her Hampshire-born English colleague, GPO telephonist Winifred, had suffered the greater loss of one of her brothers, killed in the battle of Loos in 1915. Another of her brothers, a former professional photographer, was also in France working with a Field Ambulance as a non-combatant volunteer with the Royal

Army Medical Corps. He, too, was to lose his life barely a month before the end of the War.

At the time of their enrolment in the WAAC in the summer of 1917, these two girls were already long serving 'established' Post Office staff members. Martha had been taken on as a 'learner' in 1908 and, eighteen months later she had become a fully qualified GPO telegraphist with a permanent position within the organisation. Sent by her employers at the Post Office to Dublin she had remained working there, although keeping close links to her home in Ulster.

A girl from Armagh: Martha Hanna (1891-1969)

Martha Hanna arrived in France on 22 of July 1917 in a draft which included two other young Irishwomen in this batch, one from Limerick, the other from Cork. All of them subsequently served until September or October 1919.

For Martha, the transition back to life at home in Ireland following her dispersal from the Corps had been a difficult time. It had coincided with her being struck down by a bad attack of that era's virulent 'flu, and it would seem that, when fully recovered, she had no desire to return to her Post office work in the capital city, Dublin, but instead, decided to train as a nurse in London. On her return to Ireland a few years later she made the decision to stay on in Dublin as a maternity nurse working for a City Mission that cared for the poor.

Romance may have only seriously blossomed for her when a boy she had been at school with came back into her life in the mid-1920s with the suggestion that they might start a completely new life together in Australia. George Fisher, the son of a neighbouring farming family not far from Newry, was one of the thousands of Irishmen who had seen action with the British army in the war. By 1925 he was considering an on-going Australian government scheme for the settlement of ex-soldiers in Victoria and was making plans to accept the offer of a block of land on affordable terms. The scheme was accompanied by advances of money to allow the new owners make the necessary improvements to allow fruit farms to be planted on what was virtually virgin land. The areas chosen were usually in a very poor condition – but he had knowledge of farming and while he would have understood that virgin land in Australia might seem no match to the well-tended green fields of Ulster, he was ready to have a go. This was pioneering at its best.

With her newly acquired nursing expertise and wartime experiences Martha was ready to take on a new set of challenges. Decisions were made and George left for South East Australia ahead of his fiancée in 1926. Martha followed shortly afterwards, and the couple were married in Melbourne the following year.

Showing great determination, they eventually made good because George had knowledge of farming and he soon recognised the scale of the challenge that lay ahead. His assigned plot of land lay on the outskirts of Mildura in Victoria, 336 miles (542 km) north-west of Melbourne. It was an area that had gained a reputation as a major centre for the production of citrus fruits and grapes, but there had been problems with the supply of enough water, and farmers were placing enormous reliance on irrigation from the Murray River. The methods being used to do this were not altogether satisfactory because increasing water flows from the river basin left shallow salt deposits to the surface of the land and reduced the soil's fertility.

George was soon seriously reassessing the situation that faced him. The land was not promising. He had built a house for himself and Martha but had sensibly added a small general store that sold everything including groceries. Lack of water meant he could not farm in the way he was accustomed to and a wise decision was soon made to forgo the land. The shop was dismantled; they moved it and its contents into the nearby fast-expanding town, and he and Martha set up home in the upper story of the building. Plans were made to start a family, but it was not until September 1930 that their only child, Betty, was born.

Business did well. They worked hard and, nine years, later Martha and George could afford to take a trip home to Ireland with their nine-year-old daughter on a visit to meet her two grandmothers. Little did they suspect that an unforeseen set-back lay ahead. When the Second World War broke out in September of that year, they found themselves trapped in

Belfast with no hope of returning home to Mildura until the war was over. However, George and Martha once more displayed a streak of enterprise. He took a job as an inspector of weights and measures in the Belfast area. When German bombing of the city became too dangerous, Martha and Betty went to live with an elderly aunt in Co. Armagh, who needed some care and, in a year or two when Betty was old enough to start her secondary education, she was sent off to school in Dublin, where Martha still had old friends.

They remained back in Ireland until after the war had ended, and it was not until 1946 that they were finally able to return home to Australia. Within a few years of their return, George bought another store which was in Porepunka – a tobacco growing area about a hundred miles from Melbourne. Here, their daughter grew up and – following in the footsteps of her mother – went on to train as a nurse and midwife before she married. Not long after that, Martha and George retired to Melbourne.

In 1969, the couple made another visit home to Ireland and while they were here, Martha – who was 78 by then – suffered a fatal stroke and was laid to rest beside her parents, near where she was born in Poyntzpass, Co. Armagh.

A girl from Hampshire: Winifred Dennett (1890 - 1987)

Unlike Martha, the anticipation of a life ahead on the other side of the world for English girl, Winifred Dennett, had looked to be a far more certain prospect in 1919. Attached to the 3rd Echelon of the army's HQ in Rouen for over two years in one of the telecommunication system's supervisory positions (which bore the rank of a WAAC 'Forewoman'/aka NCO), she was already engaged to be married to an Australian ex-serviceman she had met in 1915. As soon as the Armistice was announced, Winifred had sought demobilisation just as soon as possible.

Her fiancé, Hedley William (Bill) Moore, of Eaglehawk, Victoria, had seen action in the Gallipoli Campaign (1915-1916) and, although not directly wounded, his health had suffered badly. By September 1916 he had been sent home from Europe and de-listed from any further service. The couple were not to meet again for almost another three years.

Before he left Europe, Bill Moore and Winifred made careful plans for their future. As an ex-serviceman he had applied to become a registered fruit grower under a similar Australian government settlement scheme that Martha Hanna's husband, George, was to later take up. Prior to the war, Bill had worked as a baker and pastry cook. Winifred's only employment experience was as a Post Office telephonist in a well populated urban area. It was going to be a challenge – but having made the choice she was determined to join him out there just as soon as the war was over.

It was not easy for WAAC Signallers to swiftly extract themselves from their overseas service when the military conflict had ended. Their contribution to the smooth running of army communication systems had been essential but the pressure continued. Millions of men and mountains of military hardware and mountains administrative work had to be efficiently returned to the UK in a controlled manner. Because of her imminent marriage and confirmed travel plans, Winifred's request for early demobilisation was extremely fast compared to the delays suffered by others who were anxious to get away. She was sent back to London on 30 April 1919 and her formal letter of discharge was received on the third week of May. By 6 July she was able to set sail for Victoria.

When her boat docked at the port of Melbourne, she was met on the quayside by her fiancé with a horse and buggy and they set off on a slow 230 mile long journey to where he was living in the district of Piangil, in the State of Victoria. The closest town, Nyah, lay 8 miles away. Within a few months' time – by then 1920 – the pioneering pair were married at the Anglican Cathedral in Bendigo, the nearest large city. Life was going to be very different, often fraught with difficulties, but subsequently successful.

For the greater part of the past three years Winifred had coped with the challenge of working long hours in France, the inherent danger of enemy bombing attacks and the rigidity of military rule which brought little or no privacy. It was a life tightly filled by constant movement, noise and stressed-out people.

One of the first things she would have had to come to terms with was the empty vastness and silence of this new land, which, despite the upheaval of her most recent wartime experiences, was to present a huge contrast to her earlier upbringing as a daughter of a self-employed carpenter in Sandown and one of five siblings, two girls and three boys. The streets of her home in the Isle of Wight had been always filled with the throngs of fashionable visitors, bustling shops and ferry boats coming and going. Life on the far side of the world within the isolation of a tiny but vibrant pioneering community would require a significant adjustment.

For Bill, too, the Australian Government's Returned Soldiers Settlement Scheme had brought enormous challenges for someone unused to a farming life. While waiting for Winifred to join him, his first task had been to clear his allocated block of virgin land to make it ready for the planting of fruit trees. The work to prepare the ground for cultivation required cutting or ripping out bushes and shrub-land growth, usually by horses or oxen working in pairs, dragging a heavy chain between and behind them. The rough bush and tree growth then had to be burned prior to making the soil ready for the planting. There was also basic housing accommodation to be built.

As the weeks and months passed by, it was becoming disappointingly clear that all their work – and that of others in this area – was not going to yield a viable enterprise. All the planning and physical hard work that had followed was not going to be enough. Within a year or two it became obvious that many of the 'blocks' in the pre- selected locations were turning out to be unsuitable for commercial fruit-growing. Some were turning out to be too small, as was the case with the first settlers who planned to develop Nyah. Elsewhere, as outlined in Martha and George's experiences, there were problems with water supplies. For many of those ex-servicemen who went out with high hopes, there were often similar truly heart-breaking setbacks. Hard lessons had been learned.

Nonetheless, Bill and Winifred were determined not to be beaten. Winifred' soon encouraged Bill to turn to his pre-war trade. They moved to a small nearby settlement, Nyah West, opened a bakery and began to supply and deliver bread locally. Business thrived. It had been a wise move. Before long, Bill had a fully operational bakery up and running and, by the early 1930s, by then with a family of four children, the couple had rented out the bakery business and moved to the town of Eaglehawk, about a hundred and thirty miles away, where they were able to extend their activities which included setting up a poultry farm to supply eggs and chickens. Life was good.

Shortly after the onset of the Second World War they moved again – this time to the prosperous town of Hamilton, where Bill opened another Bakery and supplied the army with fresh bread for the duration. When the war was over, they returned once more to Eaglehawk, where they made further wise investments in property.

Blessed with children and grandchildren, their lives centred around hard work and family life, but it was not without enjoyable community activities such as the local Bowling Club. In due course, in much the same way that Martha's daughter may have inherited something of her mother's instinctively caring nature in her choice of career, Winifred's daughter Peg may have also been influenced by the contribution made by both of her parents during the First War. When the Second World War broke out in 1939, she enlisted in the Australian Women's Army Service and served in Hamilton, Queensland.

Unlike Martha, however, Winifred's close family ties to her home on the Isle of Wight had been broken by that time. Winifred's husband, Bill passed away in 1973 but Winifred was to live on for many more years. When she died in 1987, she had reached 97 years of age.

By Barbara Walsh, PhD.

Mary Jamieson

Mary Jamieson left her Scottish village home as a young woman, sometime after 1911, and travelled to London where she became involved in the Women's Suffrage Movement, regularly addressing the crowds at Speakers' Corner in Hyde Park.

My mother always said that she was among the first 100 women, in the early part of 1917, to join the newly-formed

Women's Army Auxiliary Corps and was stationed as a forewoman, with the 2nd Artists Rifles, at Romford OTC, Hare Hall in Essex (shown in the photo), where both Wilfred Owen and Edward Thomas had undergone their training.

She also spent some time in France, near Lille, but we don't know if this was before or during her WAAC service. From her humble village background, she seems to have moved into quite elevated and intellectual London circles, probably through her work in the Women's Suffrage Movement, but in January 1916 she gave birth to a son John, the address on the birth certificate is given as Marylebone Workhouse. The father's name isn't given.

In June 1918, she gave birth to a daughter, Mary Joan, the address on the birth certificate identified as that of the St Pancras Workhouse, she was given the middle name Joan after her godmother, a 'Lady Joan', but no surname has survived. It was quite a moving experience to see our grandmother's name, and that of our uncle and aunt, in the workhouse registers, but I like to think she had simply taken a practical approach to her situation as a single mother and booked herself in for the birth, leaving again some weeks afterwards when she was ready to go back to work.

It was necessary in those days to pay for hospital care, so workhouse hospitals were often the last resort for those who couldn't afford to pay. I have a photo of the children's father in Army uniform and must assume he was away fighting when their births were registered, unable to give consent for his name to be put on the birth register. Or maybe there were other reasons why he was unable to be identified. Sadly, he died of his wounds in 1918. Mary Joan stayed with our grandmother, but she had to give John up to friends to care for, having no family nearby and very little financial support either.

Only a year or so later, she met and married a fellow Scot, almost 20 years her senior, and went on to have a further six children, including my mother, of whom five survived. Curiously the birth certificate of the first of these children shows her name as nee Jamieson formerly Cameron but we have found no marriages to explain this.

She died aged 58, having suffered years of debilitating illness, four years before I was born. I have always regretted the fact that I never had the chance to know her.

As told by Alison Botterill

Joan Sanders

Joan was the oldest and longest serving member of the ATS. She joined the ATS at Lowestoft on the first day of its formation, on 18 October 1938, and was allocated service number W4. Another Lowestoft resident, Constance Sylvia Carlyon, had been allocated service number W3 but was released from service in 1942.

Joan Sanders was called to colours on 01 September 1939, promoted to Corporal in March 1940 at Ack Ack HQ and shortly afterwards to Sergeant. Joan was a founding member of 10th Suffolk Company ATS and began her wartime service at Landguard Point, Felixstowe working with 409 Ack Ack Battery. She had trained at Canterbury and then served in Marham, Hoo, Hadleigh, Lawford, Harlow and Wakefield.

In 1938 Joan was one of only 25 women in the Company, by 1942 some 250 women had enlisted. 1942 saw a rapid expansion of the ATS as many thousands of women joined the ranks. Joan played an important role in this expansion, participating in ATS recruiting broadcasts on the BBC.

At the end of hostilities Joan resumed her job as Office manager of W E Wiggs Agricultural Engineers of Barnaby, where her father Horace Sanders was a Partner.

Joan passed away aged 98 in January 2015.

From Lioness No.1 2015

Olive Parker

My aunt Sergeant Olive Parker ATS - with whom my mother and I lived in Exeter from June 1942 (one month after the massive air raid on the city) to September 1944 when my father was away serving in the Royal Air Force.

Aunt Olive was wounded in a later (c1943) 'hit-and-run' air attack when a bomb exploded near to the office in which she worked. I think it was a Regimental Pay Office as she was attached to the Royal Army Pay Corps in which I later served (1952-1954) in National Service.

I think the insignia might indicate Southern Command. Her sister - my Aunt Cissie - was also in the same office as a Corporal where Olive was her superior! They were of a family of eight all save one - my aunt Marie whose husband was in the Royal Tank Corps - served in the Armed Forces in either or both of the two World Wars.

Aunt Olive was based in her home city of Exeter because she had to look after her aged mother and her daughter then just finishing school. One small tale shows how kind she was. The city was full of Americans and Royal Marines so Olive with my mother decided on Christmas Day 1943 to walk into the town centre - some distance away - and invite some servicemen to have lunch with us. Food of course, was in very short supply being heavily rationed.

To my delight and amusement, they came back with four! Two Royal Marine Commandos - Arthur and Dennis - and two American sailors - Cleve from the backwoods of Virginia and Ted from the city of Chicago. The sailors were in the CB's 'Seabees' meaning they were in a Construction Battalion. This was the time a few months before the invasion in June '44. Olive heard from the Americans after the war. We think the Commandos went on to assault Northern France and they may well have been among the first ashore on D Day.

Olive made sure I knew what was going on in the war. When the siren went as it often did for German aircraft flying over at night, we left our beds and she took me out - both wearing tin helmets - to see them passing over illuminated by searchlights with the AA blasting away to no ill effect on the raiders. In the morning, the road was littered with shrapnel from the shells (hence the tin helmets) and silver paper ('window')

As told by Tony Dowland

Lucy Bowyer - Wartime memories of the ATS

It was 1941 and I lived in the small village of Wheelock Heath situated between Crewe and Sandbach in the County of Cheshire approximately 170 miles North of London. I was almost 20 years old at the time and in a reserved occupation working at a dairy product factory but decided I wanted a change and would volunteer to serve in the armed forces, a fact I kept hidden from my parents at the time. I applied to join the women's army known then as the Auxiliary Territorial Service or A.T.S. for short. It was only when I received the notification to attend for a medical examination that my parents were made aware of what I had done, and they were not too pleased. It turned out that I was the only girl from the village to join the army, one other girl joined the Women's Auxiliary Air Force, (W.A.A.F.) in the Royal Air Force. Eventually my two brothers volunteered to join the army and served in North Africa and what was then Palestine, now Israel. The strange thing about all this was that I was terrified when the sirens sounded for an air raid alert but not so when later I was actually involved in helping the anti-aircraft gunners in shooting enemy aircraft down. Perhaps we were all too busy to worry.

Having successfully passed my medical, June 1941 saw me on my way to report to a commandeered hotel in Portland Street, Manchester, there to join other girl recruits and be sent by train to Lancaster. The venue was Bowerham Barracks home at the time of the Kings Own Regiment, a formidable place steeped in Army tradition. There we were to endure ability tests to ascertain what type of work we were best suited to and of course learn the discipline and marching skills of the British Army from male instructors. Our full kit was issued here and I became W/59097 Private Lucy Evans after which we were given vaccinations and the usual injections associated with the forces which left most of us ill and wondering whether we had done the right thing in joining up in the first place.

We were up early in the morning when 'reveille' sounded and seemed to do everything to numbers having very little time to ourselves and collapsing in bed at night tired out. This went on for a month and the pay was 11 shillings per week (equivalent to 55p. today) which did not buy much. I allowed half of this as an allowance to my mother, so she had 5 shillings and sixpence (22.5p.).

Our initial training over, together with other girls we were despatched to Oswestry where there were four training regiments of the Royal Artillery (Anti-Aircraft) called Park Hall Camp. My destination was 7th Heavy Trng. Regt. and there to train on anti-aircraft instruments. Some became spotters, on the lookout for enemy aircraft, height and range finder instrument operators (this was my job) and predictor operators the instrument which decided when and where the guns should be fired. The actual firing of the guns was done by the men.

It was while I was at the camp that I met my future husband, after only having been in the ATS for one month. We met at Whittington Castle, Gobowen and proceeded to the Old Boot Inn nearby for a drink to celebrate.

Fully trained we were formed as 443 Battery/132 (Mixed) Heavy Anti-Aircraft Regt. Royal Artillery and sent to firing camp at Ty Croes on the Isle of Anglesey, North Wales, for practice purposes consisting of firing at a sleeve towed by an aircraft out at sea. What a chance for the ladies to train their sights on the men (pilots) in the firing line, so reversing the roles. Now fully operational we were sent to Paisley in Scotland in defence of the River Clyde and the shipping there. Meanwhile I was still corresponding with my future husband back at Oswestry in a different Regt. We did not see much of each other but at Christmas 1941 we decided to get engaged with the wedding planned for March 1942. Getting wedding clothes was so difficult because clothes were rationed, and coupons were required for which service people did not qualify. However, one of my comrades lent me her wedding dress and I managed to buy a head-dress which I kept in a trunk in the cold tin-roofed Nissan hut which was both our communal living and sleeping quarters.

This was a cold February 1942 and to keep clothes aired we put a hot water bottle in the trunk. Disaster nearly struck as I forgot about my waxed head-dress and some of the beads were melted with the heat, but I am pleased to say it was still wearable.

I was promoted to Lance Corporal and was married on 14th March 1942 to become W/59097 L/Cpl. Lucy Bowyer. Back then to Scotland where at times it was so cold on duty, we had to keep a hot water bottle under our battle dress blouses when about the camp, not army issue I may add! Eventually I had a posting to join 487 Battery/137 (Mixed) H.A.A. Regt R.A.at Ellesmere Port guarding a large oil refinery as my mother was not very well at the time and I was nearer home. We were not allowed out of the camp on leave until on arriving at the guard room we correctly identified the plane of the day. This was an enemy aircraft silhouette, changed every day and having individual identification marks. An incorrect answer meant you were not allowed out.

From there the Regt. was moved to London to defend against air raids and flying bombs and our battery was stationed at Whetstone in North London. Our nickname for the flying bombs was "doodle bugs" and we knew that when the motor cut out they would dive to earth and explode but we did have a success rate against them. One night our battery fired over 300 rounds, success unknown. It was a sight to be seen when the air raid alarm sounded on camp during the night and the girls had to jump out of bed pull on boots and greatcoats over army issue pyjamas, struggle to get tin helmets over hair curlers and dash to our posts to take up duty stumbling over objects on the way under the strict blackout conditions which prevailed.

I think we were there for about two years but as we were not allowed to keep a diary for security purposes, I am not sure. By this time, I was a Sgt. and my husband had been sent overseas to North Africa early in 1943. One of the benefits of being a Sgt. was being able to make ourselves a cup of tea on stand-down before returning to bed a privilege denied to other ranks. Reveille was still at the same time the next day regardless of the time being on duty on a standby. Part of our Regt. was stationed in Hyde Park near to the Houses of Parliament and Sir Winston Churchill's daughter, Mary, was an officer in that Battery. She, it was, who demobbed me when I finally left the service.

Soon we were on the move again and it was rumoured that we were going overseas as we were sent to the East coast. Only a few days there and then came another move in December 1944 to private houses which had been commandeered as billets in Weybridge. These proved to be better than the Nissan huts we had been used to and it was therefore a luxury for me and a fellow Cpl. to be able to have a hot bath at the home of Leslie Chateris, the author of "The Saint" books, in his absence, of course. However, when we came to let the water out afterwards it would not budge as the drainpipes were frozen and we left without having the courage to tell the resident housekeeper of the problem. It was very cold in the houses and we had to sieve the coal dust left in the coalhouses in order to try and light a fire.

January 1945 was just as cold but in the middle of the month we were transported to Tilbury Docks in London to board the S.S. Longford en route for Ostend, Belgium. For so many of us it was our first time abroad and experience of sailing on the sea. The journey seemed to take hours as we had to avoid minefields and we were in very confined quarters on this merchant ship. All of us were sick and so it was with much relief when we arrived at the port of Ostend as the clock was striking 13.00hrs.

There was heavy snow on the ground as we formed up and were marched to our temporary quarters in two local hotels, for two nights. I shall always remember the local children snowballing us as we marched. We then joined the convoy of lorries which were to take us to our gun site. Because of the icy conditions, one of our trucks skidded off the road and into the ditch and I was detailed to stay behind with the injured girls while the rest of the convoy carried on without us. We were eventually taken to a military hospital in Brussels where one girl was detained for further treatment. The rest of us joined a lorry to make our way to our gun site but the male driver took a wrong route and we found ourselves heading for the front line and as it was dark now and we could see the flashes from the guns firing ahead, we turned back again and the army lorry got stuck in a snowbound lane. So, our driver left us to seek help and eventually we were taken to the house of a Belgian family to be made very welcome.

There were about five of us I think and none of us could speak the language but understood when we were offered a hot drink which was really needed. We felt it was something very precious for this kind family to offer us a drink after the hardships in rationing they had undergone but I must admit my first taste of black coffee tasted like nectar. Help for us eventually arrived and we were taken to a very strange building for the night, I think it was some sort of a castle. Again, this is where a diary would have been useful in recalling things and events.

The following morning saw us on our travels again, this time to our gun site at Neerijse situated between Leuven and Brussels as our guns were being used in the defence of the Port of Antwerp then, against the bombing raids and doodlebugs.

Our new living quarters were again Nissan huts and our only source of heat was from a paraffin stove on which we also had to heat the water for our ablutions. There were four of us in our hut, all Sgts. and each day we put our ration of water in our wash bowl which was a petrol can which had been cut in half for the purpose. When our turn to wash came around, we first washed our hands and faces, other parts too and finally the remaining water was not wasted as it was used for our smalls. From this you will gather that water was a very precious commodity and strictly rationed. If we managed to get enough to put in a water bottle, those lucky enough to have one for extra overnight warmth, then this was used for the morning ablutions. Our main laundry we took to the local villagers who washed it in the village square using stones to pound out the dirt and grime. As money was of little value in these sparse times we would pay with soap and cigarettes and also barter for fresh eggs with chocolate or anything else we had from a food parcel we may have had from home.

Food parcels themselves were scarce due to rationing at home. The army arranged that at least once per week baths were made available this was in a very cold hut the water being heated outside on a field boiler and the makeshift baths only being allowed to be filled to the height of 5 inches per person. Towards the end of the queue the hut was warmer than the water!

We had to improvise sweeping brushes for the huts out of twigs we gathered from the trees bound together and then of course there were the latrine buckets to be emptied as and when necessary. This meant a detail squad being instructed to carry them to a massive pit, dug previously for the purpose then covered with sand and suitably marked "foul ground". We were allowed leave in Brussels occasionally and then we could have a proper bath in the servant quarters of the Palace there, a real luxury.

I also recall the time I acted as escort, as a senior C.O., to a party of our girls invited to an American base nearby for a dance. I don't remember much of the dance part, but I do remember the nightmare ride we endured to and from there in the Yankee 3 tonner truck.

The war finished and we joined in the celebrations in Brussels before being sent into Antwerp as a unit taking in the equipment being brought back from the front line for local storage. I remember one day being instructed to find one of the male Sgts. of our Battery and to tell him there was to be a pay parade. I found him with a party of German soldiers who were digging up the bodies of dead servicemen who had been buried in shallow graves in order that they could be properly identified and then reinterred in a military cemetery nearby. If I remember rightly, they were mainly Canadian airmen.

After a short while in Antwerp we were then flown to Germany in a Dakota aircraft and landed at Luneburg Heath and were the first ATS there.

We went again by road convoy to an airfield 26 miles S.W. of Hamburg where we were again involved in the checking in of front-line equipment as before. As we travelled along, here and there we were spat upon by the Germans. Hamburg became a place for leave but it was a terrible sight, almost utter devastation from the Allied bombing combined with the awful smell of the dead still in the ruins. We were able to eat at the places set aside for service personal but outside we would find children begging for scraps of any sort of food. The German civilians also had to scrounge and beg for food, German men even resorting to picking up cigarette ends thrown away.by troops to make a smoke for themselves. Outside the Y.M.C.A. we saw the locals picking in the dustbins for any leftover food thrown away, a very heartrending sight even for a defeated nation.

Looking back over my 4 ½ years in the army I recall the hard times and hardships and also the good times and the laughter we all enjoyed in adversity as a Regimental body of people from all walks of life. The discipline we encountered when we first joined and the strict obedience to orders at all times but what I think mainly stands out in my memory is the spirit of comradeship we all enjoyed which has endured oven to the present day when we have ox-service get-togethers. Thank goodness there was always somebody with a sense of humour to help cheer everyone up when the going was tough.

So, it was at the end of 1945 I left the service to start and set up a home ready for the return of my husband from Italy. We had not seen each other for 3 years when he came back on leave in April 1946 to return abroad before finally being demobbed in July of that year, after 7 years' service.

We set up home and both worked to bring up our three children during the lean years after the war when even then rationing was in force. It was not until about 1978 that I learned that there was a WRAC (ATS) Association for ex-service Army women so I was happy to join the Wolverhampton Branch and join up with old comrades again.

Moving to Wellington, Telford, my present home, I transferred to the Shropshire Branch in 1980. I took over as Treasurer in 1987 on the death of one of our members and also a little later became standard bearer, when the branch was able to raise sufficient money to purchase one. It was dedicated at Donnington Garrison Church in November 1988 and paraded for the first time on Armistice Sunday there. I learned of the planned 45th. Anniversary celebrations by the Burgomaster and citizens of Antwerp in September 1989 through our Association magazine The Lioness and I was lucky enough with five others who had served there during the war, to be sent an invitation.

What a fantastic event it was with all the veterans from the British, Canadian, American and many other nations taking part. The city did us proud and non-more so than the Burgomaster, Bob Cools. We were welcomed dined and feted by a grateful city and there were few dry eyes at the various venues at which we were thanked for what we did to help them during the war. I was the only woman Corps standard bearer on the parade, and I carried our county W.R.A.C. (A.T.S) standard, in a place of honour at the front for the march past. I had a remarkable experience as we formed up prior to moving off to meet a Belgian lady standard bearer carrying a Belgian Resistance standard by the name of Maria, now Mrs. Berge-De-Bakker but we were unable to say much to each other then as the parade was moving off.

Later however we met up again when we sat down for a meal in the Town Hall and she gave me a bracelet with the words that it was not gold, but it was a small token of her thanks. It was so touching as we learned from her how she had suffered under the Germans in the war. She was left for dead during a bombing attack at a crossroads and even taken to the local mortuary until somebody noticed she was breathing and transferred to hospital to be treated. She joined the Resistance when she heard English voices from the house next door and threatened the occupants that if she was not allowed to join them she would tell on them to the authorities as the voices were British airmen being assisted to escape.

She was a very brave lady and listening to her story our hearts went out to the Belgian people for all the suffering they underwent and here were they thanking us. There were a lot of hankies out, nose blowing as she talked, mine amongst them. I was again invited back to Antwerp in 1989 for the 50th. celebrations to again be given as before with all the other ex-service people there the welcome that only Antwerp can give. I met Maria again and she gave me a lovely plaque of the Liberation for my wall at home, one I shall always treasure. We write to each other on a regular basis and I deem it an honour to have made the acquaintance of such a remarkable lady and somebody so very special to me.

In my capacity as standard bearer I have been all over the country and have been guard of honour to the Queen Mother at Guildford Cathedral and lucky enough to have had a few words with her at the time.

I also had the honour to carry the WRAC standard, prior to the break-up of the Corps, at the November 1992 Royal British Legion Festival of Remembrance at the Albert Hall. I marched across the arena on my own so at least I was in step. The event broadcast by the B.B.C. T.V. was seen worldwide and a pen friend from Detroit U.S.A. saw me for the first time after we had corresponded since the war years, through the relayed broadcast on Canadian T.V.

Also, through the WRAC Association I have met and spoken to the Queen and have met the Duchess of Kent and the Duchess of Gloucester. Another meeting I had was with Group Captain Leonard Cheshire at Shrewsbury K.S.L.I. Barracks at a fundraising event and was chided by him when I told him I was in Heavy Anti-Aircraft during the war, for shooting at him and his fellow airmen on their return to home base. Tongue in cheek I did point out that they did not always give the correct identity signal of the day. He struck me as being a very distinguished gentleman.

So far, I have, paraded the standard on 87 occasions wearing my three medals, including the France/Germany Star with pride and am hoping to make it 100 - not bad for a nearly 75-year-old!

Written by Lucy Bowyer before she passed away in November 2018

Martha Tasker Watson

Martha's early childhood was spent in Kilmany Fife where she went to school both there and Rathillet. She remembers walking to school and sometimes with her pals taking the sugar beets from the fields to eat on their way. She finished her schooling and left school to become a Nanny, also working in the local Post Office at Kilmany.

Although she contracted rheumatic fever as a child and spent many periods in convalescence she decided to join up when World War II broke out. Martha joined the ATS in 1942 and although initially disappointed that she would not see service out of Scotland, she managed to swap places with a colleague who wanted to stay in Scotland thus ensuring she saw more of the world.

After initial training at Inverness, then Oswestry, Anglesey (Wales) and Wolverhampton, in 1943 she was selected as a Predictor Operator serving with 559 (Ack Ack Battery HMS Ganges at Shotley near Harwich and Ipswich which was part of the defence of London until the end of the war.

Her role saw her stationed in the gun emplacement alongside the 3.7" Howitzers, predicting the height and range of incoming enemy aircraft as they bombed London and the surrounding area. In later years she would tell me that she would still get the "collywobbles" if on a clear moonlight night looking out the back door she would say it was a "bombers moon" and expect to hear the sound of aircraft overhead and see searchlights illuminating the sky.

Although her service to the country left her with a permanent hearing problem, which was a continual source of frustration to her for the rest of her life, this was compensated for by the stories she used to tell of the exploits that the "gunners" got up to during the war. Both the sinking of HMS Hood and D-Day were memories of particular moments of sadness due to the loss of so many but there was the fun times too when she and her service pals had to shake all the caterpillars out of the vegetables in advance of a visit of the Princess Royal (Mary) to the base. She had an abiding loathing of caterpillars from that day on!

After the war she returned to Fife and resumed her career as a Nanny often working with the same families with her sister Mary. It was during these times that she met the man she eventually married - Tom Watson. Tom was one of six of a family who lived at Manorlees outside Kirkcaldy. Tom had served with 250 Squadron (Desert Air Force) as a MT Driver/Mechanic in the Western Desert in WW2 from Palestine, North Africa, Malta, Sicily and Italy. They married in Cupar in 1950.

Martha returned to the guns in 2010 after seeing a local TV presenter making a mess of firing the One o'clock gun in Edinburgh. After firing off a letter basically stating "in our day we did it like this" she received a command "from one Gunner to another" from a Lieutenant Colonel inviting her over to show them how it should be done.

Written by Martha's son Robert T Watson.

Dorothy May Hedges

In the summer of 1938, Dorothy learned that women were to be recruited into a new Territorial Service. Having long been interested in her brother's involvement with the TA, and always believing in 'going to the top', she wrote to the War Office.

In due course she was informed that a Company was planned for Tamworth - to be known as the 41st Staffs ATS Company. A day or so later she received a letter from Miss Wint who had been appointed Company Commander and a meeting was arranged. The upshot was that Dorothy was appointed Senior Leader (CSM) and recruiting began in earnest. Parades were held weekly in the Drill Hall and the Drill Sergeant of the 6th Bn North Staffords instructed the girls how to march etc.

In late August, the 41st Staffs were mobilised and reported to the Drill Hall twice a day until, on 30 August, orders were received to report immediately to Whittington Barracks where preparations had been made for the reception of Reservists recalled to the Colours.

Dorothy immediately set out to learn all she could about Army procedure from the ORQMS. In 1941, shortly after her marriage, she was sent on the first course for potential WOIs at Brockenhurst - and came top of the Course! She was immediately posted to No 17 ATS Training Centre in Lancaster with the appointment of Regimental Sergeant Major - the very first in the ATS.

No 4 ATS TC merged with No 17 to become No 4/17 ATS TC and Dorothy remained there until 1943 when she was posted to Y Signals ATS working with WOYG at Beaumanor Park where she remained until the end of the War.

Dorothy always laughed when she recalled an incident at Whittington Barracks in 1940. The North Staffords had a hockey match against an RAF team but on the day found they were three men short due to postings. Dorothy immediately volunteered herself and two of her sergeants. The Team Captain reluctantly agreed. The

RAF team could not believe their eyes and started the game showing great gallantry to the ladies. They quickly realised their mistake - the ladies were playing to win!

Back in civilian life, sport continued to play a major part in her life and she taught games and PE and umpired hockey for many years. Whilst also teaching shorthand at Tamworth College, a student, who was the daughter of an Army sergeant, said her father had told her that, 'A spot of good old-fashioned Army Drill would do the girls a lot of good'. Therefore, she asked if Mrs Hedges would please teach them how to march? So, she did - to the astonishment (and amusement) of the College Principal. The girls themselves loved it!

Extracted from her obituary which appeared in Lioness No.1 2010

Olive, The Lady Strathspey

On 6th August 2015 Olive, The Lady Strathspey (as she became upon marriage), celebrated her 105th birthday - it was a beautiful, hot summer day at the home where Olive resided in West Wittering, where she was surrounded by her many friends and family.

In 2004 Olive was interviewed by The Imperial War Museum, for the archives, and the following is an extract from that interview (which is available from their sound library):

Olive Amy Grant was born in Blowfield, Norfork to an accountant father (who served in the Engineers in France between 1914 and 1920) and a stay-at-home homemaker mother (who was a very good amateur singer). She was the middle child of three, the other two being brothers.

On leaving school she went to the local art school, since she was very talented, but had to give up after a term as her father was ill and she needed to "earn a living" – so she went to teacher-training college in London, and then taught in Northampton.

Being a teacher made it an easy decision for her to join the ATS, as she wanted to escape teaching and was, with her friends, determined to fight Hitler. She wanted to fly, but there were too many applications and they did not take any women. The ambulance-drivers HQ were in Bedford, and she had no way of getting there, so she joined the Territorial Army in Northampton. She describes the extraordinary feeling of all the women joining together to march through the local town. She did her training at Broughton – and remembered having a cairn terrier.

In July 1939 they went on camp, and this was the first time they interacted with men – who treated them kindly, and as children.

When she first enrolled it was apparent that she had no special skills, so became an Orderly (rather than a cook or clerk) – ie a dogsbody for the camp. She looked after her friend, who was Commander, as Batman – and was told to always bring two cups, so she too could enjoy a good cup of tea. The camp was very tough, with tin plates and mugs, peculiar tea and straw mattress'.

Eventually she was called up as Bombardier Storekeeper at Larkhill School of Artillery, in the Quartermaster Stores, issuing theodolites etc to the soldiers. Although still a Corporal really, in the artillery her rank was called Bombardier.

She thought she would be there forever but got tired and applied for Commission Officer Training in September 1939. However, this was delayed by an accident in which she broke her nose and both kneecaps.

Her first Command was of a platoon of Free French girls. She found them very amusing, but her commander was upset that the French girls insisted on making their skirts look "very cheap" (although nice) – but Olive said she couldn't stop them.

She was sent to Doddington Hall, in Cheshire, to Command the clerks, cooks and orderlies for the Infantry Commanders Training Unit. Each group of around 60 young men were lovely – and she was the only female in the mess.

When asked if there was ever any trouble between men and women (ie romantic liaisons), Olive replied "No! never; not to her knowledge". Women in those days just never slept with men before marriage. During the war if anyone did get emotionally involved, they would be posted along way apart.

Next, she was promoted up a rank and went on the Junior Commander course in Bournemouth to be a Captain. Three went forward for interview at the ATS Directorate in London – she thinks she was successful because she was interviewed by a 'Grant'. So, she became a Staff Captain in the War Office, handling complaints from the public in relation to women. The department was under the Adjutant General's Unit Director, Jean Knox.

She was at the War Office until August 1944 when she was posted to Italy, upon her request. On trying to find her a suitable job she was assigned to Civil Affairs and was promoted to Senior Commander. She was based at General Alexander's HQ, 'A' branch (ie Allied HQ Central Mediterranean) in Cassata, The HQ was in a lovely castle. This primarily involved working with displaced persons (not Italians), particularly after the Armistice when troops had to be repatriated to their home nations.

34

She helped repatriate German Officers (held in a villa in Capri), about 100 Russians and Poles. She had a liaison officer as she did not speak Russian, they were very poor. Each camp had their own nationalities working with them to screen their own people, but this was very tricky and it was harrowing knowing that the Russians she was helping to send home did not want to return as they would be shot, so they tried to pass themselves off as Turkish; additionally, the Poles were very desperate and sad.

Since she deputised for her male commander on occasions, she was given a higher temporary rank. She was happy at Cassata - it was nice and warm; the people were friendly, and the Italians used to admire her and say she was beautiful. Although she could not remember if there were other women there, apart from her Senior Commander, there appeared to be some in a photograph of the time. She did recall having a male batman, whose parents were dry cleaners. He used to find her eggs for breakfast in Cassata. While there she was also the messing officer in Cassata Palace.

She worked all over the Mediterranean, including accompanying Colonel Hicks to some high-powered missions in Athens, the Foreign Office and House of Commons relating to displaced Jews trying to get to Israel (as it became). She remained friends with Kenneth Hicks, her CO at Cassata, long after she left the army.

She was there for two years (1944 – 1946) returning in the summer to the ATS Directorate in the War Office, where she (along with others) insisted on wearing their overseas beret – until her commanding officer gave her the afternoon off and told her "to get a proper cap". People were still very keen on the army and they would get free bus journeys. Although she fancied being a stockbroker, she found military life an easy one, particularly for someone without a home. She didn't like teaching but did like the army and the people in it.

She now worked on policymaking for the new Women's Royal Army Corps, where she got more and more involved. She went to the Selection Committee and easily passed, then being sent to the Officer Training Unit involved with the posting of personnel and record-keeping. She was there a couple of years eventually being sent to Scotland to Command WRAC 10th Battalion, based in Edinburgh. It was here that she met her husband, who was in the Army Lands Department. She attained the rank of Major before leaving the army to marry and have a family.

By Penny Muxworthy, WRAC Association Secretary

Joy Drumey

Born in February 1918, she was called 'Joy' because her mother Jane feared that John Drumey, her husband, would be killed in France and that there would never be the joy of another baby. John Drumey did come home but died, at the age of 27, soon after Joy was born from the effects of mustard gas.

Jane Drumey was left aged 23 with a War Pension of 10 shillings a week, one and sixpence for Jack, Joy's older brother, and a shilling a week for Joy. Her mother scraped by through working two jobs; as a Post Lady during the day and by scrubbing office floors at night. Ethel, Jane's sister, helped by looking after the children when Jane had to work.

Joy remembered a gentle, loving Mum who devoted herself to her children and died early from the hard work and strain of being a War Widow and single parent in the 1920's and 30's.

Jack and Joy went to Bowes Road School in north London and left at age 14; Jack was apprenticed to a piano maker, as he was musical and good at carpentry, Joy trained as a bookkeeper as she was good with numbers.

Aged 21, doing well in her job and engaged to be married to an electrician, she was called up to National Service and trained as a Driver. As the air raids intensified over London Winston Churchill asked for 'the women to step up', to take over the jobs of men needed at the Front. Joy volunteered as a Searchlight Operator in response to this call, partly so that she might be based in London to be able to check on her Mum more often.

Thus, Joy became part of the first and only ATS Division of Ack Ack Command in the Royal Artillery, stationed on the searchlights by the big guns defending St Paul's Cathedral. Winston Churchill often went to visit the gun crews and 'the girls' at St. Pauls who had stepped up in response to his call. Joy said she was given her first pack of cigarettes by the Prime Minister and wartime leader!

The girls in Joy's Searchlight team had to walk back to their billet each morning, clambering through the new rubble of collapsed buildings and past people searching for their families. There they slept and rested until reporting for duty again the following night.

Joy worried a lot about her Mum but could rarely get back to north London to see if she was ok. She had many stories to tell of that time; of comradeship under fire, the loss of friends; of fear and bravery. She received the news that her wounded fiancée had drowned when a Red Cross ship had gone down, thought to have been sunk by order of Mussolini.

Sometimes, after a British bombing raid somewhere in Europe, she told of how a signal would come that a disabled plane was limping back home. It perhaps had damaged navigation equipment, or on only one engine, or leaking fuel. The Searchlight teams on the South coast would be on alert listening for where the plane crossed the Channel. They'd pick it up in their beams and 'point a path' towards Biggin Hill. The Searchlight team there picked up the plane in their beams and pointed it towards London. In London Joy and her team would wait for the signal from Biggin Hill and 'switch on everything' to guide the way home. Joy once explained that "when we had the plane in our searchlights overhead, we'd 'point it' towards Hatfield. The team there would pick it up and guide them in to land as best they could. We reckoned the Searchlight girls saved a good few air crews and planes, to fight again in the Battle of Britain.".

Joy permanently lost her hearing in the first waves of bombardment against incoming enemy bombers. In 1989, after 50 years of being profoundly deaf, she finally received a War Disablement Pension.

When the war ended, she went home to live with her Mum. Her brother Jack (miraculously alive after 4 years fighting in France, Belgium, Holland and Germany) returned to his wife Margaret and their little daughter Frances. Jack and Margaret had two further children, Jacqueline, born in 1947 and John in 1951. Joy always said that she would love to have had a family of her own, but her fiancée was gone, like many men he did not come home from the Second World War. Instead Joy stepped up to her new role as the world's most supportive daughter, sister, niece, Auntie and friend.

She returned to her studies, qualified as an Accountant and spent much of her career working for Haringey Council. She also cared for Jane, her Mum, and her Auntie Ethel until their death. In retirement Joy lived near Frinton-on-Sea and then moved to Kent to be near to Jack and Margaret after they too retired.

She became part of the Rockdale Housing Association community in Sevenoaks, Kent in 1990 where she lived for 24 years. Joy was 'on duty' all her life, for her family, and for her country in 1939-1945.

At the same time as the boats were landing on the D-Day beaches Corporal Joy Drumey and her team of ATS colleagues were on duty at the searchlights at St. Paul's Cathedral, waiting for news and for the next wave of bombers to appear over London.

From Lioness No.2 2014

Jean Kingdon

Sometime in 1938, Jean "signed up" in the Leigh Road Drill Hall (no the Leigh Ball Room) in Eastleigh, Hampshire. She joined the Auxiliary Territorial Service attached to the Hampshire Regiment, later the Royal Hampshire Regiment.

She was very proud of her Army Number W1554, which means she was among the first two thousand to "join up". Her unit became the 42nd Coy ATS. They used to travel to Winchester once a week for training, either in the lower barracks or in Newburgh House. Two or three weeks before war was declared, they were "called up" and they reported to Winchester Barracks. Those who could travel easily, or lived in Winchester, slept at home and worked in the barracks during the day. They did not have to work on Sundays.

On 3rd September 1939, Jean took a trip to the New Forest, with a neighbour to check on his bees. He had taken them to the Forest for the heather honey. On the way home they saw so many Don Rs (dispatch riders) and military vehicles of all kinds on the roads, that they were sure something big had happened and of course, when they arrived home, the declaration of war was confirmed.

It was back to the barracks on Monday. Jean was a clerk in Q store. National Servicemen and Territorials were being called up and she processed the issue of clothing and equipment. She could not think why each soldier was issued with 2 and a half yards of flannelette. It turned out to be "pull through" for cleaning rifles, also called "four by two", a length of flannel four inches wide, with a red thread across it every two inches. That red stripe had been introduced in the past to stop the material being used for other purposes.

A few days after the outbreak of war, they were told to report to the barracks before eight o'clock in the morning, complete with kit bags etc. They were to be posted to an unknown destination. The unit of thirty or forty women, in new shoes and uniforms, fell in behind the regiment. They marched proudly out of Winchester, behind the County Regiment. Jean said that it seemed as if the whole of Winchester had turned out to wave goodbye. It was very moving. They marched from the barracks to the railway station, where they boarded trains to where? They went to Lymington for Yarmouth and the Isle of Wight! The trains on the island were very short and some of the girls had to sit around for ages, waiting for trains to take them from Yarmouth to Newport. Thank goodness it was a fine day. Jean has memories of all troops all sitting around and singing songs like "Little Sir Echo" and "Isle of Capri" etc.

They eventually arrived at Albany Barracks (now Albany Prison) late in the evening, about eight o'clock. They were given a meal at the cookhouse which had been prepared at midday and kept hot! After the meal the ATS had to fall in, with kit bags, and they were marched to various houses, all within reasonable walking distance of the barracks where they were billeted, but only to sleep.

They had to be in barracks for breakfast and stayed all day to work. In the early days, rules were very strict: they were not supposed to go out with a male on their own, but it was permissible to make up a foursome. They were supposed to be in by 9.30 p.m. each evening and the landladies were told to report the girls if they were late in. These rules proved difficult to enforce. After some time, the ATS were moved into large houses situated outside Newport near Carisbrook Castle and they were bussed into barracks for breakfast etc.

Jean had good memories of Albany: the barracks took in "the Jersey boys", when the Channel Islands were evacuated. The Royal Militia of the Island of Jersey was the 11th Battalion The Hampshire Regiment. Jean remembered a dance in the gym with the regimental flag and that of RMIJ on show and guarded, with corks on the tips of bayonets. A lot of Dunkirk boys were accommodated in Parkhurst at the time of the evacuation.

In the Q store they worked long hours. The troops were so overcrowded that the beds were arranged alternatively, heads and feet to the wall. There was a space between the beds but less than regulations said. There were talent contests and a certain Cpl. Arthur English was very funny. After the war he gave up his job as a painter and decorator and took a job as a comedian at the Windmill Theatre in London. He became very famous in music hall and on the radio.

Albany was an Infantry Training Centre, a course lasted three months. There was an intake of 288 each month and each month 288 were posted out. One intake was all short men, less than 5ft 2ins. It was dangerous when they were drilling with fixed bayonets. (They had Lee Enfield rifles in those days). Jean remembers one of these men walking under her arm as she held a door open, she was 5ft 2ins.

Another intake could not read and write properly. Some were quite intelligent but had not been to school for some reason. They were trained to control traffic and similar duties.

At one time, when there was some kind of flag on, the troops were confined to barracks, but allowed to the cinema in armed parties, marched to and from the barracks. If Jean wanted to go to "the flicks" with a boyfriend she had to meet him in the foyer. Imagine sitting in the picture house, he with his rule, tin hat and gas mask, and you with a tin hat and gas mask. There was not a lot of room for holding hands. They were allowed out to go to some dances in the drill hall but again Jean would have to meet her partner inside and hope he was not on duty, guarding the rules in the cloakroom.

During this time, the Battle of Britain was taking place. On the Isle of Wight, the people had a good view of the "dog flights" overhead. Jean remembered that one Jerry pilot scored a "double one" on the prison clock. She also remembered a very good-looking German was taken prisoner. He spoke English without an accent and knew the Isle of Wight better than many of them.

It was decided to transfer the Training Centre to Colchester, so almost everyone was posted. Jean stayed with the depot party and was attached to another ATS Coy. For accommodation, but for messing and duty she was still with the Hampshire Regiment. There was a sergeant, a corporal, three of four men and one ATS, Jean. They all lived on the first floor of one of the married quarters, the office, mess and stores were on the ground floor. Later Jean was promoted and posted as NCO 1C Detachment at Fort Bembridge above Sandown, IOW, HQ Coast Defence Artillery. She was not happy at swapping her breast pocket badge from The Hampshire Rose, to a bomb!

There were Army, Navy and Air Force all stationed there. The Navy were in the early stages of ASDIC (sonar) and the RAF with radar. They also had a Secret Service pigeon loft, looked after by a Cpl in the Signals. The Navy, being the Senior Service, took command, the piece of lawn outside the Naval Office and the orderly room was called the Quarter Deck and no one was allowed to walk on it. The fort was entered over a drawbridge, guarded by the Navy. The RAF "Brylcream Boys all slept in civvy digs and were bussed in daily. The Navy and Army boys lived in rooms built into the hill and the walls of the fort. The twelve girls were in a hut on the barrack square. If there was an air raid they had to get up and go to the MI room. Five of the twelve girls were called Jean, so they were known by nicknames e.g. Robbie. To some people Jean is still "Blacky".

The Army and Navy shared a cookhouse; each had a stove and did their own cooking. The Navy side of the kitchen was referred to as the gallery and the Army side as the cookhouse. Each Service had its own mess hall. They used to go out and collect nettles to use as a green vegetable and winkles from the shore to try to liven up the food.

The NAAFI in the fort was run by an ATS Lance Corporal. The sudden influx of a hundred men from the Dorset Regiment meant that she needed help, with no one else on site, so Jean had to step in. She knew nothing about beer and had to learn on the spot, to pour black and tans and other mixtures she had never heard of. The beer ran out and they rolled a couple of barrels over from the Sergeants' Mess and tapped them straight away. That was another skill Jean picked up, which would become useful later on. Next morning Jean was ill. Apparently, it was a hangover caused by the fumes. From then on, Jean always hated the smell of beer.

Orders came through that all Army staff had to train either as Bren Gunners, or to fire mortars (known as blacker bombards). The CO said that any of the girls could take the Bren Gun course and five of them did, with great enthusiasm, all determined to do well. All qualified. This is entered in Jean's AB 64 which she still has (face having that on your CV these days). Some months later Jean was called to the CO's office where he explained that if the Germans landed and saw this qualification on her records, she could be shot. Jean could not believe he was serious, but he was. She decided she would rather be shot than meet a "fate worse than death" so the entry stayed.

For some reason, around early 1942 the "powers that be" decided that the fort was too dangerous a station for women. They replaced the twelve ATS girls with eighteen men. The other eleven girls asked for a posting nearer home, but Jean said anywhere would do. Her brother was at sea and her mother was a full-time civil defence worker, so being nearer home was not so important. What happened? She was posted to Winchester and the others were sent all over the place. Jean was sent to another Q store, this time in an all-female company. The ATS Commanding Officer had been one of Jean's early officers in Newport.

The story about Jean that I find so wonderful and brave, is the story of her marriage to a handsome Czech soldier called John, after a whirlwind wartime romance. When Jean became pregnant, she learned that she had ceased to be a British citizen and the Czech Army paid for her to have her baby in a British hospital. Their baby was born in May 1945. John came back from the war in late 1945 and took Jean and their baby back to Moravia in Czechoslovakia. Married life was good, but all too soon the Communist control became very tense. John told Jean that she must return to England and he would join her as soon as he could. For three years Jean waited, but John was unable to leave Communist Czechoslovakia. They eventually divorced. It is amazing that Jean reached England safely with her baby, after travelling unaccompanied through war damaged Europe. She had written to her brother and prayed that he had received the letter. She had asked him to meet her in Paris and to her great relief he was standing on the railway station in Paris. She had never been so pleased to see him. It was a very emotional reunion.

He asked how she had coped with her very young baby, all on her own on such a long train journey. "We all helped each other on the train" she told him. "In those days we all helped, you just got stuck in" she said.

Later, after twenty-one years had passed, Jean married Evan, a wonderfully kind man, who unknown to Jean, made plans for her and her daughter and himself to visit Moravia and meet John and his new family. Of course, for Jean's daughter it was a first meeting with her father. It had certainly taken a long time, but as Jean said, "All's well that ends well". Jean still wrote and kept in touch with her Czech family.

One thing of which Jean is very proud, happened long after she left the Services. As a member of the WRAC Association, representing the Southampton Branch, she was presented to the Queen. Sometime after names were submitted, they were surprised to receive a letter saying that if the selected person had to fall out, it was not permitted to send a substitute as HM did her homework. Jean thought that was a polite way of saying that they had all been vetted. Not at all, Jean was presented as a member of Southampton Branch and a JP from Eastleigh. The Queen immediately spoke about Eastleigh. It was a very proud moment.

From Lioness No.2 2011

Dorothea Colver - 31st County of London Company

Thinking back, it all started in September 1938. It was the day of the Munich Agreement and London was preparing for war. Sandbags were appearing in front of Whitehall buildings, children were being evacuated, ARP workers were getting organised. I was walking past a TA Drill Hall, near Victoria Street when the Sgt Major talked me into going inside and filling in a form to join the ATS. I told him, with some relief, that I was not yet old enough to join but he persuaded me to add a year to my age. That night Mr Chamberlain returned from Germany with his famous agreement and I thankfully imagined that I would hear no more about being a soldier and going off to war. I was wrong. An order came to report to Scotland Yard. More form filling, still claiming to be of age in spite of being told that it was a Court Martial offence to state an untruth on the form. I was then detailed to a Drill Hall in New Street, Kennington, where I was joined by one other, Mary Scroggins, and we two were lectured and actually drilled, wearing hats and high heels, always expecting more girls to join us. After the Christmas break, we two were transferred to the

Braganza Street Drill Hall, near Kennington Park, and there the 31st City of London Coy was formed. Wo were a very mixed group of secretaries, shorthand typists, clerks, domestic workers and a tailoress ranging in age from seventeen to the late forties. Our officer was a lovely young girl, Miss Rosamund Parker and she was very keen and did a superb job in training and drilling us into some semblance of a smart ATS company. There was much to learn. After a few months we were issued with our uniform which consisted of a cap, jacket, skirt, two collar attached shirts with matching tie, two pairs of thick khaki stockings and brown Oxford shoes. The "trying on" session was riotous. Nothing fitted and the caps were very odd shapes on account of having been badly packed. I took my uniform to a local tailor and he made quite a good job of altering it to fit, but no way was I going to be seen wearing it in public. I used to carry the jacket and cap in a case to the drill hall.

On the outbreak of war we were ordered to meet at Charing Cross station and eventually arrived at the Daily Express Camp at St Mary's Bay, Dymchurch, Kent. There we were attached to the 163rd OCTU (Artists' Rifles). The training staff were Coldstream Guards and Light Infantry. The ATS were billeted in the large camp pub. Sleeping quarters were in the main bar and the Orderly Room was behind the bar. There was always a heavy smell of stale beer and seaweed and damp. Although it was only September, the weather turned cold and it rained incessantly. After the thrill of 'going off to war' had worn off there was dreadful homesickness to contend with. But looking back, the things remember are the funny ones. Like the weekly bath. Having to get the soyer stoves lit to warm the water outside in a field. It then had to be poured into a hip bath and the water pan refilled for the next one.

Our first morning we were assigned to our various jobs in the camp and I had to report to the PRIs Office wearing my khaki overall to save my jacket. My overall reached down to my ankles and was belted with brass buttons down the front. Not exactly a pretty sight. The PRI was a Lt Colonel and there were also a Sgt and Cpl in the office which had only just been set up and so we all learned the procedure together. The Artists' Rifles was a very select TA Regiment. Even the Privates seemed to be known names in art and the stage etc. They were all eventually commissioned. My 'desk' was a 6ft trestle table covered with a grey blanket and sitting in the middle of it was my typewriter. It was an Oliver machine. The keyboard wasn't standard and so difficult for a touch typist and the noise it made was extreme. As I typed the table would rattle and people had to shout to one another to be heard. Eventually the Colonel said

"Enough. In future all letters will be handwritten". Seven copies of each, for all Companies, took a lot of writing.

Our meals were taken in a curtained off section of the Men's Mess. The first breakfast consisted of boiled liver and onions with bread and margarine, next day was kippers. After that all our money was spent on food and trips to Dymchurch for a meal at night.

After a month of wind and rain which made training difficult for the cadets, we were moved along the coast to Risborough Barracks. This was much better. We ATS were put into Risborough House. We had our own cook and orderlies. Cooking was done on a large coal fire with side oven, there was no gas or electric stove. We had a lovely mess-come-living room with a coal fire which was really luxury after the camp. That winter as early and very severe.

Saturday nights we all used to walk into Folkestone to attend the dance at the Leascliff Hall, one night there the band stopped playing and the manager announced the presence of sailors from the Ajax. They had been in the battle with the Graf Spee and were our first war heroes.

We were issued with gum boots and greatcoats of all shapes and sizes left over from the First World War. Mine was lined with a heavy red woollen cloth and was much appreciated as a bed cover which brings to mind the ritual of going to bed. Our bedrooms were bitterly cold particularly in the morning when we dressed. And so shirts and underwear were neatly folded and placed in the bed to be warm to put on. The skirt was folded beneath the mattress to remove creases and the jacket laid out flat beneath the mattress at the foot of the bed. Of course, shoes had to be polished, also the brass buttons, in readiness for parade and inspection next morning. We had only the one uniform and two shirts. One shirt was sent to the laundry each week and so the other had to be worn for that length of time. They were the most dreadful garments and it was wonderful when the others were later issued.

As nothing seemed to be happening on the war front, we were told we could all go on Christmas leave for two weeks. The first group of our cadets had passed out and been commissioned. The barracks were left with a small caretaker group to get ready for the next input of cadets. In the spring of 1940, we all moved further along the coast, this time to Shorncliffe Camp on St Martins Plain. The ATS once more had the COs house Underbill House, and again we had our own cook and orderlies. We were an isolated group without an officer except for pay parades. Some of our original members had been posted away, others had decided to return to civilian life. We weren't yet under Military Law and so could leave at any time. There were also some new arrivals.

Early in May the war on the Western Front really started to get serious It culminated in the Dunkirk evacuation. Across the channel we would see the flashes of explosions at night and then there was the wonderful sight of boats and ships of all sizes and description coming and going all through the days of the battle. It was the most emotional experience to see the troops landing at Dover and Folkestone. It left us feeling very depressed and pessimistic until Mr Churchill rallied us with his "fighting on the beaches" speech. Now the shelling and bombing really got severe and our Cadets were being trained under very difficult conditions. We were warned that invasion was likely and so we were confined to camp. Every night before "lights out" the cook would distribute all the food left in store. Each of us had a loaf of bread or margarine or tea etc. to put in our kitbag together with a change of stockings and underwear and toilet bag and towel nothing more, in readiness for a quick move inland. One night there was a strange bugle call from the camp, then a hammering on the front door. From my ground floor bedroom window, I saw that it was RSM Archer. He told us to get out onto the front lawn in five minutes in marching order. So, with respirators at the alert and tin hats and flowing gas capes, which had only just been issued, we made a sorry sight. We had to march to the Officers' Mess which was quite a distance from the Camp. It was a very dark night and we nervously proceeded, all the while expecting parachutists to jump out of the hedges. On arrival at the mess an elderly Lt Col answered the knock on the door. He knew nothing about an invasion and suggested that as the air raid warning was sounding, we had better jump into a trench which ran along the front of the building. In the dark it was an awkward manoeuvre getting down as it was quite deep with a thick layer of very wet mud at the bottom. The all clear eventually sounded and we saw no sign of enemy activity and so as soon as it got light we marched back to camp. The men were collecting buckets of tea and shaving water from the cookhouse and there was no sign of them having had a disturbed night at all. Back at Underhill House the fire had to be lit before we could have hot water for tea. Most of us went to bed until our breakfast was ready. We were all very late getting to work next morning. It had been a false alarm and reckoned to be good practice.

We soldiered on through 1940 and I know we did a really good job with the OCTU. I had been working for the Chief Instructor for many months and realised that the shelling, which was very frequent, cut down training time for the cadets and it was decided that the OCTU would move to Pwllheli. Our 31st County of London Coy would be split into two. Half, mostly cooks and orderlies, would go to Ripon, the other half to Chatham. The Chatham half would still be the 31st

45

Clerk for two years and it had been a really exciting job and there had been wonderful people to work with. I left my old 31st County of London with the good feeling that we had seen the war through together. I eventually landed at 21 Army Group in Brussels and was among the first ATS to go into Germany. That posting I considered to be the 'icing on the cake'.

Lioness 1994 No.2

Pat, Helen, Kay & Peggy McGrath

In 1940, the four McGrath sisters were evacuated from Guernsey before the German occupation of the Channel Islands. They arrived in Weymouth with many other evacuees. In the reception centre they met a number of the ATS who were helping there, and the sisters decided to volunteer. Very soon, after medicals and other formalities, they were enlisted and posted to Verne Citadel in Portland. After a few months they were all posted to Sandbanks, near Bournemouth.

When the islands were free again, they went back to Guernsey to be reunited with their parents and youngest sister.

From Lioness 2007 No.2
See images in centre pages

Jane Knight

On 27th September 1938 Jane heard the announcement of the formation of the ATS and immediately cycled into Aldershot to enlist at the drill hall and, being 6 weeks away from her 17th birthday, was somewhat economical with the truth about her age. Her skills as a Pitman trained shorthand typist were of great value to the ATS and she became a teleprinter operator and served in a number of small communication centres across the UK.

Following several promotions, she went to OCTU in Edinburgh and was commissioned in October 1942. On Sunday 8th June 1944, while serving in London District, she attended morning service at the Guards Chapel at Wellington Barracks. A few minutes after the service commenced, the chapel was struck by a VI Flying Bomb. Londoners had come to know that when the VI engine suddenly became silent, they had about 15 seconds to take cover. There was no chance of that in the chapel which suffered a direct hit, killing 121 military personnel and civilians and injuring 141. Jane was posted as missing but had in fact been injured, dug out of the rubble and taken home. Many years later, Jane was to write movingly of her thoughts and fears while trapped under the debris and of the eventual appearance of a guardsman above her, pulling her out.

A few months later she took up new duties in Southern Italy as part of the 8th Army. Jane became one of the first female Signal Masters and served in a number of Royal Signals units throughout the remainder of the Italian campaign. During this time, she saw the ruins of Monte Cassino which left a lasting impression on her and also came into contact with the signallers of the 8th Indian Division with whom she formed a lasting bond.

In 1946 she resigned her commission but continued in public service as a member of the little-known United Nations Relief and Rehabilitation Administration (UNRRA) which predated the UN proper. She travelled widely in former Axis occupied countries assisting with the repatriation of refugees.

After three years she joined the P&O Steam Navigation Company with whom she sailed the world many times on ships such as the Strathaird and Himalaya, working her way up to become the first female assistant purser in the company.

Jane never forgot her experience of eight years' service and in later years, she threw herself wholeheartedly into the Associations of many regiments she had served with including the ATS & WRAC, Royal Signals, Indian Signals and several of the regiments of Foot Guards. She marched at the Cenotaph for many years right up until 2008. She was especially well known throughout the Royal Signals Association and granted Honorary Membership. In particular Jane supported the three branches local to her home: Aldershot, Reading and West London. She served on the committee of the Aldershot Branch for almost 20 years, latterly holding the appointment of Vice President.

From her obituary in Lioness No.2 2010

Kathleen McBurnley - Telephonist's Memories

When War was declared, I was nearly 18 years of age and already working as a telephonist in an office in Doncaster.

The war time restrictions affected everybody including the blackout arrangements, the six-inch black line around the bath as a water level and all the air raid precautions as German planes flew over us on their way to the steel works at Rotherham and Sheffield.

We lived near to a main road and could hear the convoys and heavy guns being moved at night. The vibrations never failed to shake the house, but we became oblivious to that as long as the sirens gave us a night of undisturbed rest.

After 3 years as a wartime civilian and twice deferred from call up by the firm I worked for, I was called up in 1942 as a telephonist. Initial training at Pontefract was gruelling. I am definitely not a keep fit sort of person, but I learned to obey orders!

Then came further telephonist training on a six-week course crammed into three weeks. The final test was to connect 100 calls in half an hour using the correct army procedures.

We did this in a new school down Deanstones Lane, Queensbury. We slept in Nissen huts down a bleak hillside, swept by icy cold winds and torrents of rain.

After short stays at Newcastle and Chilwell, a huge Ordnance Depot with a large exchange, I was asked to help out at a smaller exchange in Old Dalby, Leicestershire. It is near Melton Mowbray where the famous pork pies are still made today. We worked long hours of shift work to man the switchboards and teleprinters day and night.

In the first year, we only had one day off a month and that was usually after a week of night shifts! I remember someone in authority saying, "Do it first - grumble after". In spite of everything, we always managed to laugh at our predicaments. We really looked forward to our three weeks leave every three months. My first break happened to coincide with my 21st birthday - going home was the best present I could have had.

Part of a large shed in the depot served as a dance hall on Saturday nights and for ENSA stage shows. It was also used for church services once a month. When shifts allowed, a few of us walked to Nether Broughton village church, lifelong friendships were made.

From Lioness 2007 No.1
See images in centre pages

Jessie Low

Craigie, where I was brought up, was a suburb of Perth City. When Guiding was introduced to the local church in 1931, I was thrilled to become one of the first Guides in the Company, uniform fascinated me! Then at 17, I joined the Rangers Company at St Ninian's Cathedral.

When the ATS formed, they had a local company which met in the Drill Hall at Queen's Barracks, Black Watch Depot. I joined them on 1 December 1938. I wanted to be a cook, but with no experience and as I was already a clerkess in 'civvy street', they signed me on as a clerk. Thank goodness, when I saw the facilities cooks worked with, both inside and outside the kitchens.

The initial training evenings were mostly drill in 4s at that time. I had learned that in the Guides - left, right, together - but I was soon smartened up - 1-1, 2, shoulders back, chin in, arms straight by your sides, heels together, toes apart. Drilling in civvy shoes was no good so we had to go to Norwell's Shoe Shop in the High Street where they had a consignment of proper army shoes, brown and really heavy. We were then ready for our drill lessons.

The Black Watch went to camp at Barry Buddon that year. Some of the local ATS would have liked to accompany them but the Black Watch were having none of this and we had to spend the day in the barracks for instruction. I was sent to the RQMS who showed us around his stores with all the uniforms and the necessary documentation. He gave us a coffee break, sent us home for lunch and finished the training session at 3 o'clock! Not what I was used to in my normal work, I can tell you!

When I got home from work on 31 August 1939 there was the OHMS letter stating that I had to report to Queen's Barracks next morning at 8.30am. When I arrived, we were detailed where our place of work would be. Five others and I were sent to a hut where there were long tables on each side. We were given a pile of attestation forms to complete for each reservist reporting for duty.

On Sunday 3 September the Hut Sergeant allowed us to listen to his wireless and we heard Neville Chamberlain tell us that we were at war with Germany. Lights went out all over the country. Reservists reported for duty over the next four weeks. We completed their forms and sent them to the stores to be kitted out. In the meantime, our own uniforms arrived comprising a tunic, skirt, cap, two khaki shirts with collars attached, one tie and two pairs of khaki lisle stockings. Underwear and an extra skirt came later. Washing was difficult as we were on no account to wear civilian clothes. No washing machines then!

Barrack routine was the order of the day, but we were allowed to wear Black Watch tartan skirts when we were off duty. They were tailor-made, with 4 pleats. North Inch Perth 1941. With our Black Watch tartan skirts In the meantime, Balhousie Castle was taken over by the ATS as a billet. As NCO, I had to do duty one weekend in six, night duty once a fortnight and evening duty once a week. This meant that, after checking late passes at 10 p.m., I had a long walk of about 45 minutes in the blackout to get home. I would be frightened to do that now! Girls had to be in at 9pm. with two late passes a week which allowed them to stay out until 10pm.

Perth was alive with people in uniform. The Record Office took over Sharp's School. We had to report to the Black Watch RSM Drummond at 8.30 a.m. each weekday morning for drill. Several male squads were drilling at the same time and we were certainly put through our paces. So much so, that we were deemed smart enough to go on the monthly church parade to the West Church (now St Matthew's) in Tay Street. We marched down Atholl Street and up the High Street to the sound of the pipes and drums.

I became the Chief Clerk in the RASC office, stationed in the newly built Queen's Hotel in Leonard Street. Then, in October 1942, I volunteered for general service, was promoted to CSM and posted to a Hvy Ack Ack Bn at Oswestry.

This was the unhappiest month of my army career. Having travelled in a packed train from Perth, changing at Crewe, surviving on mother's sandwiches, I was met by the Bombardier who took me to the Sergeants' Mess where I could buy a drink and a snack over the bar. I had to share a bunk with a permanent Staff Sergeant. Of course, I had to have the bottom bunk - what a welcome! The following morning a male CQMS issued us with our operational kit - battledress, boots and gaiters. "What size shoes do you take?" I said, "Sevens", so he issued me with size nines! This happened to all of us. The girls had no idea how to wear boots with gaiters. By this time most of them were in tears. The ATS RSM took our first parade. She was the most forbidding woman I have ever encountered.

After a month we were sent off one night to an unknown destination. This turned out to be a firing camp at Whitby. The operational staff were training every day climbing up 199 steps to the cliff top, where they fired at balloons being towed behind aircraft. 39 Training Camp Whitby. CSM Dunsmore in combat kit at Royal Hotel After training we were moved every few months from Whitby. We went to Wilmslow onto Harwich, Caldecot, Cardiff, Ipswich and then to

Shoreham-by-Sea. This was where some of the troops were getting ready to embark before the final push on D-Day.

I was then posted to Portland Bill and was able to celebrate VE Day in Weymouth. With the war in Europe over there was no more need for Ack Ack batteries, so I was posted to the RAOC at Beeston, a clothing depot where 'demob suits' were being issued. Then I volunteered to go abroad and was posted to Klagenfurt in Austria in 1947 as part of the Army of Occupation. I remained there until 1949 when I was posted to Aberdeen as RSM with the TA, covering Dundee, Aberdeen, Inverness, Wick and Thurso. Our annual camps were held at Cultybraggan Camp, Comrie, and it was there that I met my future husband and where, after our marriage, we would eventually live for a number of very happy years.

From Lioness No.1 2009

Joan Awbery

War was going very badly in 1941 I thought it was time I took a hand in it.
Went to the Recruiting Office in Cambridge to offer myself to the WAAF. They were just about to close for lunch and told me to come back in the afternoon. The next door being ajar I found it to be the ATS recruiting office! Good fortune had smiled on me! Nov'41 called for medical. Calling up-papers arrived in Jan '42
with instructions to report to Talavera Camp, Northampton with the minimum of baggage.

Nissen Huts, communal feeding, washing of mess-tins and irons in communal tub of warm greasy water, hard beds, nights spent with thirty or more snorers, groaners and teeth-grinders under scratchy blankets Tortoise stove not lit until 5pm and just got warm by lights out time.

All this during the coldest winter for a decade. Out on the barrack square in snow in civvy shoes and bits of ill-fitting uniform, under the eagle eye of men Sgt Majors learning drill and saluting. Breaking-in time but hardships endured with the comradeship engendered and natural cunning in evading the worst! Even life-long friendships made.conditions greatly improved by the time we left after our six weeks training. and scattered throughout the country.

I had volunteered to be a driver, but in the frost and snow opted for office work, with shorthand and typing to offer. Asked where I would like to be posted, said Scotland - sent to Cambridge, 25 miles from home, to where I biked on my days off with my washing and the unexpired portion of the day's rations.

Life was quite cushy -interrupted by the night's fire-watching duty and hearing the distant sound of bombs, none dropped on Cambridge, fortunately. constant sound of bombers going out from local airfields.

One night a distant explosion disturbed us, and, in the morning, it was reported an ammunition train had blown us near the station at my home town. Rumours were rife that the town was obliterated, and I was taken home to investigate. The station and surroundings were no more, and the driver and fireman killed but no casualties in the town due to their bravery in getting the blazing wagons into the countryside.

In Cambridge, billeted in big old houses on the Madingley and Grange Roads beautiful rooms divided with plywood sheets into small spaces for offices. Here employed in Eastern Area Sub-Command as P.A. to a particularly unpleasant Brigade Major. After complaining, my next job was with the Army Kinema Service - training films and one recreational film taken out to lonely outposts of gun and searchlight sites along the coast of East Anglia. They were transported by a 'Tilly' with a projectionist and a mechanic in case the film broke down, (which it could be guaranteed to do).

During these times monotony was relieved by attending three-week WO and NCOs' course at Nevilles Cross, Durham and a lively week in and out of gas chambers on a course at Winterbourne Gunner on Salisbury Plain. Once having to go overnight by train to Glasgow Police Station to bring back an absconded ATS girl.

After VE Day I was posted to Harpenden on admin duties then in 1944 to Embarkation Camp in Bristol. After many false stops and starts finally off from Tilbury Docks, wallowing about on the Channel in convoy with overnight journey, no sleep, having started off from Bristol at 3 a.m. Arrived at war-damaged Ostenee given a meal where the Belgian owner proudly displayed the signature of Mary Churchill, who had been on the draft ahead of mine.

Then to Brussels for remaining months of the War in the BLA Legal Service as secretary. Billeted in the local Barracks, then for a short time in a house which had been the German SS HQ! VE Day in Brussels something to write home about! The day after, parades of returning Belgians from their forced labour and concentration camps, each parade headed by a band and hordes of local residents. Services in Cathedral and noisy and frightening demonstration all over the city - for the return or the rejection, of King Leopold.

Life fairly primitive in the barracks but we had the use of hotels converted to luxurious clubs - the Monty Club, the YMCA, the Canada

Club - where we could have baths, hairdressing and substantial meals - Brussels being a Leave centre.

A week or two later my first-ever flight - in a Dakota, sitting on kit bag to Germany. The thrill of crossing over the vast Rhine about which we had heard so much. Sight of bombed towns below. First to Harford then to Rhine Army HQ in Bad Oeynhausen, still with the Legal Eagles. Then their offices were moved to Bad Zaluzflen, a lovely small Spa town where I was the only ATS - billetted with the circumspect ladies of the Control Commission, just out from England. To visit my pals in Oeynhausen I had to seek a friendly armed soldier to accompany me. The locals not at all pleased to see us, we had probably turned them out of their homes for offices But we had friendly German cooks and maids - far better meals than army ones!

Had the chance to see other parts of Wesphalia accompanying my Major to duties in other towns. Going on leaves in Paris, Brussels, the Hartz Mountains and the Mohne dam. After signing on for another six months I was demobbed in Guildford in July 1946.

Written by Joan Awbery for this book.

Amy Maund - Transfer to the Military Police

My service life started on 04 December 1942, having reached my 17th birthday the previous March. Typical of the teenagers at that time, I wanted to 'do my bit' for the war effort. Needless to say, my parents were not too happy, but I finally persuaded my father to sign the necessary documents for me to join the ATS.

So, on 04 December I duly set off for Glen Parva Barracks at Leicester, never having been away from home on my own before. I met up with girls from all parts of the country and, with them, soon settled into Army life sharing a hut with twenty-two others. We had bunk beds with what were referred to as 'biscuits' for mattresses, three square blocks, not very soft, which had to be anchored with the bottom sheet. If this wasn't done correctly, they would come apart during the night not very comfortable! Of course, we soon got used to them.

We did our basic training at Glen Parva, drills etc and were kitted out with our uniforms. Everything was off the peg, so, as you can guess, lots of alterations were necessary. We must have looked a motley crew going in one side of the building in civilian clothes and coming out the other side in an assortment of ill-fitting uniform and civilian clothes. There were some funny ideas of what fitted; part of our issue were blue striped pyjamas. I was quite tall but, when it came to my turn, I was given the same size as someone about the same height as Pat 5' 3" and hers fitted! Incidentally, she and I became very good friends. She came originally from London but now lives just outside King's Lynn and we have kept in touch over the past fifty plus years.

During our month of basic training we had interviews to decide what job we would eventually be allotted. I had joined with the idea of becoming a driver, only to discover after having committed myself to service, that I was too young. After various tests it was decided that I would be trained as a telegraphist attached to a Heavy AckAck Battery. Pat was also selected for this and so, after our basic training, we were both sent to Arborfield, just outside London, to commence the second part of our training. Here we had another issue of kit so, having up until then worn my own civilian ones, I got my pyjamas changed. We were issued with trousers, battle dress, boots and gaiters, so we felt we were really in the Army. I was always getting into trouble because I couldn't keep my trousers tucked properly into my gaiters, the reason being that the trousers were not really long enough for me. At Glen Parva I had been provided with a hat that had a wavy brim and no matter what I did with it, pressing it, putting weights on it overnight, it just would not stay straight. I thought at the second kitting out I would be able to change it, but no such luck, I was stuck with it.

The training as a telephonist consisted of learning the Morse Code, both by lamp and key. I never really got the hang of it. We were shown how to take a field telephone to pieces and reassemble it. We were very proud to be able to do this but, when we eventually got to our gun sites after training, we were absolutely forbidden to tamper in any way with the telephones! We had to call in the Royal Corps of Signals if we had any problems, so, a typical waste of time, that part of the course.

Whilst at Arborfield we were visited by Mary Churchill, the then Prime Minister's daughter. She was an officer in the ATS. This gave us a morale boost as, by then, we were all feeling rather homesick and, speaking for myself, wondering why I had volunteered. Being near London, Pat and I were able to have a couple of weekends at her home which was a very nice break for us.

Somehow, I managed to get through my telephonist's course and Pat, and I were eventually posted to 632 HAA Battery. The battery was made up of two sections. Our section went to Bude in Cornwall and the other half to Weybourne in Norfolk. These camps were practice firing camps, mainly for the men manning the guns and the girls who operated the rangefinding equipment. There were eight of us telephonists, but we did not have a lot of work to do. We were at Bude for a month, during which time another girl and myself were sent to Portsmouth to relieve some ATS on a site where there had been several raids. Consequently, they were in need of a rest. The Germans must have got word that we were there because in those two weeks we never had one alert! Then it was back again to Bude where the rest of the battery had completed their training.

Where to next? Well, typical of the Army we were sent to Helensburgh overlooking the Clyde, quite a journey. When we got there, all fired with enthusiasm, our training over at last and ready to really do something to help the war effort, it was to find that it was a nonoperational site. In other words, to the outsider it looked like a normal site, but the guns were made of wood. Each day drill went on, normal routine as if we had real guns, but we knew differently. I celebrated, if you could call it that, my 18th birthday there. Remaining there a month we all felt rather fed up, it was March and the weather was so cold. Thankfully, the other girls I was with were a jolly crowd and kept our spirits up.

One day word went around that we were going overseas. No-one seemed to know where to but we had to have our photographs entered in our AB64s the Army Service passbook.

It finally transpired we WERE going overseas but to Northern Ireland. Great secrecy surrounded our move; we were not allowed to write or 'phone home'. Although, thankfully, I was not aware of it at the time, there were German submarines operating in the sea between England and Ireland, hence the secrecy because a whole battery of service personnel were being transferred. So secret was it that the people of Helensburgh went to bed at night with us still at the camp and got up in the morning to find we had gone. That was the theory at least. We were all lined up at the station in the early hours of the morning waiting to board the train for Stranraer when some bright spark in our group realised that is was April the first and we wondered if we were part of a hoax. Not so; after a very rough crossing when most of the girls, including myself, were seasick, we arrived at Larne. We finished up at a camp south of Belfast, an operational site, so some of our training was at last put to use. We were not far from Dundonald where the people made us very welcome and various activities were laid on for our off duty times.

After a spell there our battery was then moved to McGilligan Point, the northernmost tip of Northern Ireland. The river Foyle separated us from the Irish Free State which was neutral. We on our side of the river had to maintain complete blackout while across the river from us was a blaze of light. I still had my horrible hat and one very windy night while walking through the camp it blew off. I thought good now I've lost it and can get a replacement. No such luck. Someone found it and of course it had my name in it so I was still stuck with it, wavy brim and all.

While in Northern Ireland, I had a sudden urge to change my job and applied for the Military Police. I had to go before a selection board and when asked why I wanted to go into the MP, I said it was because my father was a policeman. They obviously considered this a reasonable answer, so I was duly transferred to Belfast and did a month's probation which involved going out on patrol with a fully qualified policewoman, or Redcap as we were known. The life in the police was a complete contrast to Ack Ack life. We were a unit of girls in a large requisitioned house in a very nice suburb of Belfast off the Antrim Road. I completed the probationary period and, in March 1944, was sent back to England to attend the CMP Provost course at Aycliff in Durham. There were about a dozen girls on the course, together with men. We were taught all kinds of things, traffic control, unarmed defence, how to immobilise vehicles, plus, of course, the inevitable paperwork! The course lasted a month and, if I remember rightly, all but two of the girls passed. The passing out parade was hilarious. As you may know, a Redcap automatically became a Lance Corporal. We were also issued with different hats, stiff peaked hurrah! At last I got rid of my awful hat. They had a removable red top and we also had armbands with 'MP' on. Well, we girls went proudly on parade with our armbands, only for most of them to finish up on the ground we had not yet learnt the trick of putting a bent pin in the armband and hooking it on to our stripe. I was posted back to Northern Ireland to start life as an MP and it was a very happy time. We were like one big family in that house.

Work in the Police was very varied; we were often sent out on detached duty, two of us for about a week or fortnight to another part of Northern Ireland where there were numerous ATS camps. We usually stayed with a civilian family and were welcomed into their homes as if we were part of the family. Larne was a favourite place of mine. We had to see that the girls arriving by boat got the right trains to their destinations. One of the highlights of my time in Belfast was when the King and Queen and the two Princesses visited. It was a long tiring day for us as we had to be on duty, but I wouldn't have missed it for anything. I was able to see the Royal Family quite closeup. Our final job about midnight was to check that all ATS personnel had got away to their various camps. The iron in our house was constantly in use because we always had to be immaculately turned out, more so that day. Some people thought we had special uniforms, but our issue was exactly the same as others, we were constantly pressing uniforms and polishing shoes. We used to send our collars to the Chinese laundry, so they were really stiff.

During my time in Belfast I met Ted, my husband. He had been busily chasing Rommel up and down the desert and when he arrived back in the UK he was sent to Belfast. He too was in the Military Police and so occasionally we managed to get special duties together. One such time was when General Alexander came over to Belfast. He attended a performance at the Opera House. After seeing him inside we had free time until he was due out again, so this was one of the occasions when we were able to combine work with pleasure.

The Spiritual side of our service life was not neglected. When in the Ack Ack battery we were lucky to have a Christian as our Commanding Officer. He set aside part of one of the Nissan huts as a Chapel where we could go for private prayer. In the Police we had a Padre's assistant, a lady, Jesse Scott. She was a lovely person; she came from Southern Ireland and her father was at one time the vicar of Bray but I don't think he was the original one mentioned in song! Whilst in the ATS I was confirmed and Jesse took me for my first communion in St Anne's Cathedral, Belfast. Jesse and I corresponded although we met up only once since my leaving the services. One Easter, Jesse, two or three of the girls and myself went out and gathered masses of daffodils to decorate the Chapel in the barracks in Belfast. Ted and I always said it would have been nice to have had our wedding there, but it would not have been practical, besides it was not licensed for weddings.

It was a time, on looking back, that had its bad moments, but these were outweighed by the comradeship and, being a teenager when I joined up, I think it helped me to grow up. I certainly have no regrets.

From Lioness 2002 No.2

Vivien Stride - 496 Mixed AA Battery RA

The Battery was formed at Arborfield and then sent to Practice Camp at Weybourne. I should think none of us will ever forget being on a Norfolk beach from am until it was dark in January, with only half an hour indoors for the midday meal. We froze!

We were supposed to go to sites at Cardiff, but they were not ready for us, so the men were sent to the Fun Fair at Barry and the girls to Llantwitt Major to live in St Donat's Castle. I am sure that everyone will remember arriving there, accompanied (for reasons best known to himself) by the BSM. On the journey to the Castle, he invented a particularly nasty ghost for the Castle, and as the owners had given instructions to absolutely clear everything out before we arrived including light bulbs most of the girls would not go upstairs that night.

We did a lot of nothing much as, of course, we were completely non-operational but lots of drill in the dry swimming pool and a scramble to get to the little local cinema before the RAF at St Athan took all the seats, were our main activities.

When we were finally reunited with the men, we were still non-operational as there were only 4 wooden guns! The CO did his best go get the real things with no result; finally, the Site Commander took things into his own hands. He bought some pretty green paint for the 'guns' and planted daffodils round the gun pits. Obviously, some 'Brass Hat' must have passed and noticed this, and a rocket arrived from the Regiment, but also our GUNS. At last we were ready for action!

We had a song which went
Hurrah, hurrah the 496 are we
Hurrah, hurrah, the whizzbang Battery
Why should England tremble when she's got such girls as we
Up with the good old AntiAircraft.

Lioness No.2 1994

Irene Parkes - My war service in the ATS

Irene was born 12 March 1922 in Edmonton, Alberta, Canada, the youngest of 5 children. Her father joined the Royal Canadian Army in 1914 at the outbreak of the First World War; in 1918 he was gassed at the Battle of Ypres, returning home shell-shocked, and spent the rest of his days in Canada farming his smallholding in Edmonton, saved up for and purchased by his wife. He was a changed man on his return, very bad-tempered and "awkward" to quote Irene.

In 1936 everyone returned home to St Helens, Lancashire, Dad, Mum, Evelyn, Irene and 2 brothers. In 1943, she received her call-up papers, along with her 21st birthday cards, and was posted to an all-female camp just outside Warrington for 3 months for basic training. According to Irene, this consisted mainly of injections and learning how to salute. The girls weren't allowed out into Warrington "in case they caused trouble".

Irene was given the choice of the ATS or the Navy, it was the ATS for her. After her basic training, Irene was posted to Camberley, Surrey, where she passed her driving test and learned how to drive an ambulance; within 2 weeks she was teaching other girls how to drive a 15-ton truck. Her pay was 8 shillings a week. Cleaning and maintaining the truck was part of her job too. Even until she stopped driving in her late-eighties, Irene did basic maintenance on her own car. She also successfully taught her own children to drive.

The girls at Camberley lived in Nissen huts, 30 girls to a hut, with one pot-bellied stove for heating. There was an ablution hut with 15 washbasins, so it was "first up, first washed". There was always hot water and many of the girls stripped to the waist to wash, observed most days by the chap who kept the boilers in good repair! Irene remembers him as a small, skinny man, and also remembered that his presence did not faze the girls - none of them took any notice of him at all.

Her C.O. at Camberley was a member of the Wellesley family, and it was only in her later years that Irene saw a picture of the Duke of Wellington and realised that her C.O. was a female version of the Duke, she was the image of him. The C.O. kept a little dachshund, and other dogs who dared to approach were kept away by the judicious use of a whip.

The Camberley girls were often invited to dances held at the other 2 male camps nearby, Canadian and Polish. As no-one ever wanted to drive, Irene would volunteer, she remembers waiting over an hour for one of the girls to show up, much to the annoyance of the other girls who didn't want to be late back to camp.

News came that the then Princess Elizabeth had decided to join the ATS and would be coming to Camberley. There was a big re-shuffle, and many of the "ordinary" girls were posted to other camps. Some were allowed to stay to whitewash the stone path to the main house and generally clean round and litter-pick before the Princess came.

Irene herself was moved to Edinburgh and stationed at Leith Barracks, which were very old, but clean. Her job there entailed driving officers around, she never knew who until it came up on the board. Some officers were good, and some bad. Irene drove one particular officer to a function where they stayed overnight. He decided that Irene was a driver with benefits and after dinner he insisted on a very reluctant Irene having a drink with him. He persevered, but to no avail – when bedtime came he found himself at the other side of a firmly locked bedroom door, with a chair under the handle to be on the safe side. He was very apologetic the day after, asking Irene not to report him! Eventually Irene was allocated to

Major-General John Walker, who was a doctor, and Irene was promoted to Corporal.

The HQ was in Edinburgh Castle, but the Maj-Gen had a private house, and Mrs Walker waved them both off every morning. Irene says that the Major was the nicest man she ever met in the Army, he treated her like a daughter. He would say to Irene "only salute me when anyone important is around", e.g. on the occasion when King George VI and Queen Elizabeth dined at Holyroodhouse, the Maj-Gen was invited (but not his wife) and he instructed Irene "Parkes, give me a good salute", when she dropped him off and picked him up.

Irene mentioned that her vehicle flew a red flag when Maj-Gen Walker was in, otherwise it was taken off. Other soldiers had to salute the car if he was in it. While watching "Foyle's War" in recent years Irene has spotted mistakes in that Sam – Foyle's driver - should always have gone around the back of the car when he was in it, and didn't!

Irene mentioned that 2 of the daughters of the Bowes-Lyon family were stationed with her at Leith. As a general rule they kept very much to themselves, except once when Irene's trick of darkening her very pale eyelashes aroused their curiosity enough for them to ask her "Why do you do that?" She also remembers Lady Fiona Campbell being at Leith, Irene describes her as a "lovely girl, no edge to her at all".

As D-day approached Irene became a Don-R, a despatch rider, taking messages to other camps as telephone communications weren't considered safe. Of course, all the road signs had been removed in case of invasion, so it wasn't easy. For this, she used one of two motorbikes, a Triumph 250 or a Matchless, both kick-started. The Matchless was so heavy that she had to rest it against the kerb to get it going.

Irene thinks that she may be the "last woman standing" of the girls she served with in the war. She went on to marry a St Helens man - John Winstanley - after the war. John himself was mentioned in despatches, and together they started up and ran a very successful business in St Helens until retirement.

As told by Irene Parkes for this book.

Iris Fenn

On 14th May 1943 I caught the train from Brighton to Guildford to start my initial army training at Queens Camp. My friend Mary Cowling had joined up earlier and become a Dispatch Rider. I was hoping to do the same. At Haywards Heath another girl joined the train, she was also on her way to Queens Camp. We made friends immediately and her name was Olive Perrot.

On arrival we were issued with our uniform which also included a thing to clean the brass buttons, penknife, scissors and sewing kit called 'Hussif' - Army name for Housewife perhaps. Kit inspections were quite common. We were then shown to our billet which was a spider hut (so called because of the way the huts were arranged, like the legs of a spider). There were ablutions which we thought was a strange name for baths and toilets. Our NCO was a Cpl Gearing who was very friendly and became popular with us. The first weekend we were all confined to barracks. We had to have dreadful vaccinations and the moaning and groaning was pathetic. We felt so ill and many girls wanted their mothers! Most of the girls were my age, around 18 years old.

The next 3 weeks we had to get down to the serious business of training - marching on the parade ground, route marching, running in gym kit - I began to feel very fit. We needed to get used to army food. The dining hall was very large, and I thought the "breadless days" were not too bad, as we had ships' biscuits instead and the raw cabbage was a bit chewy. An officer came to each table to ask, "any complaints?" The outdoor life was making me hungry, so I had no complaints. There was a NAAFI canteen on the camp, also a "Sally Ann" (nickname for Salvation Army canteen).

A few Free French girls had arrived at Queens Camp with us. I did not think they were very strong. It was usually one of them who fainted on the Parade Ground in the heat. We sat out on the grass and had Army discussion groups - which became very tense. The French girls blamed us, our country for "letting them down" in the War. We felt quite indignant considering what our soldiers had gone through at Dunkirk. It was very heated so the 'powers that be' stopped the discussion groups. However, we had a concert at the end of our 3 weeks, put on by ourselves. One of the French girls sang Ave Maria - she had a lovely voice and it was beautiful and so I hoped all had been forgiven.

Olive and I went into Guildford when we had any time off. One day we plucked up courage and took a boat on the river. The funny

63

thing was we somehow acquired 2 extra passengers. The boat man was not very pleased.

I needed to get past the selection board if I was to become a Dispatch Rider, like my friend Mary Cowling. It was not to be. They said I was too light at 7 1/2 stone, but I could become a driver. My new friend Olive and I were sent to the Driving Centre at Camberley for 6 weeks training. There were 15cwt trucks, Utilities (Tillys) and 3-ton Ambulances. If we went on the road in the mornings, we did mechanics or first aid in the afternoon, and vice versa the next day. We learned the 16 61 tasks on the vehicles and decontamination in case of gas attacks. I still have my notebook about it. We learned how to quickly change a wheel. The trucks were put up on 4 blocks, so the wheels could turn while we practised changing gears. The trucks and ambulances had crash gearboxes. We had to learn how to double de-clutch. The Tillys had synchromesh gears, so they were easier to cope with.

When out on the road there were no road signs for us to find our way. Our map reading consisted of 'turn left at the King's Head or Queen Victoria. Public houses had become signposts. Someone told me there was a signpost pointing out to sea which said "Bath". This was to confuse Jerry (the Germans) if they were to invade us.

We had many lectures in a Nissen hut. The floor of the hut was made of material like lumps of coke. In the heat of summer, the fumes rose up so that we felt gassed. It was difficult to stay awake. There were pieces of machinery all around on tables. I found it very interesting to learn about the internal combustion engine. On our time off Olive and I used to visit the Blue Pool at Camberley for a swim. We met some Free French soldiers there and had a chat with difficulty.

One of the last things at Camberley was to pass our driving test. I had my test on an Austin K2 ambulance which I passed. Having finished the course, it was time to receive our postings to our various units. Before we went there, we had some leave.

My favourite vehicle was a Ford truck with a V8 engine. It could have gone a lot faster if the workshop mechanics had not put a governor on the carburettor. It would cut out at a certain speed. There were Army petrol stations in many places. We just filled up and signed, then we made out the work ticket and added the mileage. The vehicles were very thirsty, 12 miles to the gallon was quite usual.

There were a few breakdowns. One time, I had to deliver a Morris Pup ambulance up North. My journey was on the Great North Road. I had filled up with petrol at Stevenage and not knowing the area I did not know where there were any more petrol stations. As there was only one petrol tank on a Pup, I ran out of petrol on a very spooky moor outside Doncaster. After some time an Army lorry came along and rescued me. I delivered the Pup and had to return by train. That was alright until I came to Waterloo. The last train for Dorking had gone and I spent an awful, cold night locked in a waiting room covered by a piece of coconut matting.

Another breakdown happened on the return journey from Hastings. The lights went out and the officer just sat there while I had a look at the fuses. Luckily, I found the dud fuse and replaced it with a spare. I had been taking an officer, and sometimes his sergeant, around the area visiting families of men serving abroad.

Another very embarrassing breakdown happened right in the centre of Dorking where the main street divides into two. Our trucks had 2 petrol tanks which needed to switch over when necessary. I missed it and fluttered to a stop. I knew what to do as it was a way I had of starting up in the morning. I had a little bottle on a string which I dangled in the full tank. I lifted the bonnet and poured the petrol into the carburettor. Then I took the starting handle and gave it a quick flip up from the bottom (keeping thumb same side as fingers to prevent accident). Only this time I had quite an audience. A whole row of Canadian soldiers were leaning on railings, watching from a high pavement. When I started up the truck a great cheer went up.

I did have one or 2 boyfriends but nothing serious. I had been writing to John, who I met when I was 16, but he never returned from Arnhem in 1944.

Up in the hills from Reigate towards Kingswood was a secret underground place called Radio City. On the other side of the road was an old quarry where the homing pigeons had their lofts. These were looked after by the R Signals. It was really thrilling to take these birds to the Ashford area of Kent for release. They were in training for D Day. We asked for water at the oast houses so the birds could have a drink first. I was concerned in case any were lost but the R Signals soldier said, "If they don't come home, they are no use to me".

I first heard about Vis, Flying Bombs, on the Brighton Road outside an Army Camp. I was waiting to meet 3 tanks as I had 75 "Flimsies" - 4-gallon tins of petrol, for them. The sentry on the gate told me about these pilotless aircraft Hitler was sending over, with a 14ft wingspan. The tanks never arrived so I had to return with my load of 'Flimsies'. At St Margarets the "Buzz Bombs" started to come over regularly.

The bus station had watchers on the roof. We had to dig trenches in the garden. The ground was very hard. Our trenches were only about knee high and we soon became fed up with crouching in them. We then went under our beds instead. When the engines stopped on the Buzz Bombs, it was very nasty wondering where it would land.

I did come upon a tragedy one day which was near the Surrey/Kent border. A house had been hit off the main road and it had been used by the ATS. Fortunately, the drivers had all left for work, but the people left behind were killed. It was upsetting to see, amongst all the rubble, a gym shoe.

I have seen a map of Southern England showing where the Buzz Bombs fell, and it looks as if we were hand-picked as a target

By Iris Fenn in Lioness No.2 2012

Hanna Kennedy

I was called up into the ATS on 15th January 1943 and did three weeks basic training, learning to march, drill etc at High Leigh Hall, Knutsford.

From there and after my first leave I progressed to the driving school at Gresford, North Wales. It was an eleven-week course, map reading, First Aid, mechanics, then the dreaded driving test which I passed after eight weeks. My Instructor then let me take her to Liverpool, where I lived, to tell my mother the good news. It was the first time I had driven through the Mersey Tunnel.

My first posting was to Whitchurch Bristol driving for 666 Mxd HAA Battery, but very shortly we all moved by train to a firing camp on the coast at Aberforth. We were there for three weeks.

We then moved back to Bere Alston on the edge of Dartmoor. This was a beautiful place and the people were very kind to us. A few months later we were off back to the Bristol area at Westbury on Trym but shortly after that 666 Battery were disbanded and we all went our separate ways.

I was posted to 102 Signals Unit at Silver Hill between Hastings and St Leonards where we felt the full force of the doodle bugs all the time. A few weeks later we moved on to Orford in Suffolk. By this time, I was driving an American Jeep which I was allowed to use off duty although I don't think that the officers were aware of this!

Ted our MT Corporal was very good to us. We were still there when the war ended in June 1945 and Records reminded me that two years earlier, I had volunteered for overseas service. I was moved with others to 8 a camp in East Hampstead Park outside London. A month later, after all our injections, embarkation leave etc, together with about 250 more ATS, I boarded Dunarta Castle not knowing our destination, We threw our pennies on to the quay to ensure we returned, and we set sail for what was rumoured to be Durban, South Africa.

After a week of a very seasick full journey we docked at Naples. Disembarking we were fed, fitted out with KD and despatched by lorry to Caserta. We were only allowed off camp if the person we were going out with signed us out and in again. I was issued with a 3 ton Canadian Dodge to drive and loved it, especially finding my way round Naples area.

If I was on duty at the weekend, I would sometimes transport people going on leave to Rome on the Saturday and spend the night in a room provided by the Nuns in one of the beautiful churches there. On Sunday mornings I would pick up people returning from leave and take them back to camp. If we were off duty we could travel, by lorry, for a shilling (5p) return to Sorrento on Saturday morning. For 2 shillings (10p) you were able to get a bed and all meals at the WVS hostel.

Our unit then moved to Padua, so still driving, I had to find my way about all over again. My friend and I, returning from a journey we were making, once spent a night at Mestre outside Venice. We stayed in a big house which was a sort of stopping off place. There were no locks on the doors, so we slept with "one eye open".

Being a driver, I saw a lot more of Italy than other service people did, Sorrento, Capri and inside the Vatican. I even rode with an American soldier on the back of his motorbike and visited the ruins of Pompeii. We used to dance every night in the Caserta Palace, where the Peace Treaty was signed in 1945. I also saw the balcony in Rome where Mussolini met his gruesome death.

My friend Vi and I were friendly with two Americans who were stationed on the opposite coast of Italy. They said that they flew over to Caserta at weekends which, of course, we did not believe. Eventually they took us to the airfield and in their little 4-seater plane flew us over and around Naples in a splendid air tour.

I was chosen with others to take part in General Alexander's farewell parade. We had to march with a Scottish Pipe Band in front and an American Band behind us which made it difficult to keep time!

In October 1946 I became the wife of one of the men in my unit and during the winter I developed a bad bout of bronchitis. I came off driving and worked in the ration store, nearer to my husband. There were several couples getting married at that time, so the Army equipped and opened a small hotel called Battaglia, run by a sergeant called Steve. Each couple had a bedroom and sitting room and

8,000 per shift. As we became proficient and passed the test to become postal workers first class, our pay was raised from the basic shilling [5p] a day to 14 shillings [70p] a week.

Sometimes we worked on the airmail roads and at other times the surface mail. Mail from all over the UK was collected several times a day from the two railway stations: the LNER Victoria station, now a shopping mall; and the LMS Midland in Carrington St. The postbags were delivered to the appropriate offices: the surface and airmail bags to Hickings, and the parcels bags going to their appropriate offices around the city.

In Hickings, after the mail bags had arrived and had been opened, their contents, consisting of bundles of letters, were sorted into skips. The skips were then taken to the 'roads' as the sorting aisles were called. Each road was made up of about 10 frames, 5 on either side, and each frame consisted of 48 pigeonholes.

The ground floor was mainly given over to surface mail and the first and second floors to a mix of surface and airmail, where each frame was allotted to a particular theatre of war. For instance, there would be several individual frames for the Middle East Force (MEF) Central Mediterranean Force (CMF) South East Asia Command (SEAC) India, North Africa, etc. as well as the Colonies and small islands once coloured pink on our Atlases.

To make identification of the different theatres easier, the frames were distinguished one from another by different coloured labels. Within the frames, the pigeonholes were labelled with the various regiments, unit and squadrons in that particular battle zone, or the many training centres abroad, especially the RAF. Wherever there was a serviceman there would be a Field Post Office close by.

The Royal, and Merchant Navy's mail was dealt with by their own Post Offices. (The responsibility for their mail eventually fell to the Royal Engineers in 1962).

While we were sorting, every so often there would be a shout from a Senior NCO, either Sgt Major Sam Sewell or RSM Cooley, "MEF mail going out, get moving!" This meant that cut-off time for the dispatch of surface or airmail for that Zone was approaching and we would have to work at top speed to ensure that all the mail was sorted, tied into bundles, labelled and placed into skips for the men to collect.

We girls were continually harassed by the male NCOs to work even faster, and woe betides any slackers. I learned a lot of words I had previously never known! Sappers took the skips to the ground floor and sorted the bundles into the relevant mail bags, which were then tied down and sealed with lead seals. These bags would not be opened until they arrived at the Field Post Offices overseas. The bags were then put onto trucks and taken to one of the 2 railway stations in the city.

At the stations, the men had to wait for a specific train and load the sacks into the parcels van and pick up any incoming mail from the civil post offices around the country, and so it started all over again.

Airmail in those days went down to an airfield in Eastleigh, Hampshire, and from there was flown to its destination.

The surface mail went either to the ports of Liverpool or Glasgow, depending on the destination overseas. In the office we were under the command of the REPS officers and NCOs, but out of the office our own ATS Admin Officers were responsible for dealing with our well-being and meting out punishment to those who offended, such as not wearing our caps outside, or failing to salute an officer.

We were under the same regulations as the men, no relaxing of the rules because we were the fairer sex! Sometimes there would be a conflict of opinion between the male and female officers, but generally it worked well.

Some of my colleagues worked in the parcels offices dotted around the city, and like us they worked day and night. Initially some girls found it difficult to flick the parcels into the correct gaping open mouths of the mailbags which were hung on huge frames, and they had to spend some time learning the technique, but, as usual, in the end they were more dexterous than the men. There were also some specialised smaller offices dealing with registered mail, and parcels not properly packed. The latter would be repacked and sent on their way.

The saddest job we did was returning mail to the next-of-kin of servicemen who had lost their lives in the fighting, or on troop ships lost at sea, in particular after the debacle in Malaya and Singapore in early 1942. Mail that had already been on its way by ship had to be returned to Nottingham and we had the sad task of sending it back to the next-of-kin with covering letters. It was a particularly harrowing job.

Another office where the ATS worked with the REPS was the Location's Section, which was highly secret. This was where details of the movement and whereabouts of every unit in the British Army were kept, and only a few people worked there. Information came in from the War Office, the Air Ministry and the Postal Section HQ of the various expeditionary forces. To ensure that such important details were not lost, a duplicate set of the locations was kept elsewhere in Nottingham.

When a draft was about to be sent overseas, the men were given a code known as the 'Draft Indices' which was printed on their

The morning parade in the office was like something out of Dad's Army. I never knew what reply I would get from some of the girls. It certainly would not have gone down well with our female officers, had they been there. As for our male officers, they mostly ignored us so long as we did the work: only the NCOs treated us the same as the men and could be terrifying! We hated 'em!

Our off-duty hours were well catered for. We had our own ATS Fife and Drum Band who marched with us on special parades. They did a good job and were always smartly turned out. We also had a very good dance band formed by a few men who had played in dance bands pre-war. Some of the girls were very good singers and dancers, and along with some of the Sappers, put on really professional concerts for us. There were also Sports Clubs for the men and women, and football and cricket teams. Nottingham had plenty of cinemas and a good theatre to visit, as well as the dance halls, and as two of my friends and I had our bicycles with us we often went for cycle rides out into the lovely Nottinghamshire countryside.

In 1945 we were moved out to a deserted Ack Ack camp at nearby Clifton Village. We were housed in prefabricated iron huts with outside showers, wash basins and toilet facilities. Heating was from a coke stove in the centre of each hut which filled the place with smoke. Sometimes we had no fuel to keep it going and so we were forced to pile greatcoats onto our wooden beds to keep warm at night. This was quite a shock as previously we were in requisitioned houses built just before the war.

In each of our huts there was a Rediffusion loudspeaker and we were lulled to sleep by the velvety tones of a man's voice from AFN Munich, Stuttgart, singing "Out of your Dreams" from Oklahoma. Then an unseen hand would switch it off at about 11pm. We were bussed into work each day, but in February 1946 Nottingham was flooded rendering the roads impassable, so for a couple of days we were unable to get into work. We didn't mind that of course.

After Germany surrendered in 1945 some of the REPS serving there were sent back to England and were transferred to Nottingham. They worked beside us, filling the places of other postal workers going abroad.

The largest contingent of REPS was sent out to the Far East to join the Forces being assembled to recapture Burma, Malaya and our Far East possessions.

As demobilisation got under way after the end of the war, the married girls and older men, some of whom were 60 years old volunteers, began to leave and National Service men arrived to carry on the good work in peacetime.

I was demobilised on March 1st, 1946 after over 3 years in the Army Post Office and went back to my civilian job. Looking back, I can say that all in all it was a satisfying job, perhaps not as dangerous as that carried out by the brave Ack Ack girls.

We have had a thriving Army Post Office Association since 1985 and though the numbers are diminishing, it is still going strong. In June 2004 we celebrated the 60th anniversary of 'D' Day and the Normandy landings and in 2005 the end of the war in Europe and Far East, with several ceremonies in Llandudno where our APA reunions are now held.

We ladies and gentlemen may be old in age but are still young at heart and cherish our comradeship of those sometimes sad, but mostly happy years. I still have friends from those days, and we correspond with, and sometimes visit each other. Happy memories. With special thanks to Captain Simon Fenwick who encouraged me to write this article.

From Lioness No.2 2012

Doris Goss - The Welsh Guards' Girls

There were a dozen or so of us, members of the ATS, stationed at Sandown Park to support the Training Battalion Welsh Guards. We lived in a beautiful house in Esher, which seemed less luxurious when the bombing started, and we had to sleep on mattresses on the ground floor. However, the Welsh Guards had to live in the stables at Sandown Park racecourse, their wartime training centre. We were there to do office work to ensure the smooth running of the Battalion.

The officers in charge were Lt Col Tom Oakshott, Maj F Ellis and Capt Dai Llewellyn. I was a Shorthand Typist and sat on the third row of desks in the Orderly Room (now the top of the racecourse grandstand). The office was controlled by "Ack" Harris, a cheerful, loud voiced Warrant Officer, who kept an eye on everything and everyone.

On Wednesday morning we had Gas Mask Drill, when we had to continue our work wearing a bulky mask. This was particularly hard on Peggy, our telephone Switchboard Operator, who could neither make herself heard not clearly understand the incoming calls when masked. Every Wednesday she would beg Ack harris to let her take the mask off. The more she pleaded the more he insisted she wore it

We had to practice speed writing blocks, writing each letter without taking your pencil from the paper. Difficult on As, B's, F's, G's etc, and as you were working a few letters behind the sound, if you lost the rhythm, you had to miss a few blocks before you could pick it up again.

Then there were Q codes to learn by heart. There were hundreds. Each one meaning a different instruction, so that stations could talk to one another using only 3 letters, Example QSA what is my signal strength? Reply QSA 2 QSV (quick send vies). The first one would then send a series of Vies (di di di da, di di di da) while the second one would tune in better. QTC - have you a message for me? QSU - revert to alternative frequency, and if you did not know it, woe betide you, you had lost your group.

There was also German procedure to learn and then the most dreaded Electricity and Magnetism. The work was all done by men up till then, and we had to take their exams. Of course, if they were out in the front line in India, Burma etc, they had to do their own running repairs. It was, and still is, a complete mystery to me. Ohms' Law etc and circuits, but I managed to pass it by learning it word for word, and as we had engineers on site to repair any faults, we were never called upon to put it into practice. I finished my course first, passing both the B3 and B2 exams and was posted to Beaumanor, and billeted in a requisitioned house called Rose Cottage. I was with another three in the dining room, which had French windows onto the garden, and an open fireplace for which we were always scrounging coal in the winter, there being no other heating. Marjorie came down on the next intake but was billeted at Carats Hay.

We were intercepting German traffic, a very wearying and nerve-wracking job. Your designated group was usually to be found buried under loads of static, loud music and voices. If you were on a group long enough, you got to know his individual style and the rhythm of his sending. Recognising the tone of the morse key was a great help every midnight. They changed their call signs then, and if you recognised your operator with his new call sign, you noted it on your log pad, and the Intelligence Corps could then build up a table of predicted call signs, which lasted for a month, then it all started again.

There was one group, 408kcs, that I was regularly put on. Many groups all operating on the same frequency at the same time. Bedlam. It was covered by four sets, two across the aisle from the other two. You had no time to log the chitchat between them, just pick out a C barred, da di da di da, (start of the message) from the jumble and, as you were writing, keep an eye on the three other sets, to see if their pencils were making the same strokes as yours. If so, you dropped it and picked up another C barred, and so on ad infinitum. Not many people liked covering that frequency, but I did because you were kept busy.

Night duty was the worst, Germans didn't like working at night, and you were forbidden to knit, read or write letters. You had to keep your hand on the dial and sweep the frequency all night for nothing.

When VE Day came most of the ATS were posted away to different Army Units, but I and a few others were selected to stay and learn Japanese Morse, a very different kettle of fish!!! Seventy-six letters or symbols instead of 26, and a completely new set of hundreds of Q codes to learn. We intercepted this from Beaumanor, and I thought that it couldn't be very important if we could pick up the signals from halfway
around the world. I found out from the talks at the reunion weekends at Bedford that it was extremely important. The main cities of Japan communicating with their Foreign Embassies, and obtaining much vital
Information.

When VJ Day came, no let up for us. It was work as usual, as it had been on VE Day. But four of us decided enough was enough. We hitchhiked down to London, joined in all the celebrations in Trafalgar Square, Buckingham Palace etc and in the early hours of the morning were picked up by Troop Carriers and taken to Clapham South Tube
Station where, deep below, we were given a bunk bed for the princely sum of 1 shilling. I still have the ticket. We hitched back the next day, but were immediately put on a charge, fined one day's pay and 3 days cleaning duties or 'fatigues' for missing one shift at Beaumanor. It was worth it and I still have the Charge Sheet, which I nicked from the notice board before they removed it.

The huts at Beaumanor were built in a rough semicircle, with the village green and cricket pitch in the centre. Forbidden to use this village green as a short cut to the greenhouse disguised NAAFI, as it would never have done to have made a footpath right across the middle of the cricket pitch, we had to walk the long way around for our breaks. It was very eerie on night duty, with Red Caps and Alsatian dogs looming up in the darkness. The huts were all camouflaged outside to represent a village, with barns, cottages, shops and even a cricket pavilion with a dummy clock tower on top. They are still there to this day, kitchens and bathrooms added, and bunk beds, chairs and tables installed.

They are used for educational holidays for the schoolchildren of Leicestershire living, as we did in wartime, with rations, sandbag filling, stirrup pumps, gas masks, tin helmets, and of course learning about the Codes. The J is still there on my hut, and WOYG is still to be seen on a door of one of the troop carriers' workshops. The secrecy made us like family, we could only talk about the work to one another and it made us very close, which still persists to this day.

From Lioness No.2 2002

Ann Pope

When war was declared I was 21 years of age, orphaned, and living with my elder sister in Dundee, where I had been born and bred, and from where I had not strayed far. I held a responsible job, classed as a 'reserved' occupation which meant that whilst my friends were called to the forces, one by one, I stood enviously by, confined to a civilian office.

Life was suddenly and violently changed. All windows were blacked out, clothes and food were rationed, fear and sadness pervaded as lists of casualties began to appear in the newspapers. Bombing started, the German pilots navigating along the shining river Tay to find the surrounding airfields. Sirens wailed and people fled to the air raid shelters or hurried on duty in the Home Guard and firefighting posts.

Being a seaport, Dundee was suddenly invaded by foreign sailors in strange uniforms French, Polish, Belgian and Dutch. Submarines docked in the harbour. It was rumoured that the brave Polish sailors never brought back any prisoners from their operations.

The horrors of war, the blitzing of London, the Battle of Britain were made bearable by the inspiring broadcasts of Winston Churchill, avidly listened to by every household. Times were bad.

In 1942 I was released from reserve and, after passing a medical examination, I was drafted into the ATS and sent to Dalkeith Barracks in Edinburgh for basic training known as 'square bashing'. I was given a number, an ill-fitting uniform, allotted a bed in a large barrack room, vaccinated, inoculated, drilled and tested for ability. Everything was suddenly communal, and I was a very raw recruit. But we were all in the same boat and soon made friends. Meals were eaten in a huge mess room, in the corner of which was a huge bucket wherein to scrape the leftover crumbs from one's plate. By the bucket stood a watchful officer and once, when I brought a half-eaten meal for disposal, this officer, clearly outraged, demanded to know 'Why have you not eaten this good food?" I pointed to a large snail on a lettuce leaf. "You should be ashamed of wasting so much food' was the reprimand. Never again did I complain.

Finally, having been tamed and conditioned for life in the army we were each informed of our fate. I learned I had been chosen for the work of 'special wireless operator' but no one seemed to know what that entailed. So, it was with some trepidation that I set off alone for New Brighton where I joined other members of a new squad.

In the morning we were issued with tickets marked 'Reykjavik' which caused great consternation until we were told this was to 'fool the enemy' in case of an accident at sea and we were bound for the Isle of Man. I, who had never been far from home, thought this was an overseas posting!

After a stormy crossing of the Irish Sea we disembarked looking strangely green and unsteady on our legs. We were billeted in a row of empty hotels along the seafront at Douglas. I was in 'Lancaster' and soon settled down to a course of training for our future task, that of intercepting wireless communications from the German Army, thus providing vital information to the hallowed Bletchley Park, the secret headquarters of Intelligence.

I was thrilled and eager and with the rest of the squad worked and studied with a will to complete the intensive training course set for us. The island was beautiful, set in an emerald sea and we had it all to ourselves no tourists, no rationing, just the inhabitants and interned Germans and Italians and us. The Germans were hidden away inland and we never saw them, but the Italians used to watch us from behind their wire fences as we marched along at 'attention' and with Latin gallantry they called out 'Hello pretty girl'. We dared not laugh or turn to look for we had been drilled to Guards standard by Sergeant Major Paddy Quee with such strictness that, if in the wind a hat blew into the sea, not a muscle moved. We had been trained to wait for the command 'at ease' before daring to show signs of life or even death!

We spent the next months studying hard and when we passed our exams and were deemed ready I had the offer to stay on in the island as an instructor but, full of ambition to go 'on ops' and win the war single handed, I chose to move on. I was sent to the Y station at Garats Hay in Leicestershire to join the operators at Beaumanor on 'A Watch'. Then I discovered the fascinating and exciting work of the interceptor. I am to this day grateful for the chance. We worked in eight-hour shifts in huts (very draughty round the legs), each of us in front of a huge business-like wireless set, each with a prescribed task but not knowing the location or importance of our quarry. We sat in pairs, listening and taking down German messages sometimes through loud interference designed to thwart us. Our worksheets were collected throughout the shift and spirited along the channels of classification and urgency, eventually to reach Bletchley Park. We could only guess at the value of our work.

Thanks to the capture of the famous Enigma machine we were well briefed for the approach of D Day. What excitement when we arrived on duty to be told 'this is it!'. And all happened as predicted as if by magic.

On occasions, one of us would be given the task of 'search', trolling the airways for signals of particular interest, and on such an order I had one of the most memorable experiences of my life. Searching round the dial I recognised a very urgent signal which I reported at once to my superior. Suddenly the room was charged with excitement. 'Hold that signal at all costs' I was instructed and so held on like grim death to enable it to be traced and, to my surprise, I was thanked heartily. When I returned to work the next day, I was met by an anxious 'Can you find that station again, it has been lost'. I did have the good luck to find it and everyone seemed pleased and relieved. The result was a summons to the Colonel's Office to be thanked and congratulated on saving many lives. I had found Rommel's headquarters, just outside Paris! I walked on air for days, but the frustrating thing was that, because of the vital necessity for secrecy, I was unable to tell anyone of my good luck.

I look back with pride on those historic times in Y Group which I would not have missed for anything in the world.

From Lioness No.2 2002

Charlotte (Betty) Webb MBE - From Bletchley to the Pentagon

The year 1941 is a long time ago, but I still have vivid memories of my service as a member of the Auxiliary Territorial Service (ATS), attached to the Intelligence Corps at Bletchley Park (the Government Code & Cypher School) and at the Pentagon.

Having signed the Official Secrets Act to the effect that I would not divulge anything which I heard, saw or read about within Bletchley Park in the course of my duties, my next thought was "How do I do that?" so I said to myself "Betty, you must comply – just do it".

In the Mansion at Bletchley Park, Major Ralph Tester had some offices above the Ballroom, and it was there that I was shown my job of registering the incoming Morse code messages as they came in from our signal (Y) stations, in their hundreds. The only part of those messages that were in the clear was the date and the callsign. The rest was simply groups of five letters or figures, all sent out in Morse code. Every message was carefully recorded on a card index so that the code breakers could refer easily to any particular one. I found this rather boring at the time but now realise that all the less interesting tasks were VITAL to the whole process of code breaking.

One rather tricky task I was given was to type out an officer's scribblings of translated messages so that they made sense because he not only wrote from top to bottom on a page (as you do!) but then he would turn the paper round sideways and every possible which way – you name it. Maybe he liked to save paper! All very trying.

My most interesting duty was paraphrasing translated Japanese messages for onwards transmission, to whom or where I knew not. That was why I was posted to the Pentagon (May/June 1945) to continue paraphrasing Japanese traffic after the end of the war in Europe. At Bletchley Park the work schedule was long and tiring, especially for those employed on the machines. 0800 to 1600, 1600 to midnight and midnight to 0800, the latter being the most draining. Most of us found that having a meal at 0200 upset the digestive system!

Until January 1944 civilians, Army and Air Force personnel were billeted with families in the neighbour villages and towns and Women's Royal Navy Service members lived mainly in mansions such as Woburn Abbey (the country seat of the Dukes of Bedford). After that date the Army and Air Force personnel were housed in a newly built camp within walking distance of Bletchley Park. The Bletchley Park team was made up of men and women from all walks of life – landed gentry, aristocrats, university alumnae, well known figures and a mix of ordinary people like myself. I found this mix of people incredibly interesting – an education in itself especially for me after my quiet childhood in the depths of the English countryside. In free time we had the opportunity to join in many recreational events such as the Bach Choir, a gramophone group, a madrigal society, musical evenings and occasional plays – all organised by inmates. It amazes me how those taking part had the energy to fit in all this social programme with their onerous workload, but they did and I am sure it maintained a healthy balance between work and play. Also, there were dances especially after the group arrived from the USA bringing food and drink that we had been dreaming about for such a long time.

When we all moved into the camp, we were accommodated in freshly built, very basic huts meant for 18 people but often having to house more. We had a bed, a barrack box, a few hooks and a shelf each for our personal belongings. Heating was by two coke stoves, which gave off some pretty awful fumes, so we avoided lighting them unless absolutely necessary. Sometimes, face flannels would be frozen stiff overnight. The ablutions were VERY basic. We stood on duck boards (wooden slats) at the wash basins and there were baths but as water was rationed, we had to queue for our turn – usually sitting on a concrete floor. We did not complain - we were a happy lot. After all we had a very special job to do.

Never in my wildest dreams could I have expected this posting. The war in Europe was over so I expected demob and home. Oh no not for me, my section head called me saying, "Sorry Betty, you are to be posted to the Pentagon". So I went off to the holding unit in London to await instructions to join a ship for the USA. Due to a mess up (not mine) I missed the ship and eventually travelled by Sunderland flying boat from Poole Harbour via Ireland and Newfoundland into Baltimore and after 22 hours arrived by train in Washington D.C.

The enormous roads – everything really, took my breath away especially the Pentagon building itself with its 32,000 staff and the central court - big enough for General Eisenhower and his entourage to drive round in tanks when he returned from Europe where he had been Supreme Commander of the Allied Forces until the end of the conflict there. Security in the Pentagon was understandably very tight. We had to show passes and identity both at the doors from the concourse leading to the ramps and again in order to be allowed to enter the offices we were assigned to. And, if you bought shopping during the lunch break, the guards searched it before we went back into the offices (very embarrassing when you have bought some nice undies).

As at Bletchley Park, I was a minor cog in a major wheel and therefore not privy to the details of the whole operation. However, in 14th October 1978 (the veil of secrecy being lifted in July 1975) I attended the first gathering entitled "Quite Special Intelligence Reunion" addressed by Professor S H Hinsley OBE, President of St John's College Cambridge, followed by a discussion chaired by Brigadier R P Erskine-Tulloch. After that almost every year further reunions were held where attendees were invited to give their stories of their service at BP and/or the outstations, and through these stories along with referring to the many publications of the subject, I have now been able to piece together the jigsaw.

In September 1994, quite by chance, I was invited to give a talk about my part in the BP story to a Probus Club in Norfolk. I was petrified but they seemed to enjoy it. Lately the public's interest has grown and the importance of its role in winning World War 2 has been more widely acknowledged. So far, I have been privileged to address over 150 clubs and groups, giving them an outline of the importance of the work carried out at the Government Code & Cypher School at Bletchley Park and encouraging them to visit our National Museum and Archive (Home of the Codebreakers) which is now a first-class heritage attraction.

Written by Charlotte Webb MBE for this book.
See images in centre pages

Irene Burman - Happy memories of Edinburgh, Camberley & Windsor

In 1942, I did my initial training at Glen Parva Barracks in Leicester and my most vivid memory was having to do PT in our khaki knickers! I then went to No 1 Motor Transport Training Centre at Camberley and already being a driver, I trained to be an instructor. My first posting was to No 3 MTTC Dreghorn Barracks in Edinburgh where we took over from the men of the RASC who went to Burma.

We trained on 30 cwt Bedford lorries that had frame covered canopies which jutted out 6" either side behind the cabins. The students never allowed for this and going along Princes Street the side mirrors were often taken off the trams many an accident report I had to make!
How different Princes Street looks now.

After a year, No.3 MTTC was disbanded and I went back to Camberley where I spent the next three years driving, instructing and as a spell as a mechanic. We had a 16-task system which I had to teach the students, each on the care and maintenance of the vehicles.

On a theory paper, one question was, "What do you do if your lorry gets stuck under a bridge?' One student answered, 'Jack up the bridge'!

When the students passed their driving tests, they were allowed to drive through Windsor Great Park on their own. This was usually on a Saturday morning, but they had to leave their logbooks behind as I had to make them up for the week. Two students hadn't left them and, as I was on a weekend pass, I thought I'd better go and find them. I had a motorbike to do convoy training, so off I went on my bike through the park and, not being able to find them and coming to a sharp bend, my bike went up a bank and I was thrown into the middle of the road. An American soldier who was quietly taking pictures of the Castle came to my rescue and taking off my crash helmet his first words were "Gosh you're a Gal"! Luckily, I was not hurt and was able to ride my bike back to camp without the logbooks!

Her Majesty the Queen completed her ATS training whilst I was there and when the course ended, she was presented with a clock made in wood by the workshop people; on one side of the clock was a truck and on the other a field ambulance. I often wondered if it ever stood on her mantelpiece.

After we disbanded at Camberley in 1945, we had to clear the camp and we found a few bicycles that were left behind so we loaded them into a field ambulance and sent them to a worthy cause.

I was then posted to Southampton to the RASC as a mechanic and I did inspections on vehicles and lorries up to 5 tons and on test drives I found it very hard going with crash gear boxes and no power steering! My granddaughter Hannah is now serving in the British Army and was at Sandhurst at the same time as Prince William. It was wonderful to attend Sovereign's Parade and to see Her Majesty the Queen take the salute at her grandson's commissioning. Hannah has just completed a posting to Afghanistan where she served in the front line with the Grenadier Guards. I am so proud of her.

From Lioness 2008 No.1

Dorothy Foster - Memories of the Middle East

At the outbreak of war, I was a shop assistant in Brighton and did my share of fire-watching on the rooftop over the shop. With a friend we decided to join the Forces if we could be kept together. We joined the ATS having first tried the WAAF, but they would not guarantee we would be kept together.

We were attached to the Royal Corps of Signals and were very proud of our badge. We were trained at Chester for six weeks learning about electricity and magnetism, how to repair Field Telephones and work the current type of telephone switchboard. After training our first employment was in the gun operations room doing plotting with 34 AA Brigade at Sutton Coldfield, Birmingham from 1941 to mid-1944.

Returning from sick leave I was informed that I was fit enough to be conscripted to be posted overseas which was quite a shock. I spent a few weeks in the camp awaiting further instructions and eventually one morning on the Notice Board we were all informed of our destination - Palestine, The Holy Land. One group was bound for Haifa and I was delighted to find myself in the other group bound for Jerusalem.

To a girl who had always had a connection with the local Church in Brighton to find myself going to such a Holy place was a relief and overcame the original disappointment of having been conscripted to go overseas.

By this time, I had been promoted to Corporal, was a 37 Supervisor at the GHQ switchboard in the King David Hotel and was billeted at Allenby Barracks on the Bethlehem Road. As we were in a relatively hot country, we were issued with KD uniforms (which needed considerable starching and pressing), decent underwear and stocks, sandals and short socks - what a difference from the UK khaki uniforms!

So started a quite amazing couple of years. Within a few days of arriving at Allenby Barracks the Sergeants invited "us girls" to a party and some eight or ten of us sat around a table in the corner wondering what the evening would bring. At another table was a group of "civilians" and the Sergeant Major introduced us. It transpired that the "civilian" who invited me to dance was a Palestine Policeman but because he was in CID HQ in Jerusalem, he always wore civilian clothes. My "civilian* named John took me around and about so that I saw so many exciting places and "happenings". The Holy Sepulchre, the Stations of the Cross and a multitude of interesting things and places in the Old City; dancing under the stars and within trellised gardens of tavernas. The Church of Nativity in Bethlehem and the local shops selling all sorts of mother-of-pearl covered bibles/prayer books etc.

Also, further afield with a late-night visit to the Dead Sea and waiting to see the sun rise over the Jordanian mountains across the Dead Sea. Even floating in that saltiest of water which in those days was much higher than nowadays. Within six weeks I became engaged to John - something which the ATS Officer confronted me with and wanted assurance that this was "genuine" - it certainly was, and we have since enjoyed and celebrated our golden and diamond wedding ceremonies! I am often asked to tell about some of the more bizarre happenings and one in particular seems to hold the attention no matter how often it is heard. Allenby Barracks was situated on the road from Bethlehem to Jerusalem and if I was travelling into Jerusalem to meet with John, I would catch the Bus (No 7 I believe), with a Jewish driver. These buses had a long seat beside the window just inside the door and opposite the drivers position and it was always my intention to sit on this seat as near to the door as possible just in case I wanted a quick exit for any reason. On one occasion on the seat immediately inside the door were two Arabs, nothing unusual thought I, and sat down. The one next to me was quiet but the other was arguing furiously with the driver in Arabic so I was quite ignorant of the subject of the conversation. Two or three stops after I had boarded, the Arab who had been speaking so forcibly stood up, caught hold of his friend and carried him off the bus and carefully laid him down on the pavement, still berating the bus driver. Now I understood - his friend was quite dead! I had been sitting next to a dead Arab man, for about ten minutes! When I arrived at my stop and got off John said, "Whatever is the matter? You look quite scared". When I told him, he almost collapsed with laughter and then explained that probably the reason for the argument was that the live Arab was not going to pay a fare for his friend as he considered him not to be a passenger but luggage!

It was not all fun and laughter, however. There were some hair-raising times. You never knew from day to day what might happen, a bombing, a shooting and one day I recall counting up to 20 coffins, all of Palestine Policemen being carried to the Cemetery on Mount Zion.

Another day John and I were in the cinema in the German Colony, Jerusalem and the film (a Western, I think) included a lot of shooting. As usual in such circumstances we sat at the rear of the cinema, often with other friends, but it was not until we left the cinema that we realised that there was actual shooting going on outside. With bullets ricocheting around us we literally laid down in the gutter, crawled along to the end of the road and quickly entered another friend's premises which were above the local Police Station.

One other memory will always remain. A comparatively small, though elderly, Arab walking down the street carrying a grand piano on his back - true. From time to time one witnessed similar strange and interesting things and looking back 60 years what one remembers most vividly are the good and happy times even the celebrations on VE day when nearly everybody had rather more to drink than usual!

My time came to go home to the UK and John's contract had also expired but he had no knowledge of how long it might be before he was able to go on UK leave. I travelled to Ismalia only to find that no troopship was waiting for me and that it might be some weeks before a sailing date was available. I considered that being in Egypt and John in Jerusalem was not ideal so requested to go back to Jerusalem. I was told that I could only have a rail warrant for one way and opted for the return from Jerusalem to Egypt. The only way back to Jerusalem was to go to the entry/exit point where the Military Police

Inspected everyone's "papers". I asked if I could wait for transport to Jerusalem and given the OK and waited. A Lieutenant in the Royal Signals came in for clearance to Jerusalem and I asked him if he would be good enough to let me accompany his convoy. He agreed and so I crossed over the Sinai desert in an Army convoy.

As soon as I arrived in Allenby Barracks in Jerusalem, I telephoned John who was amazed that I was back. That trip was an experience, crossing the desert at night needs to have been done to understand the thrill but anxiousness which it carried with it.

Eventually we both travelled back to the UK. I arrived home first and, as agreed, visited John's parents in Oxford. Whilst I was there a radio announcement informed us that a ship had docked carrying a mixture of personnel for the end of the War celebrations and a number of Palestine Policemen. John's father was sure that he would be home in a day or so and, sure enough two days later - a knock on the door. I was ushered into the pantry and after John's parents welcomed him back, I came out and completed the ideal homecoming. A marriage was arranged in Brighton very quickly and "That's that".

From Lioness 2007 No.2

Doreen Walden - Behind the Wire (or Exodus)

During the last two years of the British Mandate for Palestine, I was a member of Palestine Coy ATS in Jerusalem. It was a small company, comprised of about 60 girls, and the only ATS company left in Palestine. Half of the unit were in Signals and we manned the switchboard at the King David Hotel on a 24-hour basis, it being HQ for the whole of the country.

Most of us were volunteers from GHQ Cairo, seeking refuge in the Promised Land, though after the closure of GHQ Cairo, a few arrived from the Canal Zone in Egypt. We were billeted in Allenby Barracks on the outskirts of the city in what had, in days of yore, been the married quarters of the Army personnel, a pleasant camp, though now surrounded by barbed wire. It was manned by Arab labour so there were no "extra duties", except in the Company Office where we had to do the occasional evening stint to check everyone into camp at 11 pm.

We were a fairly cohesive bunch and, being a small unit, everyone knew each other. After the blowing up of the King David on the beach. Sadly, for the camera man, the tide crept in behind us and we were cut off from the shore in water 12 inches deep. We were in swimsuits which was OK but the small photographer in his best suit, and carrying a large camera, had to be carried back to dry land, with much laughter.

In 1941 volunteers were needed for radio location training. I volunteered and was sent to Oswestry on a six-week course. I became Number 1 and joined 513 MDX H.A.A. Battery at Newcastle 'Tyne Johnny".

From there we went to firing camps in Scotland and North Wales for further training. It was pretty tough and very active during the raids.

Maintenance work on the power unit was no joke during the winter but it had to be done. At one time we were issued with fur coats with no zips or buttons. You had to put them over your head like a jumper. They were very claustrophobic and a hazard when rushing to get on duty during an air raid. They were soon re-called. There was plenty of good company, friendship and NAAFI entertainment.

In 1943 volunteers were wanted for the Military Police, guess who volunteered? I did my police training at Blackdown and Aldershot, then posted to Manchester and later to Northampton. My duties were varied in the extreme. I was part of the Guard of Honour when HRH The Princess Royal visited Manchester and I also acted as escort to POWs landing at Tilbury.

Early in 1944 my unit was due to be posted to Egypt. My mother begged me to apply for a transfer as I had one brother wounded who had been taken prisoner of war at Arnhem. Also, my younger brother had been wounded at Monte Casino and was in hospital in Italy. I got my transfer and was sent to the RAPC in Maryleborne Road, London. After a while RAPC was transferred to Whitchurch. I was demobbed from there on 3rd December 1945.

After the war I worked as a civil servant and then for the NHS. I retired at 60 and my daughter decided that I needed a hobby and bought me a spinning wheel. I have learned to spin, dye and weave and have created numerous items for my family and for exhibition with the Spinners and Weavers Guild. I am now nearly eighty-six and still spinning, a little slower, but the wheel keeps turning.

Lioness 2006 No.1
See images in centre pages

Pat Goodman - Service with 70th (Searchlight) Regiment

In the week of the Munich Crisis - September 1938, I and with many others, queued up in Procton Park in Brighton, where I was living at the time, in order to enlist in the ATS. When I reached the grizzled old First World War Sergeant he said, "You can't join because you are in the ARP" pointing at my badge. Undeterred, I went to the back of the queue took my badge off and was duly accepted.

During the next twelve months we met weekly for drill and instructing and were formed into two platoons with some being made up to Sergeant with immediate effect.

That summer a few of us were selected to join the Royal Sussex Regiment on their summer camp. Initially, I had not been selected. However, one girl was unable to go and I managed to get into her uniform so I went. It was a tight fit - but I made it. We went for a week and I just loved it.

I was W/2546 Volunteer Goodman known as "Goody". Our CO had served in the Great War. Initially we met in the Royal Engineers' Drill Hall. Later we transferred to the Drill Hall of the 459 Battery, 70th (Sussex) Searchlight Regiment RA TA. We continued happily throughout that year, though the war clouds were definitely gathering.

One day in late August, on my return from the office, my mother handed me an OHMS envelope. I was told to report to the Drill Hall the next day. My mother was very anxious (as if I was going to be thrown into the front line she knew not where). The day dawned and I was so excited. Joining the rest of the Company we spent the whole of the day having medicals etc. The Southdown Coaches were waiting to transport us. Finally, we were all off and travelled to our destination which turned out to be Ditchling only 5 miles away!

We were billeted in the village and spent our days under canvas except when we were in the cookhouse. This was part of an old chicken house with a field kitchen with those great metal drums for potatoes etc smoking away.

It was a very wet autumn, so we lived in wellies. Our CO said we would only be there for a few weeks then all go home. Our pay would be 30/- a week. We didn't go home, and our pay turned out to be ls/4d a day. Initially we had signed on for 4 years then when that expired, we were asked if we wished to be released or to stay on for the duration. Of course, we all opted to remain for the latter.

On Sunday 3rd September 1939, I was at the village crossroads on sentry duty - the CO was in the office in a nearby cottage. Most of the villagers were at Church when a policeman came by on his bike. He was blowing his whistle and had a placard on his

I passed out as Sgt D.C. (Detachment Commander) and given my Detachment. My site was Streatham Sports Pavilion. Our huge S/L slap in the middle of houses. Don't know how the residents managed to get any sleep. Night-time being the time we were out in action.

I shall never forget our first 'Take Post'. We were now on our own – a handful of girls and I do mean girls, 18 years old (that being my age the rest around that). Illuminating our first German plane was mind blowing; we didn't have time to feel scared. Then the guns opened up on our target and that was that, bits of debris flying everywhere.

Our other Detachments were scattered around the capital, Morden, Clapham, Mitcham and Wimbleton where our T.H.Q. was.

We were sorry to leave our comfy site, but it was decided to move the whole Regt comprising 495 Battery, 301 and 342 further away from the capital, with the aim of stopping the German planes en route, before they hit London, but now we liaised with Fighter Command.

Our fighters would shoot down German planes once we illuminated them. We never found our life boring! The German fighters would dive down and strafe our very powerful beam. My site was now situated beside (of all places B.H.Q.) Swakeleys, Ickenham, Middx. This meant we were always under the watchful eye of our O.C. Major Soloman.

I was then promoted to Troop Sgt at our T.H.Q. Harefield Middx. Wasn't long there when the Major asked if I would come into B.H.Q. and be the Sgt Major. The female Sgt Major was retiring, the male Sgt Major was being posted and I was to take over from both (aged 21!!). Sgt Majors at this time were admin trained, but I was operational. It made sense, and I accepted.

Before I left T.H.Q. a buzz-bomb dropped near the Camp, flattened a farmhouse close by killing the farmer and his wife. They had been so good to us, allowing us the use of their phone. The blast had sucked all the walls out of our Camp. Luckily no-one was hurt. Gen Sir Fred Pile came to visit with us and to survey the damage. I found him easy to talk to.

My new job entailed going around all our sites (495 Battery) and instructing. Whilst at Greenford we had our first initiation into coping with a buzz-bomb. We hadn't a clue what to do with this terrifying object. Our expensive equipment was useless. The guns were useless. These flying bombs flew so low, guns couldn't cope. We knew we were in great danger, but it missed us and crashed on a supply depot full of armaments and many, many A.T.S. In the meantime, we still had to cope with the bombers coming over.

I was in London when the first rocket was dropped on the city. We all thought that a gasometer had blown up! These were massive bombs and again nothing could stop them.

We as a Regiment were the first in the field to work with radar equipped Searchlights and the only all women Searchlight Regiment in the world! We 'took action' in all weathers at all hours. Sometimes when we had had an exhausting night in action, we would be called out once more, but this time not enemy action. We had 3 mins to get up, get the huge generator going to supply power. No need of radar this time. Our orders were to illuminate our Searchlight beam towards a given aerodrome. This enabled very badly shot up B26s American Flying Fortress to get safely back. They used our beam as a flight path! I have often wondered if they realised just who worked this massive beam!

Lioness 2018 No.2

Hetty Eames - Searchlights & Footlights

I was called up for service in the ATS in 1942. My first posting was to Pontefract in Yorkshire. After much training and a spell at Leeds University, where I passed all my exams for the Searchlight Regiment, I was posted to Rhyl in Wales along with 200 other ATS.

We were sent to a very large camp called Bodelwydon, near Rhyl. Twenty of us were separated from the rest and trained apart. We were called the special 20. However, my time at Bodelwydon was one of the best of my life.

Whilst I was there, an officer called Brian Price, the actor PC 49 of TV fame, put on a big show in the camp theatre. He asked for recruits to join the show, so I volunteered and was one of his dancing girls. He managed to put on a wonderful show just using the troops. He even sent to London for our costumes, they were beautiful and arrived in a very large Theatre Basket. One number was Spanish, the other Russian, a wonderful show. Brian tried to get me into ENSA but I couldn't be released after being chosen for the special 20.

From Bodelwydon we were sent to Rickmansworth in Hertfordshire. We were then put into groups for Searchlight sites around the London area. I was stationed at a site behind the King's Arms on the Al in Borehamwood. I also took a PE course, as there had to be a PE instructor on every site, I passed all exams.

Lioness 2002 No.2

Dorothy Leed - Where Was I?

Born on 25 November 1921 in Cathcart, South side of Glasgow. I moved to the village of Eaglesham on the edge of the Fenwick Moors in early 1939, this is the village where Hess made his crash landing, we heard and saw his plane go over our house and the aircraft landed in a field nearby I was there at the site soon after and actually got some small parts from the plane!

All this before my call up papers in the Summer of 1942. Training at Glencorse Barracks Dalkeith then posted to HQ CMD (Central Midland District) Royal Leamington Spa to join G Corps Intelligence Branch working on maps, Kings Regs etc and typing until early 1944 when things were changing and I was posted to join HQ MWD (the new MidWest District at Shrewsbury.

I had nowhere to go for a time strangely, then "report to Camp Commandant at HWQ MWED Shrewsbury". He had no place for me! No one had, but I got a desk and typewriter in "Q" at last and involved in moves and transport.

Then out of the blue one day, I was called to the Camp Commandant's office, there, he said "speak to no one, a car is outside to take you to a place of work of vital importance". Sure, enough a "FANY" driver shut me in the canvas back of a jeep on an unknown journey. I reckoned I was still in Shrewsbury and I knew the feel of roads etc.

We stopped and she appeared to help me out. I had no idea where, as the car was reversed into an enclosed "tunnel" corridor. I was greeted by an officer who took me to a "cubicle" containing a desk and typewriter. "Have you had tea?", "No.", "Come this way". I was led along this man-made tunnel, put into a cubicle with table and chair. Tea was brought to me. The officer came and said "come you are not required for 4 hours" and put me in a cubicle with a bed!

After that it was an NCO who escorted me back to the typewriter cubicle, who gave me a Top-Secret envelope which contained my "work". You had a bell to ring for help or to go to the toilet as you were escorted. I never saw anyone else but presumed there were other typists along these corridors. From the constant darkness and strange smell, I took it I was in a crypt or cellar of a church etc. I never found out where or who else was involved.

I was there for several days and nights. You ate or drank when told, you worked when told and you slept to order! I gathered, roughly from the contents of the work sheets it was orders for movements of troops, supplies and all sorts etc. I knew the code names of exercise and code name of beaches; places were OS numbers for maps! Finally, a thank you from officer and put back in jeep. The driver knew my billet address. Arrived, helped out night, stars out "what time is it?" 4 am. I can't get in I have no key! We threw stones at the window of my mate's bedroom. Luckily, she heard and opened. She and the rest of the office (and the landlady) all concerned for me. I had disappeared so mysteriously and all I was allowed to say was I had been doing some top secret typing. I know not where.

Only when D Day was reported could I then reveal I had been giving the orders for movement of troops and for supplies to them.

Later the GOC in C Western Command Lt Gen B G Horrocks came to the HQ to personally thank me. I had been picked out for my speed and accuracy of typing apparently!

Lioness 2005 No.2

Winifred Goodbody

My friend Stella and I joined the ATS on Thursday 9th September 1938, the day King George VI proclaimed that the Auxiliary Territorial Service was formed. We went straight from work at Stoke Newington to the recruiting office at Park Lane Tottenham opposite the Spurs Football Ground. The Sergeant asked me when I was born? I said 4 April 1920. He did not believe me and said, "You only look 16. Have you got your birth certificate with you?" I asked him if he carried his birth certificate with him? He said no, I said I don't either. We had forms sent to us and had to pay 6d for a Doctor's Certificate to say we were in good health.

We started training at Hornsey Drill Hall North London. The Drill Hall was in the process of being built so it was a case of mud everywhere. The roof was open to the sky and had no doors, so it was cold inside. After a few weeks the roof was on and the doors appeared. We attended every Wednesday evening, parading under the watchful eye of The Regimental Sergeant Major from the Grenadier Guards who the officers called Henry. He was over 6 feet tall and broad. He soon had us marching around and called me out to be the Right Marker! We carried on training every Wednesday evening. During the summer of 1939 we were issued with our long overalls, most of us could not see our feet when we put them on. We were not allowed to cut any off so we had 8inch hems.

September 27,1939. We met up with Hendon Platoon on Paddington Station to start life in the Army at Central Ammunition Depot Bramley. We were lined up when the Section Leader was told to look for a girl with an honest face, the same Section Leader who issued my uniform. She kept looking at me until the officer came to inspect, "What's your name child?", "Goody Ma'am", "right I want you to look after this case, it's a typewriter". When we got off the train at Paddington the Officer called out has that child got the case, I replied "yes Ma'am". Same enquiry getting off the train at Reading and getting on the train at Reading and getting off the train at Bramley. We then boarded a coach to Bramley Camp. When we got inside the camp the Officer said, "Where's that girl with the money?" Blank looks all around. The Officer then said, "You girl. You have the case of money" I said "No I have got the typewriter, the Officer replied no you're carrying £200, the pay for the next few months. Remember we were only paid 9 shillings a week.

I was a storewoman, and spent six weeks learning to be an amendment clerk and stocktaking in HM Stationery Office, which meant I was locked in. These documents had not seen the light of day since around 1919.I asked for a duster.

Every morning I was allowed out for a break, I was asked how I was, I said "Not so dusty" so the name stuck! I was transferred temporarily to the Ammunition School of Instruction but stayed for over 3 years. I was in charge of all the books, 5 in a set for the Ammunition Examiners' Courses, Ammunition Storemans' Courses and Officers' Courses. I had to help the ledger clerk at times. I used to help in the laboratory and had the only pair of brown laboratory shoes marked Dusty. I also had the job of cleaning the wonderful collection of shells built up over the years at the school by Mr Lee.

I was a trained first aider, stretcher bearer and fire NCO. This meant our gang was on duty at least one night a week. We used to sit on top of the air raid shelters and watch the German planes fly over us to London and pray that our families were safe. Being fire NCO meant I was taking fire drill every evening after work.

When Princess Mary, The Princess Royal (the King's Sister) came to open our new camp, Nissen huts and ablution block, we were the Guard of Honour for Her Royal Highness. ATS Guard of Honour

We had to keep our rooms spotless to show new girls how to clean etc and our room was chosen to be inspected by Her Royal Highness. My friend, Vi now a Sgt was in the escorting party. The Princess wanted to know what polish we used to get such a shine, Vi said "Issue polish, Ma'am and Dusty's balaclava!" which took some explaining.

The CSM had caught me one day. "Goodbody; you haven't brought any wool yet?" I said I wasn't any good at knitting, so I was given large size knitting needles and bundle of khaki yarn which was in reality dyed dish cloth yarn and a pattern for a balaclava. I knitted and knitted, and the more I knitted the longer the garment became. It would have covered a two-year-old completely. What to do with it was the problem until Vi said we could wrap it around and around the bumper (floor polisher). So, we did, hence the highly polished floor. Princess Mary saw the funny side.

On one occasion we all went home on Easter leave, I had my arm in a slin as I had chemical blisters on my hand, Gwen and Amy had collided with each other on their bikes so Amy's knee was heavily bandaged as was Gwen's ankle, Duffy had just come out of hospital so was very white and shaky, Ivy had hurt her hand and Vi had an eye patch. We were getting off the train at Paddington when an elderly lady said, "oh poor girls they must have come home from overseas", it spread amongst the passengers waiting to board the train, who parted leaving space for us to walk off the platform. Vi nudged me and said, "don't you dare say otherwise". Everyone clapped us, our faces red.

Lioness 2005 No.2

Mabs Merritt - Life in a Nissan Hut

Day began with Reveille at 6.30 am, the 0/Sgt bellowing "Come on, let's have Yer outside in 10 minutes". Having crawled outside we would be subjected to 20 minutes of sheer cruelty, jumping up and down, arms flailing all over the place. PE was followed by a mad rush to the ablutions, this was a delightful building situated at the extreme end of the ATS billets. It comprised of a line of wash basins, 4 bath cubicles and toilets facing these. The floor was concreted with duckboards lying on top. The only heating was the water that came from the taps, and that was not always as heated as one would expect, therefore your ablutions took only the minimum of time.

Breakfast 7.30 followed by bed barracking, which meant folding your sheets and blankets in a certain way. Each blanket had a narrow label on which was your name and number, having folded the said blankets and sheets in the correct fashion, one blanket would be folded around sheets and the other two blankets, the label showing and strictly in line. This bundle of bedding went to the top of the bed, next went your respirator and steel helmet, below that, water bottle, followed by tin plate, mug and knife, fork and spoon. Last of all were your walking out shoes, all polished of course. Dress uniforms were hung up in front of your greatcoat, the sleeves of both had to be tucked into the back, buttons and brasses had to be gleaming at all times.

8.15 am 0/Officer would inspect barrack rooms and at 8.30 we had to be outside for Battery Parade and inspection by the CO. You were then detailed off to your various duties.

The operational sections for the day would proceed to the Gun Park or Command Post, where maintenance on instruments would take place. These sections would be on Standby and Look Out. The sections not on standby would be doing fatigues or drills, some would be in the cookhouse or cleaning windows, white washing stones or anything that didn't move. Those unlucky perishers who had committed some trivial offence would be detailed to clean the ablutions these were "lawi loo loos" and of course there were those who spent a shift peeling spuds.

The best fatigues where when on guard duty, this kept you away from prying eyes, the Guardroom being on the perimeter of the camp. Most fatigues would finish at lunch time and usually meant you would have a pass out from 1400 to 2359. Those on pass would be inspected before being given this pass.

Having got out of the camp, you would then either walk through Porthkerry Woods to the delightful town of Barry, or walk to the end of the lane which was about a mile of desolation to the main road, hopefully to catch a bus, or thumb a lift, be it private car, military lorry, dust cart, coal lorry. We've been in them all.

The nearest town was Barry. What can one say about Barry? Not a lot! Here was the station, the flea pit, some chapels and Thomson Street which was out of bounds.

The nearest town of any size or substance was Cardiff, which offered more and varied diversions. Sometimes we were allowed 24-hour passes. We had a pretty little scam going we would get platform tickets in Cardiff station, board the London train, give the tickets up at Paddington, when the volume of passengers passing through the ticket collectors didn't have time to notice. We would do the same thing coming back. We would catch the midnight train back to Cardiff and then puffing billy back to Rhoose and be in camp in time for roll call.

There were times when the C/O would be bloodyminded and stop all passes for operational exercises. The RAF and Navy co-operated in these and they would last all day and at the conclusion of an exercise the O/C, one Major Bishop would assess. The old devil was never satisfied and forever reminding us that the Civilian population needed and expected our protection, Yeah! Yeah! Yeah!

Things did get hairy sometimes when there was a spate of Air Raids and we would be in action most of the night. I remember one particularly nasty night, someone somewhere decided to shine a searchlight battery on our site, of course the raid started. The searchlight belched it hideous beam skywards and the Hun, not only was he being shot at, but his plane was being lit up. He didn't like that, so he got his machine gunner to shoot down the beam of that dastardly searchlight and out went the light, the Hun was able to continue on his way. I think the aforementioned searchlight took itself off, I know not where.

As D Day approached all leave and passes were cancelled and camp placed on High Alert, and the only way one could get out of camp was for medical reasons. There were some crafty people in my section, one day 4 of them asked me to get them on the medical list to have their eyes tested at Llandaff Hospital, which had a military wing. I though what's good for them is good for me too. So, with the help of the Medical Orderly, we obtained the necessary documents and off we went, we had a lift in the Ration Wagon. Arriving at Llandaff we saw the optician one by one, I was the last one in. Having done his duty the officer said "Corporal, you and your squad have half the error in your eyes that I have in mine. Clear off, enjoy yourselves and don't be late returning to camp". From yours truly a smart salute and "Yes Sir, thank you Sir" and a hasty retreat.

Once, while on leave I had the need to go to a civilian dentist who removed a front tooth. On returning from leave I visited the Army Dentist in Barry, to ask for a tooth to fill the hole in my facial orifice "did I" said he "have difficulty in chewing?" "No, I do not" said I "well then" said he "if it doesn't interfere with chewing, the Army couldn't be expected to supply me with a tooth". Feeling rather put out I found a civilian dentist and had to pay the £1.10s for a replacement tooth.

It is a well-known fact that you should never volunteer for anything in HM Forces. There were certain ways of volunteering for benefit, that was courses, because if you passed courses you got an extra 2p or 4p a day, thus I went on courses for Gas, Aircraft Rec', Military Discipline and Education and almost doubled my pay.

About 3 months after D Day our Battery was sent to take over an 8-gun site near Sidcup. This was a very dangerous area being on the flight path of the VI, Doodlebug Rockets and later the V2. Up till now we had only Aircraft to deal with, this was something very different. Very often the Doodle Bug flew too low for the larger guns to fire, this meant the lighter guns came into play. The plotting of Doodle Bugs was very difficult because they came in droves and would pop up all over the plotting table, but from the numbers that were sent over really very few of them got through. We worked closely with the RAF.

Hairy though it was, there were some hilarious moments, one night there was a stonk on, the Doodle Bugs were coming in numbers the Claxon started blaring, this meant everyone not on duty were to get themselves into the nearest slit trench. Some girls were so eager to get into a trench they went into the first one at great speed and landed on top of 3 female officers.

Another night we were in bed when a stray bug came over. The girl in the bed next to me, who was a Scot, muttered "praise the lord to keep its engine running". At that precise moment the engine cut out, there was an almighty explosion, doors shook, windows caved in, beds danced, women swore, it felt that all hell had been let loose. Fortunately for us the thing blew up in the empty field next door. Another came over by itself the next day, we got it as it came down.

The onset of the V2 was awesome, you neither saw them or heard them until they exploded on impact. There were all sorts of theories of how to deal with them, intelligence found out that a V2 Rocket took 3 minutes from Launch to impact, this was what we had to work with. The idea that we were told was that if we could work out the angle, height and range of the rocket, so that the guns could elevate and fuse the shells and all sites fire at the same time. It was thought that maybe the V2 could be destroyed before landing. It was a huge job because it involved all guns ringing the London Area.

The powers that be were worried about the morale of the population, for 14 days we practised, 24 hours a day, at last the drill was perfected and we awaited orders for firing from high. In the event the theory was never put into practice because the launch site was captured.

During this time, we were very lucky, about 10am one morning when most people were in the NAAFI a V2 exploded in the air over our Camp, shrapnel was falling everywhere, it was very fortunate that there was no one outside. Ten minutes earlier and there would have been numerous casualties.

The winter of 1944 was very severe, at one point all our boilers packed up, there was no heating, no hot water, food had to be cooked on field kitchens, and we went to bed almost fully clothed. This condition went on for almost 2 weeks.

VE day arrived to the joy and relief of everyone, all work was suspended except for the most essential, we were all invited by tho locals to the village hostelries and we graciously accepted. Back at camp some Gunners had produced a horse from who knows where, anyway the C/O was being conducted from the officers' mess and was being helped onto the back of the nag. The nag was given a slap on its rump and of it went trotting around thc site with Major Bishop hanging onto its mane. The officers mess was raided once again and out was escorted the Second in Command, he was manhandled to the roof of the Radar cabin and was rotated violently. Great fun, but it all ended the next day and we were back to normal spit and polish.

During the summer of '45, there being no further use for Anti-Aircraft Batteries, we were disbanded and posted to various other units. I was posted to the Provost HQ in Buckingham Palace Gardens near Victoria Station. The Provost HQ occupied 3 large houses; on arrival I was interviewed by the female Provost Marshal. She invited me to go on a Provost course and become a Red Cap, this meant that I would have to relinquish both stripes and at the end of the course get back one stripe and a red topped cap. I respectfully refused, stating that my rank was substantive and could only be removed by Court Martial or at my own request, which I was not prepared to do. She seemed surprised that anyone could refuse to join the Elite Corp of Military Police, with a sniff she said I would have to go into admin and be in charge of the rations. As I only had a few months to go before my demob I didn't mind and as it happened turned out quite to my advantage, and also to the Cook NCO and the Clothing NCO.

Knightsbridge Barracks was the ration depot where I came to know a Free French Sailor and we would swap my onions for his sugar, jam for cheese etc. Needless to say, the cook was quite chuffed, and showed her appreciation in many culinary ways. The clothing NCO and I worked closely together too, when a lorry full of used ATS clothing lost a bag, we retrieved it, sorted it, and took ourselves off to Chelsea Barracks and renewed the lot. I was able to have 3 greatcoats which I was able to take home and when demobbed took them to any Railway station where you get £1.10s each. The final day of my war service came on February 26th, 1946!

Lioness 2004 No.1

Frances Nunnally - "After All the troops have to eat!"

Across the space of 78 years, I still hear the voice of the then Prime Minister Neville Chamberlain on the radio saying, "This country is now at war with Germany". My heart sank as he spoke, war for me meant that there would be no more postal service between Britain and Austria, cutting off communication with my family. For I was an Austrian Jewish refugee having reached England just a few months before. My parents, in Vienna, had managed to find an English family that would take me in, helping with housework and childcare. After mum and dad put me on a train in Vienna, I never saw them again, they perished in the Holocaust.

In 1941 I was able to join the ATS. My platoon consisted mainly of refugee girls like myself. But Although we now proudly wore the British uniform, we were still technically "Aliens" having come from what was now "enemy territory". So, we could forget about deciphering secret code and tracking planes, buy went to work feeding the troops. We worked in cookhouses and mess halls of "Gibraltar Barracks" a large training centre in Bury St Edmunds. We lugged big iron pots of food that weighed almost as much as we did and took turns washing dishes after each meal.

Oh yes, an enormous prehistoric, dishwasher groaned through the chores of "doing the plates". But once a week these had to be washed by hand in hot soapy water, then the mess hall tables had to be scrubbed squeaky clean...not to forget about the floors!

Winter was tough as we slept in unheated barrack rooms, while snow piled up on the parade square outside. We piled greatcoats and sweaters on top of our army issue blankets to keep warm.

While serving in the ATS I made many wonderful friends. We all worked hard, played hard and prayed. Then suddenly it was all over. The costliest war in history came to an end and we returned to civilian life.

But for us refugee girls' victory and peace meant the beginning of a new challenge - to find out what had happened to our families. The search led to Auschwitz, Trblinka, Bergen-Belsen and other death camps. I learned that my entire family had perished.

As life went on, us ATS girls, married, had children, worked jobs and remembered. My years of service in the British Army will always be with me. True, our battles were fought in the cookhouses of Britain, but I do feel that I had a small part in helping to win the war. After all, the troops had to eat!

Written by Frances Nunnally for this book.

Mary Walker - The Singing Fire Controller

I did my initial training in 1942 in Pontefract Barracks and well remember one of the Drill Sergeants shouting 'Now, come on Ladies, stick those chests out, you've got a hell of a lead over the men'.

I was then posted to 575 Battery Royal Artillery to train as a Radar Operator at Portland Bill where I remember seeing all the planes, bombers and gliders being towed over the Channel towards France around D-day.

At this time, I was an Operator of Fire Control on the Transmitter with a Head and Breast Set switched on. Things were a bit quiet and I was waiting to be relieved. I forgot I was live and started singing at the top of my voice. The names of the song I've forgotten but it included the word 'Rendezvous'. My relief opened the door and I said, 'Hello, is it mealtime?' and a voice in my earphones said, 'No my dear, it's Rendezvous time'. I'd been singing to the whole of the Command Post! I was expecting a rocket for this but the Officer in charge said he thoroughly enjoyed the performance!

After this, in 1944,1 was posted to a Gunsite in a village near to Brussels. When the war ended in Europe, I was transferred to No. 2 District Censorship Station in Bruges for a while. Then I went to Bonn where I met Charles Walker, a Grenadier Guards Corporal, who later became my husband.

Lioness 2005 No.2

Betty Templeton - South Africa & Egypt

I was conscripted into the ATS in late April 1942 when I was 20.I did my basic training at Pontefract Barracks where we had the honour of being inspected on our passing out parade by HRH Princess Mary, the Princess Royal. I was then posted to the Clerical School in Strathpeffer in Rossshire (where I was billeted in the Highland Hotel), to do an intensive three-month clerical course.

Afterwards it was home to Leeds for a short leave before my first posting. The journey from Strathpeffer on the slow train was quiet but the overnight journey from Edinburgh was quite eventful as after midnight I was able to say, "It's my 21st birthday". As the train was packed with service personnel, we had a tremendous party! However, it was a bit of an anti-climax when I arrived at Leeds to find the trams had not started running and I had to sit in the station for over 2 hours before I could get home.

My first posting was to Preston in Lancashire as a Clerk/Shorthand Typist at a RE Supply Depot. Volunteers were being recruited for overseas postings, so I quickly added my name to the list. Within two months I had been accepted and was sent to a Holding Unit in London to be kitted out with tropical uniform and was told very sternly that we must not mention this to anyone.

On 16th January 1943 we travelled to Liverpool where we embarked on a troopship. Whilst waiting to be escorted through the dangerous waters of the Atlantic (all the ships of course being blacked out) we witnessed a number of terrifying raids on Liverpool and I realised how lucky I was. The ship was the SS Volendam, an ex-Dutch Cruise Liner, striped of all luxurious fittings, but four of us were lucky enough to get a cabin with two portholes whereas the majority were below decks. We had one or two scary experiences when the accompanying destroyers dropped depth charges but in the event all the convoy survived.

As this was my first long sea voyage, I was rather apprehensive, but I found my sea legs fairly quickly. During the morning we were kept occupied with various lectures (and of course boat drill complete with "Mae Wests"). The lectures included how to avoid sunstroke, (a punishable offence), being careful of what we ate and drank, the danger of mosquitoes, and most importantly, how we should comport ourselves in a foreign country. But we did relax in the evenings and a few of us got together with the men and formed our own concert party. (I had a good singing voice in those days). There we also 3 ENSA parties on board so we were never short of entertainment.

The journey to Durban took around 6 weeks, partly because our ship was the slowest in the convoy (we were always being chivvied by the little corvette) but also because we had to go a long way out into the Atlantic to avoid enemy submarines. We were in Durban for just over three weeks waiting for another ship to take us further on our journey a real holiday as we were billeted in a lovely hotel on the seafront!

As a clerk, each morning I helped out in the South African Army Post Office sorting the mail. The afternoons and evenings were mostly free, except for further lectures and drills. The weather was glorious, and we spent the afternoons on the beach and the evenings in the open-air cinema or we were sometimes invited to dances. This may sound rather frivolous, but we were told by our officers to make the most of it as conditions would be very different when we reached our final destination.

However, the dream ended all too soon and we found ourselves on another smaller and less comfortable troopship. There were also three battalions of raw African conscripts who had only received the minimum basic training and were quite unused to discipline. By this time the heat was almost unbearable and although we changed into tropical gear, it was not such a comfortable journey. It was also quite weird and rather scary to hear the African drums throbbing at night and the chanting, when we were miles out to sea. During the day there were compensations such as watching the dolphins and flying fish and there were some spectacular electric storms.

We arrived at Port Tewfik in Egypt three months after leaving England and were taken by army lorries to the Kasr el Nil Barracks in Cairo. (These barracks had been condemned after the First World War!). It was there I had my first horrifying experiences of bugs. The place was alive with them and three times a week I had to dismantle my bed on the balcony, stuff all the corners and crevices with cotton wool soaked in paraffin and set fire to them. The smell was horrible. It was not a pleasant experience, but it was amazing how quickly one became blasé, and also to using the obligatory mosquito nets because the barracks overlooked the Nile.

I was sent to work in the office of the Director of Ordnance Services and on the first day had to sign the Official Secrets Act as they were already planning for the invasion of Sicily and later Italy. I think for the first time I really felt part of the war and was at last doing something useful.

During the summer months I worked from 8 am to 12 noon and from 5 pm to 8 pm in the evening, seven days a week. Working with me in the office were men of the Royal Army Ordnance Corps and also two Lebanese girls. We were under intense pressure at all times as it was vitally important that the necessary equipment be available at short notice.

After work there were always various invites to mess dances etc for which transport was provided there and back. I joined up with a Royal Signals Dance band and we played at various Services Clubs and Camps in the area. On these occasions I was given special permission to wear civilian clothes. These were sent out to me by my sister in law who also sent me the latest dance tunes and songs.

I was also lucky enough to get a ticket for a concert by Nelson Eddy when he came to Cairo to entertain the troops. Naturally I visited the Great Pyramids of Giza and Sphinx whilst in Cairo. After being in Cairo for a year I developed Bronchitis due to the barracks being on the banks of the Nile and I was posted to Alexandria on medical grounds.

At first, I was billeted with 502 Motor Ambulance Corps, a Unit of voluntary lady ambulance drivers (similar to the First Aid Nursing Yeomanry in WWI). They had just come down from the Western Desert and were fully occupied in re equipping and servicing their ambulances in preparation for their next assignment in Italy. Their CO in the meantime was acting as ATS Area Commander and I was her Clerk/Shorthand Typist, giving me my first stripe.

When they moved out, I was then attached to the Legal Depot at the HQ Barracks and also acted as Shorthand/Typist to the Brigadier, (which got me two stripes). Eventually I was promoted to Sergeant and took charge of the office where I remained for the rest of my time in Egypt.

I was still in Alexandria on VE Day and we had a big parade along the sea front and celebrations well into the evening. The journey home in September 1945 was much quicker as this was via the Mediterranean. I travelled on a very old troopship and had to master the art of sleeping in a hammock. As you can imagine the first efforts were hilarious!

I was finally discharged in December 1945. Many experiences were rather frightening, and I had to cope with conditions not previously in my imagination, but I do not regret any of the time spent serving with the ATS and I was proud to be working alongside so many other dedicated people from other services. When the TA was restarted in 1947 I joined 15th AA (Mixed) Signal Regiment at Gibraltar Barracks in Leeds where I met my husband who had joined the Royal Signals in 1938 and we were married in 1948.

Lioness 2004 No.2

Gwenda & Vera Gillham - Biggin Hill

About 8 of us ATS arrived at Biggin Hill in August 1942 from 131 HAA Regiment at Alverstoke which had been sent overseas. We formed No 2 Platoon D Company, 11 Group. We were billeted in houses taken over for the WAAF with whom we shared until more ATS joined and we were given our own houses.

The Operations Rooms were away from the aerodrome. The first one was Towerfields, a house near the Mark, in which was situated the plotting table surrounded by a dais. RAF Officers sat opposite their table and Army Officers overlooked both tables. Our table next door had a huge map of the south east of the country, showing all the gunsights and searchlights. We received our information from the RAF radars and passed the information on to the Dover gun sights ~ a very special line.

Our first top secret operation involved the raid on Dieppe. We were all very upset when we heard it was a failure as we had been in touch throughout.

The RAF Commander at Biggin Hill, Sailor Malan, was a very fine man, not above giving any of us a lift to the Ops Room. After a while we were moved to the Rookery which had been modernised and provided much better conditions. It was a very busy time; we had many a near miss from the German bombing raids around the Bromley area.

Just before the invasion began, we were joined in the Ops Room by Americans, who were newly stationed at the aerodrome.

As the flying bombs became more intense the guns were moved to the coast and the barrage balloons inland. We were bombed out of our house and had to return to Biggin Hill but were to sleep in surface shelters across the aerodrome ~ no fun at all. Eventually we were moved to a school in Lubbock Road and slept in Chiselhurst Caves.

During 1943 my sister, W/246571 Vera Martin joined us at Biggin Hill. In August 1944 when we were en route to a gun site near Sittingbourne we were hit by a flying bomb. My sister was killed instantly, and I survived with cuts and bruises.

Lioness 2004 No.1

Alison Hill - A Gunner's Travels

I volunteered for the ATS in March 1942. In April I went to Cambridge for my Medical. On 17 April, having passed A1, I was on my way to Northampton for my Basic Training (marching, immunisations etc). Whilst we were there an order was issued that we were not allowed to go to bed on a Monday night before midnight! We could clean buttons, shoes or enjoy a singsong in the Garrison Theatre, but no bed!

After three weeks, five of us were posted to Devizes as Operational Fire Controllers (OFCs). But at the time we had no idea what that stood for. Arriving at the camp we found we were to operate the radar; in other words, we controlled the guns. After two weeks of theory we went on to the sets. In between lectures about radar, we had instruction on plane spotting and lectures about gas. After eight weeks we passed out as OFCs. We had also passed the gas test.

Richmond Park was our next posting this was to an eight gun battery. 435 Bty had been formed in 1941, but now it was going to be divided, so they needed more personnel. Over the next few months A & B sections went around relieving other batteries to go to firing camp.

This was about the only time I did guard duty. Why did the men have guns at night, but we only had sticks in the daytime? We had been taught to use guns.

Next stop Walthamstow Avenue. When the battery left here for Buckhurst Hill the OFCs were sent to different batteries as we had no radar on the hill.

My friend and I went to Croydon, not as radar, but testing the teams who came there. Radar came to Buckhurst Hill, so we were back with our friends. Having been off radar for some weeks when the rest had a trade test, I wasn't ready, so I went on a course at Chelmsford for three weeks and passed.

Then it was our turn for firing camp. We went to Weybourne, then back to Buckhurst Hill for a few weeks, followed by another week at Walton on the Naze. While we were away, the two halves of the battery changed sites, so we returned to Waltham Abbey.

During our time there I celebrated my 21st birthday. The ATS officer sent for me and presented me with a cake. The cooks had iced a slab of cake for me, it tasted so good!

At the end of our time here we were expecting something to happen but did not know what. On the journey to our next site, Manor Park, we got mixed up with the "D" Day boys. People were giving them sweets, sandwiches, drinks, even money, but when a lorry load of girls passed by, they looked amazed.

Whilst we were on this site the V1s arrived. We used to get 'Take Post". Ten V1s are over Dover followed by another ton. All clear, stand down. Before we could reach the manning hut where our Radio Moe was making us a cup of cocoa, it was 'Take Post" again, ten followed by another ten. This went on all night. We never got our cup of cocoa that night and for several nights after.

Next to this site was a Bty of 64 guns manned at night by the Home Guard. What a din when they fired! But what a picture watching the flashing of the Ack Ack shells, tracer bullets, flashes from other guns and searchlights.

After leaving Manor Park, we had a few days back at Waltham Abbey. Then they decided we were bringing the V1s down on important places, so we were moved to Horley under canvas. It was while we were there that the V2s started. One landed in the next field to us at breakfast time, what a clatter of tin plates and mugs when we hit the ground!

A few weeks there then, one hot sunny Sunday in August, we climbed in the lorries and made for St Leonards. After going up seven flights of stairs, seven times with our kit, we had another flight to go up to the cookhouse for stew and cabbage! Next day came another order we had to move everything down to the cellars, as it was not safe to stay up high.

Then, when the V1s and V2s moved away from the South Coast we came back to London to Chingford. As the battery was going overseas, Ann and I were posted to 534 Bty who were stationed on Dengie Marshes, Tillingham. It was in November, we came away from brick-built barrack rooms with five blankets, to tents with duck boards floating in water and three blankets. However, we moved into the Nissan huts just before Christmas, what lovely fires we had, but no water. We were allowed one bowl of water for a dozen of us to use. As we were all OFCs in one hut it was very thick after we had all used it!

After VE Day we moved overnight by train from Essex to Whitchurch, Bristol. Here we were sorted out for different jobs, as the Ack Ack was no longer needed in England. I was sent to Clifton to work in the Army Post Office at Nottingham. Early in September my future husband came home after four years in the Eighth Army as a Desert Rat, so I applied for leave and we were married on 22 September 1945. My sister was also in Ack Ack, in 531 Bty. We used to meet in London when we could get a 24 hour pass together.

Lioness 2003 No.1
See images in centre pages

Nell Armitage - The Dawn Patrol

100 Girls... part of the first batch of women conscripts in Britain were chosen to be part of an experiment to operate a Searchlight site manned by women only. Training was at Kimnel Park (Wales) by male Staff Sergeants. The experiment was secret, as we were to use Radar to locate enemy planes location.

After training complete, we transferred to 10 sites, situated north, south, and west of London. We were engaged in the defence of London, and we worked with the RAF and not the guns.

At this time, we became part of 495 Battery, 93rd Searchlight Regiment. I was stationed at Farnham Common, and was the mechanic responsible for the maintenance of an ancient WWI Thornycroft Searchlight truck, which provided the power for the radar and the searchlight.

During the time I was there, a newsreel was taken of the girls at Farnham Common and shown at all cinemas in Britain for a week. There were also pictures and articles in all the papers and magazines.

We called ourselves The Dawn Patrol, as we rarely went to bed before dawn. We had to do night guard duty, with only a police baton and a whistle with which to protect the radar, searchlight etc. Girls were not armed in those days.

I recall, quite vividly, our accommodation which was very basic. The ablutions consisted of a shallow, metal sink, with 2 cold water taps and a couple of hooks on the wall. Next door, the latrine was something from the dark ages. Two pans with a board with two holes suspended above. We were rostered to empty the pans. Two of us would carry the pans to a far corner of the site, where we would dig

Maj Gen Sharon Nesmith - Foreword
Cpl Rebecca Brown RLC Crown Copyright©

Dame Helen Gwynne-Vaughan - Page 3

McGrath sisters & Peggy Messenger - Page 48

Kathleen McBurnley - Page 50

Charlotte (Betty) Webb MBE - page 82

Maureen Walsh - Page 91

Agnes Russell - Page 121

Alison Hill - Page 112

The WRAC Band - Page 150

Anne Workman - Page 170

Catherine Corley - Page 170

Pauline Grundy - Page 127

Marie (Sammy) Simon - Page 185

Mary Woollard MBE - Page 186

Ali Brown - Page 190

Rowena C Naile MBE - Page 199

Major Caroline Constantine - Page 201

a hole, empty the pans, wash them (Phew) and return them to their resting place.

I also recall that, whatever we had to do, we gave it our best shot. We were a closely-knit group and proud to have been chosen to defend our country in this way. I was very happy there, but, unfortunately, a driver for the ration truck was needed, and I was transferred to Troop HQ, and then later to Battery HQ.

Lioness 2004 No.2

Eileen Mander - The Day I Met Monty

In August 1941 was serving in Germany. I was an ATS driver in 721 Car Coy at Rhine Army HQ, Bad Oeynhausen. An important conference was about to take place at HQ and Monty was to host it, at that time he was CIGS (Chief of the Imperial General's Staff) and nearing the end of his term of office.

It was a wonderful opportunity to see him and, hopefully, to get a picture of him. So, I set forth with my newly acquired Voigtiander camera and secured a position at the front of the crowd, all set to snap my hero.

There seemed to be hundreds of officers from all parts of the British Zone and I began to doubt that I would even see Monty, let alone photograph him. Then, suddenly, there he was, walking along the path where I stood. He was accompanied by Lieutenant General Sir Charles Keightley and they were talking quietly together, having turned aside from the mainstream of officers, who were heading towards the Kurtheater where the conference was being held.

I fumbled with my camera trying to focus on them but without success, as they were constantly moving. Then, Monty spotted me and fixing me with those steely blue eyes he walked towards me and stopped. For an awful moment I was scared that he was going to ask me how I came by my German camera! I would not have dared to lie to him. I got it on the black market for 400 cigarettes.

I snapped to attention and saluted rather difficult with a camera in one hand. I need not have worried, although he did glance at the camera. He knew it was a German one. He asked me a series of quickfire questions about my service and I answered in quickfire reply. The adrenaline was fairly pumping by this time. Then he said, "Did you get your picture?" "No Sir" I replied. "Why not?" retorted Monty. "Well Sir, every time I get you in my sights you move on".

Monty threw back his head and laughed the allusion obviously amused him but I could have bitten out my tongue!

Monty turned to Sir Charles Keightley, who had been listening to all this, and said "Well Charles, I think we can stand still long enough for this Auxiliary to get her picture, don't you". Sir Charles readily agreed and the two of them posed for me, Monty giving me a kindly smile, those blue eyes twinkling.

The picture taken, I saluted smartly and thanked him. He nodded, smiled and said "Carry on" then turned away and walked towards the entrance of the Kurtheater. He was soon lost to sight, but the memory of that brief encounter stays with me. I got the picture of a lifetime and felt proud enough to burst!

Lioness 2003 No.1

Enid M Holmes - The Reluctant Recruit

During the war when Ernest Bevan, Minister of Labour, announced in the House of Commons that women born in certain years would have to register for war work and that single women would be conscripted into essential services, the Women's Armed Services, Land Army or Munitions I don't recall giving it much thought. So, when the registration for my age group came up I gave the Women's Services as my preference, confident it wouldn't apply to me as I was in a reserved occupation, or so I thought!

Several weeks elapsed but our family's concerns were elsewhere for the Japanese had invaded the Far East and my brother was stationed there. As the weeks passed, the news from that area got worse and worse and on 15 February it was announced that Singapore had fallen. A week or so later we received an official communication from the War Office stating my brother had been posted "missing".

Within the next few days a buff coloured envelope, summoning me to attend a medical at Edgware Health Centre, dropped through our letter box. On a Friday morning, realising what I thought would never happen was now a distinct possibility, I duly attended. On being passed A1, I was informed that I would be conscripted into the Women's Services, a prospect I faced with some dread, for I was shy with strangers, lacked confidence and was torn with doubts on so many things. How I envied those girls who seemed to have plenty of chat, especially with the opposite sex. A fortnight later another envelope arrived with my call-up papers, railway warrant etc instructing me to report to Glen Parva Barracks, Leicester on 27 March. I gained some notoriety at the office, being the first girl to be called up, and many girls who had never spoken to me before actually did so.

On a dull March morning off we set. I was miserable, knew I must not cry, although I felt like it, fearing to upset my father and aunt. On approaching the steps to the main line station, a strange sound greeted us and, on arrival at the top, we realised what it was. There were masses of people, mainly women, many of them in tears. It was quite horrendous, for girls in those days did not enjoy the freedoms of today. I boarded the train, found a seat and bid my family goodbye.

After all these years I can still see their small figures on the platform smiling and waving. We gradually began to relax, and chat and the crying ceased. We were met at Leicester by ATS personnel and directed to waiting transport. On arrival we were directed to the cookhouse, having been issued with an enamel mug, one knife, one fork and a spoon. We were then ordered to a large hall for the completion of masses of forms. Hours later we arrived at our sleeping quarters, a long barrack room containing 26 two tier bunks for 52 girls. I found I'd been given a top bunk, with a Corporal underneath not a happy prospect I felt.

Saturday dawned, you queued for everything, to wash, to go to the toilet etc. Ordered into line, we were marched to breakfast where every piece of food was slapped on to the same plate, the cooked items together with butter and jam. By the time you found somewhere to sit the butter and jam had joined together by floating in the eggs and bacon. We were then marched along to the stores to be issued with our kit, two uniforms, one greatcoat, two pairs of shoes, four shirts, two ties and four sets of underclothes. The knickers khaki of course were the type worn by our grannies and were referred to as "passion killers", very voluminous with elastic around the waist and at the end of very long legs! We must have looked a sight, skirts had to be regulation length of 16 inches from the ground, so that when on parade, the skirt lengths were in a straight line, ignoring that the girls were all shapes, sizes and heights. The skirts needed to be altered and we had to wear overalls, again only one size and length, until they were finished.

Back in the hall we were informed we'd be receiving our inoculations that day and would be confined to barracks until Monday evening. Both arms were used for these injections which meant you sometimes could not raise them above your elbows causing much amusement. Forty-eight hours without anything to do. Nothing to read how I wished I'd brought a book. The awful feeling of homesickness

117

reared its ugly head. A radio continually blared out a favourite song of that time, "I never said thanks for the lovely weekend", which didn't help matters.

Monday afternoon was our first taste of drill. Assembled on the barrack square we could see, in the distance, the Drill Sergeant Major with the usual ram rod back and cane in hand strutting across his precious square. Barking out commands accompanied by the usual expletives, there was a sudden break in the ranks as three girls unbelievably walked off. Calling us to a halt he marched purposefully after them demanding an explanation. He was politely informed that they were not going to be sworn at. He took their names and resumed his drill. The next day another Sergeant, an ATS, appeared. The drilling recommenced. So continued weeks of FT, drill, marching backwards, forwards, every way and which way, aptitude tests and interviews.

Would we like to do Ack Ack? Certain jobs were not available to me for I was too short. Anyway, they discovered I was a shorthand typist and that was that. After the initial three weeks training, we were due for 48 hours leave prior to receiving our postings. We were faced with the prospect of being separated from the friends we'd made in these last weeks and of forming others at our new postings. Assembling in the large drill hall the following Monday, names began to be read out. The process took ages until you began to wonder whether your name was ever going to appear.

It did 151483 Holmes, EM Strathpeffer. Wales, I thought. Wrong again! Scotland. We were instructed to take down the train times and when and where to change trains. I got as far as Inverness and gave up. On Tuesday morning we collected our sandwiches at breakfast, said our farewells and set off for the station. We tried to swing our kit bags on to our shoulders without success. It was to be a couple of years before we were issued with kit bags with handles and even then, the handles were too short. You had to make your kit bag narrower in the middle in order for the handles to meet. We had no alternative but to drag our kit bags along complete with gas masks and tin hats.

The first train change was at Leeds. So, began for me a magical journey. It was springtime, the green hills of Yorkshire, the fields with their stone walls and frolicking lambs delighted me. I'd never been north before. This was in the days before television and distance travelling being available to all, so such scenery was new to many of us. We were sitting opposite two Tommies who gallantly looked after us, grabbing cups of tea when the train stopped. Without them we would never have made the tea bar. It was now afternoon and we had eaten our sandwiches. The soldiers were to leave us before we got to our next stop, Glasgow. The lovely scenery continued and reaching Glasgow late in the evening it was still daylight.

A lorry awaited the 20 of us, our first experience of trying to board it. With straight skirt and short legs like mine it needed a heave from someone on the vehicle and a push from the rear to enable me to clamber on. We had had to change stations and were dropped off at the station for the Highlands. We settled down, sitting anywhere to await the train's arrival. We scrambled on and there were the usual drunks about, speaking what seemed to us a foreign language Scots! Another stop was made at Inverness some hours later and a further wait for the train to Dingwall. The train was unheated, and we snuggled together to try and keep warm. Leaving the train at Dingwall it was now the early hours of Wednesday morning and it was snowing. There was a canteen what heroines those women were.

All these years later I can still recall the lovely warm Scottish voice. "Oh, you poor wee lassies, you look so tired and cold". So we were, but with her motherly care and bowls of soup we soon warmed up. It was a short journey from Dingwall to Strathpeffer and at 6.30 am, in snowy conditions, we dragged our kit bags up the station steps to the path to the Ben Wyvis Hotel where we were to report. We had finally arrived some 20 hours after setting off. The Commandant of the Clerks School was appalled at the time we'd been travelling and at the lack of rations issued for our journey. We were ordered into breakfast and then informed we were to find our rooms and relax until lunchtime. We were famished and when we finally sat down with our plate of porridge and cooked breakfast, discovered the porridge was made the Scottish way, with salt. I've never eaten it since.

Four of us were to share a room in the attics of the hotel with wonderful views over the valley with the mountains in the distance, at that time covered with snow. It was now April with double summertime, a wartime regulation, it hardly ever got dark in the Highlands during our stay. We were to undertake a course lasting 10 weeks working from 9 am to 7 pm with Saturday afternoons and Sundays free. We were formed into small squads and ordered to elect our own Squad Leader, all very democratic. Often you find there is one person who may be anxious to assume such a position. We had one, Daphne, she had visions of becoming an Officer, but I don't think she ever managed it. Each squad marched to the various hotels for the lessons we were to have. After completion of the course you sat an exam, and, if successful, obtained tradeswoman's pay of one guinea a week.

Strathpeffer had at one time been a Spa. It was a lovely place situated midst beautiful scenery; I recall taking myself to task because

I felt so miserable with homesickness as I gazed from the attic window watching the snow gradually disappearing from the mountains as the weeks went by. It was a lovely spring with the Scottish cattle in their long shaggy coats staring at us as we wandered through the fields. Unusual for Scotland there was a drought during our stay. Our weekends were spent walking through the countryside and going into Dingwall, a pretty Highland village. There were the usual Saturday evening dances, with French Canadian and Norwegians who were employed logging in the nearby woods.

Shortly before the end of the course a group of us was informed we were to be posted to Chilwell, an Ordnance Depot outside Nottingham. How we were chosen we never knew. What a rude awakening. It was a huge place, like a town on its own. Discipline was harsh. The vast area was staffed by the military with some hundreds of civilians not the happiest of environments, especially as they enjoyed many more privileges than we did. Imagine our horror when we learned we were to go on another course of a few days to recognise various parts of engines, what the heck had we been on a Clerks' Course for? We decided to write to the CO at Strathpeffer acquainting her of our situation. We all signed the letter, subsequently we discovered if there are three signatures or more on a petition it is mutiny! Ignorance is Bliss!

We had a miserable time, having completed the short course of a few days, we had to do night work, copy typing and to endure the unkind comments of some of the civilians who seemed to think they were hard done by because they had to work with us.

My first long leave had been due in June but had been cancelled until later that year. However, I was allowed 48 hours leave in late June. It was apparent to my father and aunt that I was unhappy, although I didn't mention it. I remember laughingly asking my aunt if she would hide me if I deserted and they sent the Military Police for me.

Returning to Chilwell on the Monday morning, four of us were informed we were to be sent to HQ Northern Command at York. Had the CO managed to pull strings we never did find out. I was so worried, as were the others, that the powers that be might change their minds that I didn't write home until I was established at York. And so began for me one of the happiest periods of my life.

Lioness 2002 No.2

Agnes Russell - WAAC, QMAAC, ATS & WRAC!

"I BELANG tae Glasgae" sang a tuneful Scots comedian, and so does 58-yearold Staff-Sergt. Agnes Russell, who has now entered on the last lap of a long and unusual military career.

She first donned the voluminous, ankle-length skirt of the Women's Army Auxiliary Corps in 1918, and she has just gone to the Women's Royal Army Corps Training Centre to which she brings the experience of an old soldier and an immense knowledge of Quartermaster's stores.

Like many old stagers, she is shy of talking of her experiences. She has worn the cap-badges of the W.A.A.C., Q.M.A.A.C., A.T.S. and W.R.A.C.; she has acquired five medal ribbons and a certificate of merit from General Sir Alan Cunningham, but these are but the bones of a long career in which administrative ability and devotion to duty have always been evident.

Her soldiering started in the King Street Barracks of the 3rd Reserve of the Gordon Highlanders at Aberdeen, where she immediately found her niche in the Quartermaster's Stores. Eighteen months later she embarked, curiously enough, in the City of Aberdeen for France. She still gives the galley staff a rather belated pat on the back for baking their own white bread at a time when everyone else had to put up with a grey-black, glutinous variety. She was destined to work with the American Expeditionary Force in the South of France and, while there, worked as a Record Office clerk. Her chief memory of that time was that she found the American system of working without regimental numbers was more than a little confusing. She was still there when the Peace Treaty was signed and, like everyone else, found the subsequent celebrations rather exhausting.

Her next move was to Wimereux, near Boulogne, where she worked for the Camp Commandant until, in February 1920, she returned to London to be discharged.

Nineteen years later, after a spell as a dress machinist in Glasgow, February 1939, saw her back in the uniform of a volunteer in the A.T.S. Seven months later she was embodied. Amongst other places she was stationed at Boroughhead, Bogside, Ardrossan, Peterborough and Woolwich. Then she went to Ashchurch as S.Q.M.S. to take charge of the clothing store of a R.A.O.C. unit.

Her present engagement ends in two years' time, and Staff Russell has no idea what her future out of uniform will be. Old soldiers have a way of taking care of themselves, and we hope she will never let us lose sight of her.

Lioness 1950 Nov-Dec

Editor's note: Agnes is also mentioned in the February 1954 Lioness alongside a picture of her receiving the British Empire Medal.
See images in centre pages

W/6811 Staff-Sergeant A. G. RUSSELL Those who can should look up their Lioness of November December, 1950, wherein they will read of the already long and distinguished service of Agnes Russell, who has served for all the time possible between 1918 and the present day and has worn in her time all four badges (counting Q.M.A.A.C. as two) of our Corps. We picture her receiving her B.E.M., one which we make so bold to say, was never better earned. We offer her our congratulations and best wishes.

Mary Soames OBE

Mary was born on 14 June 1916 in Finchley, London and was the only child of Holly Berry and Harold Hickson. She adored her parents but rather lived in fear of her strict, domineering father whose tremendous influence carved out how Mary lived her future life.

She enjoyed an idyllic childhood during the 1920's and attended St Ronan's School, Hadley Wood in Hertfordshire where she attained her school certificate in 6 subjects. She went on to Clark's Secretarial College in Chancery Lane for a 9-month Shorthand and Typing course – so impressed was the Vice Principal with Mary that he took her on immediately as his assistant secretary. She stayed there for 2 years before moving on in 1935 to do more secretarial work for William Richards & Son, a firm of Adjusters, where she stayed until enlisting into the First Aid Nursing Yeomanry (FANY).

Mary was encouraged to join the FANY by her cousin with whom she was very close. Her Aunt and Uncle lived in Hanover Square and Mary spent a lot of her time there, so it was not surprising that the two cousins decided to join up together in November 1938. They trained at the Duke of York's HQ off the King's Road and Mary's first posting was as an Ambulance Driver based at the Royal Albert

Docks attached to 19 Field Regt RA. From there Mary was posted to the Motor Transport Company at the Tower of London.

Many remember Mary regaling her story of driving a brand new requisitioned Red Ford V8 Bakers van with the words 'Luxury Super Loaf – Sliced and Wrapped' engraved in gold lettering on the side and Mary leaning out of the driver's window shouting to the guard at the gate 'Sliced and Wrapped' as she swept past them with a flourish of her hand. That was her favourite story and we heard it so many times in recent years as her memory began to fail her but she never forgot 'sliced and wrapped'!

On one occasion Mary reported to a male officer and said 'your car is waiting outside sir' to which he replied 'where's the driver?' Mary very indignantly replied ' I am the driver!'

She also spent some time based at FANY HQ as an orderly and as a driver with No 2 Driver Training Company in Wrexham, North Wales. She rose through the ranks very rapidly and after a mere 3 years she was promoted to Warrant Officer Class 2.

Knowing Mary as we all do, it won't come as a surprise that throughout the war she enjoyed a great social life in London, partying and dancing through the night at the Berkeley and Savoy Hotels; in one particular restaurant she and her colleagues were known as 'the pretty soldiers' and were always treated to free drinks!

The FANY Motorised Transport Companies came directly under the control of the ATS, so it was not surprising that Mary was soon singled out as a potential ATS officer. She passed her Officer Training interview with flying colours and attended her ATS Officer Cadet Training Unit in Windsor from where she was commissioned on 6 th November 1942, winning the coveted Sash of Honour (the award for best overall officer cadet) and became Subaltern Mary Hickson ATS.

Mary's postings as a commissioned officer took her all over the UK and to Bad Oyenhausen, Rheindahlen and Berlin in Germany. In 1949 the ATS was disbanded and the Women's Royal Army Corps was formed, and women officers took on the same ranks as their male counterparts.

Mary enjoyed all her postings but especially Berlin where she was responsible for 35 female clerks and where she had a wonderful flat, 2 hausfraus to look after her every need, and a driver. She had Army HQ appointments in Scotland and Shrewsbury and a variety of Quartering and Staff appointments at Bicester, The War Office and later on in the MOD.

She was an extremely popular Officers' Mess member, sometimes being the only woman in the Mess which, of course, pleased Mary! She always volunteered to look after other mess members' dogs when they were away, and her love of dogs remained with her throughout her life. Her devotion to her widowed mother knew no bounds and wherever she was serving, Mary drove home in all weathers to Finchley at weekends to visit her. When she was stationed in Scotland, Mary took her mother to live with her in her flat in Kelvinside.

Her penultimate posting was to the WRAC Directorate working for the Director of the WRAC. During this tour, Mary who was by now a senior Major, was awarded the MBE in June 1961. Her final posting was on promotion to Lieutenant Colonel and was to the Army HQ in Aldershot as Assistant Director WRAC.

Living in Government House Officers' Mess at the same time as Mary was one Lt Col Arthur Soames of the Gloucestershire Regt and the rest, as they say, is history! Mary and Arthur were married on 7 November 1964 at Aldershot Garrison Church and Mary retired from the WRAC on 24 February 1965.

Thus, began the second chapter of her life as she took up residence at Highlands, Upper Old Park Lane, Farnham and which was to last for the next 50 years. Mary's transition to civilian life was met with the same drive, commitment and devotion that she had given to her military career. She literally hit the ground running and took on the responsibilities of running Highlands with its extensive garden, looking after Arthur, Jessica and Tristan, not to mention her beloved mother and Arthur's mother, cooking and entertaining, and finally still finding time to undertake various charitable works not least the Chairmanship of the ATS and WRAC Benevolent Fund Grants Committee.

Mary chaired this committee for 25 years during which time she presided over the disbursement of £2.2 million to 18,000 beneficiaries She was also instrumental in obtaining a National Lottery award of £200,000 to supplement the Benevolent Fund; her commanding performance for the Lottery Assessment Board was so compassionate and convincing that there was no chance that the charity's request would be turned down.

Generations of WRAC Officers and Warrant Officers will remember Mary as Chairman of Grants where she always showed great perception, compassion and understanding in considering the diverse and needy circumstances presented in the casework; they would also clamour to be at the December meeting to enjoy her famous mince pies and sherry! Mary was awarded the OBE in 1999 for her significant contribution to the ATS/WRAC Benevolent Fund.

After she retired as chairman of the Benevolent Fund, Mary became a very active Life Vice President of the WRAC Association, never missing Council meetings or Association functions. She was a stalwart of the Aldershot Branch of the Association holding various office within the Branch. Mary also worked tirelessly for the Camphill Village Trust, a UK wide based charity which provides a home within a supportive community environment for the disabled. She supported two Camphill centres both based in Gloucestershire and raised thousands of pounds through her annual plant, pottery and home cookery sales at Highlands and by having a stall at the Alton show. Not only did Mary raise money for the Camphill Trust but she also gave its disabled and handicapped adults Respite stays at Highlands teaching them cookery and gardening skills.

She epitomised the phrase a bon viveur; she was a marvellous hostess and a wonderful cook who was never happier than when she was sat at the head of the dining table at Highlands dishing out generous helpings of her home cooked fare. She enjoyed her wine and was guaranteed to be great company at any social gathering where her mischievous sense of humour always came to the fore. She loved her beautifully established garden and tending to her plants in the greenhouse and enjoyed sitting outside on the patio soaking up the sun with one of her many beloved dogs nearby.

Mary was a remarkable woman and a great contributor who dedicated her life to the service of others. She was non-judgemental, constantly seeing the good side of people and was a shining example to so many of us. She loved life, enjoyed parties, flirted outrageously and adored dogs. She had enormous energy and warmth and her kindness, thoughtfulness and generosity knew no bounds.

From the obituary written by Sue Westlake MBE in Lioness 2015 No.2

Christine MacKinnon

Chris MacKinnon joined the ATS in WW2. She met and married a bomber pilot who, she said, was the image of John Mills, the actor.

Sadly, her husband's plane was shot down during a raid and Chris received that dreaded telegram advising her that her husband was 'missing in action...' Chris learned from other men on the same raid that several of the crew had bailed out of the doomed bomber and they were convinced that there were survivors. The telegram of course, made no mention of possible survivors so Chris set out to establish her husband's fate only to be met with "doors closing in my face".

Undaunted, Chris (in her ATS uniform of course) and her mother in law presented themselves at the Air Ministry but were denied entry. After several visits, they somehow managed to get past the guards and found their way to the most senior officer. He refused to see them so they took over the two seats outside his office and refused to leave until he agreed to answer their questions. Faced with such determination, he eventually relented. However, he was unable to establish the names or the fate of the crew members who were seen parachuting from the plane. Chris never saw her husband again.

Later, whilst involved in Army PR, Chris was required to keep a packed suitcase in her London office as she was often called away at a moment's notice. On one memorable assignment, she found herself in Aden with a publicity crew who were gathering information and photographs for various recruiting publications and it was there she met a young servicewoman whom she would encounter again later in her career. Of that period, Chris always said that her greatest thrill was when she was required to look after' her hero, Charlton Heston, at a PR function.

Chris was persuaded to come out of early retirement and return to uniform to take over as the Army Careers Officer, Women's Services, at Blackheath AGIO in the 1970s. It was there that I met her for the first time and it was there that she met again that WRAC girl from Aden. Chris met each of the three WRAC members of staff, Sue Marcroft, me, and the third Recruiter who promptly reminded her of the last time they had met: "Ma'am, do you remember filming in Aden, when you insisted I stand on the very edge of a sheer drop? Another inch and I'd have been killed!" A moment of thought and Chris remembering the incident said "But Sgt Clewlow, it made such a good picture, don't you think?"

Chris MacKinnon brought to the job of ACO a great sense of humour, support for her staff and a social calendar never before experienced in that office! Later, she took over as ACO of an integrated office, taking over from Col Tommy' Thomas, RCT when he moved to the St Albans office. Further reorganisation of the London offices and Chris moved to the post of ACO CLRD but she kept her links with her former colleagues and her social activities continued of course.

Lioness 2003 No.2

Pat Earls

Pat completed her early education at Wesley College in Dublin and in 1940, just after the start of WW2 at the age of 18, and while on a visit to relatives in Northern Ireland, she joined the ATS. She had not discussed this career move with her parents, but she was always proud of the fact that her father had served with the British Army in France during World War 1.

In the immediate post War years, Pat served in several parts of Germany with the Allied Control Commission and was working with the Americans and French during the Russian blockade of Berlin in 1949.

Pat returned to UK and was commissioned in 1954. She continued her active service until 1963 when she was appointed as Army Careers Officer, Northern Ireland. Pat's friendly nature and affinity with young people was obviously recognised, for in 1973 she was appointed as Women's Services Liaison Officer which involved visiting some schools in Southern Ireland. This period in Pat's life also coincided with the height of the political troubles in Northern Ireland, and Pat was commuting on a daily basis from her home to various military establishments.

Her office in Belfast was bombed on two occasions by terrorists and following the assassination of a fellow colleague in the recruiting service, Pat was obliged over a period of years to take special precautions for her personal safety. She did this without any fuss and seldom referred to the matter.

Pat retired from the Army in 1982 after 42 years' service including 18 as AGO Northern Ireland. Throughout her life she was a keen motorist and was one of the first women motorists in Northern Ireland to pass the UK Advanced Driving Test she was still driving her car after her 86th birthday.

Lioness 2008 No.2

Pauline Grundy

Pauline went to Goldsworth School in Woking in 1929, and then in 1932 to Guildford County School of Girls where she gained a London School Certificate in Physics, Chemistry and Mathematics. In 1940, after the outbreak of World War 2, she received training in analytical chemistry at Woolwich Polytechnic and went to work in an explosives factory, before returning to Woolwich Polytechnic a year later to study Engineering and Telecommunications in preparation for Officer Cadet Training and a commission in the ATS as a 2nd Subaltern.

In 1942 she went to the Army Radio School to be trained for work on a "top secret" system that was the forerunner of Radar and, fully qualified, was then posted to anti-aircraft batteries in Southern England. Her duties were to maintain the Radio Direction Finding systems on the Heavy Antiaircraft Artillery gun sites.

Early in 1944 she was posted to the War Office initially as a Junior, and then Senior Commander attached to the RAOC. In June 1953 she was awarded the MBE "in recognition of special work at the War Office, being one of the first batch of girls to be trained as radar officers".

In 1954 Pauline attended Staff College, and in her CV at the time, added as an afterthought "Prefer to work in London". So in October of that year she was posted to HQ British Troops Egypt where she was appointed to the newly created job of Liaison Officer with the Egyptian Army on the strength, as she put it, of "stretching a few points about her proficiency in French and shorthand".

There she continued to indulge her love of amateur dramatics, having been in several plays with the War Office drama club back in the UK. In Egypt she joined a local drama group and almost immediately met Douglas, a tall dashing RAF officer whom she married in 1957.

Pauline was one of the last WRAC officers to leave Egypt in 1956 during the evacuation. She was posted to GHQ Middle East Land Forces in Episkopi, Cyprus and flew there with the General and Chief of Staff in the Commander in Chief's private plane.

In Cyprus, Pauline completed her three years of overseas duty and resigned. After Douglas left the RAF, they lived in South America for several years and even after Douglas died in 1983, Pauline continued a very active travel programme taking her literally all around the world. She spent her last in the Queen Elizabeth Park Care Home built on the site of the WRAC Centre in Guildford.

Lioness 2008 No.2
See images in centre pages

Dame Jean Rivett-Drake DBE - Director WRAC 1961 - 1964

Jean Rivett-Drake gave 25 years to the Army and as long again to public service in her community in Sussex. Tall and with a keen mind and wit, she was nothing like her army nickname, "Puddleduck", which was derived from her name instead.

Jean Elizabeth Rivett-Drake began her military service in the 1930s with the First Aid Nursing Yeomanry (FANY). Women were also being recruited to drive military vehicles and that was Jean Rivett-Drake's forte. In 1940, she transferred to the ATS.

The war years, with their acute sense of national endeavour, highlighted her personal strengths, her leadership and organisational qualities in particular.

Commissioned in 1942, she was a Captain by 1944 for the start the preparations for D-Day and the invasion of Normandy in June that year.

Eagerness to get ashore in France once the Normandy bridgehead was secure became a national obsession and none were more eager than the women of the ATS Continental Group NorthWest Europe, responsible for the support of 21 Army Group. It was the first ATS element to arrive in France.

Jean commanded a company in this mixed transport force equipped with 3 tonne vehicles responsible for delivery of ammunition, fuel and a huge range of supplies. Alternative demands for ammunition or petrol for the Allied tanks to continue pushing the front forward, kept the transport companies working around the clock. Exhaustion was commonplace but Jean's care for her drivers was intense. During this time she was mentioned in dispatches for her services and appointed second in command of the group as it became part of the British Army of the Rhine in July 1945. Jean battled with the constant turnover of drivers and staff to meet demobilisation demands and the necessity to train new arrivals.

She was appointed MBE for her services with the continental Group in 1947. With her name known and her competence firmly established in the war and its immediate aftermath, the Army offered her a career of challenge and opportunity.

She was accepted for a regular commission in 1949, the year in which she became an acting Lieutenant Colonel. She was appointed Commandant of the WRAC Warrant Officer and NCOs' School at Liphook in 1949.

Thereafter, she moved quickly up the promotional ladder. She went to Singapore in 1954 as Assistant Director Far East Land Forces. This was during a troubling period in the Far East. The

Singapore military base, with stockpiles in support of contingency plans to resist any further Chinese expansion in South East Asia, required WRAC staff in many roles. Throughout the command, there were close to a thousand women under her care.

On appointment as Director WRAC in 1961 she set herself three priorities for her tenure in charge. These were a widening of the range of WRAC trades and specialities so easing the pressure on manpower following an end to National Service in 1962; replanning WRAC redeployment worldwide, as detachments were withdrawn from some theatres and established in others; and a smooth move of the WRAC depot and training regiment out of Guildford and back again, to permit construction of a new purpose built barracks.

Before retiring in 1964 she was an honorary ADC to the Queen during her time as Director and was appointed DBE. She returned to Sussex, where she had grown up with her family before the war, here she became a JP and later chairman of the bench at Hove. She served on Hove Borough Council and was a great supporter and eventually president of the Brighton Youth Orchestra. She was Mayor of Hove and a Deputy Lieutenant for East Sussex.

Extracted from her obituary in Lioness 2000 No.1

Dame Mary Pihl DBE - Director WRAC 1967 - 1970

Mary Mackenzie Anderson was born in Sutton, Surrey. Her father, Sir John Anderson, introduced Anderson Shelters when he was Home Secretary and Minister for Home Security during the Second World War; he was created the 1st Viscount Waverley of Westdean in the 1952 New Year's Honours. Educated at Sutton High School and Villa Brillamont in Lausanne, Mary had travelled widely even before going to school in Switzerland. Her father had been Governor of Bengal and, because her mother had died when Mary was only 4, she carried out many representational duties although she was only in her late teens at the time.

Mary Anderson joined the ATS in 1941 and was commissioned in 1942. Several postings in Scottish Command followed leading up to her appointment as ATS Group Commander for Highland District based in the Headquarters in Perth.

In 1949, she became APM WRAC and had responsibilities in UK and BAOR. After a tour as DAD WRAC Lowland District based in

Glasgow, Major Anderson was posted to the War Office in January 1950 as a GSO2 in the TA Directorate.

Major Anderson's next posting was especially significant. Her post with the Signal Division in HQ Allied Forces Northern Europe, Oslo, from June 1955 until February 1958 included responsibilities as the custodian of the encryption codes used by that NATO Headquarters. During this time, she was awarded the MBE. This appointment also encouraged her great interest in travel and allowed her to become an expert skier: a skill she retained well into her seventies. She began a lifelong affinity with Norway and met Frithjof Pihl whom she would later marry after leaving the WRAC.

After Oslo, Major Anderson returned to the UK and was appointed as OC Officer Cadet Wing at the WRAC School of Instruction. She served there until June 1960 and her contemporaries remember her as a very fair OC who was an accurate and shrewd judge of character. She showed great interest in the welfare of the Cadets and ensured that they were given as much advice and support as possible at the start of their careers.

On promotion, Lt Col Anderson went to Chester as AD WRAC Western Command and then to Cyprus until 1963. On return from Cyprus, she was promoted again and became Deputy Director WRAC at MOD until December 1964. During this tour, she ensured that the WRAC took over more roles to alleviate manpower shortages following the end of National Service.

A tour as Commandant of the WRAC Centre followed until August 1967 when she was promoted and appointed Director WRAC.

Brigadier Anderson retired in 1970 and was advanced to DBF. Dame Mary became a Life-Vice President of the WRAC Association in July 2000. Those who served with Brigadier Anderson remember a very able and intelligent officer who took her responsibilities very seriously. An exacting staff officer who expected others to share her high standards, she was also very concerned for the welfare and conditions of those under her command. Her junior officers especially remember her as someone who encouraged them to express their views and enjoyed lively discussion with them.

In July 1973, Dame Mary married Frithjof Pihl who had been an active member of the Norwegian Resistance in Nazi occupied Norway during World War 2. For several years, they spent six months of each year in Norway and the other six months in UK. Dame Mary became a fluent Norwegian speaker: a skill she never lost although she used to complain that it spoiled her ability to speak French!

Lioness 2006 No.2

Eileen Nolan

Eileen was born in Bournville, the estate created by Cadbury for its employees. Her father was a technical advisor in the company and Eileen worked there in sales and advertising before joining the ATS in November 1942.

After initial training in Halifax, she attended an NCOs course at Pontefract and remained involved with training until attending OCTU in Windsor in early 1945. Second Subaltern Nolan was commissioned in April 1945.

In 1946, Junior Commander Nolan was posted to Guildford and, in 1948, she moved to B Coy, 12 Battalion at Prince's Gate, Kensington, London. She commanded some 300 women who worked in the War Office in Hobart House. During that time, she also led the contingent taking part in the Festival of Remembrance at the Albert Hall.

In March 1952, Captain Nolan went to Kingston, Jamaica, commanding WRAC and locally enlisted servicewomen, and returned in March 1954 to attend the WRAC Staff College at Frimley.

Following that, her initial staff appointment was as Staff Captain 'Q' at the War Office. Her responsibilities included the movement of freight to and from the Middle East. This was over the period of the Suez Crisis which often meant around the clock working in the Ops Room.

In 1957, Captain Nolan was promoted to Major and a year later was in Tripoli commanding the 90 strong WRAC contingent and filling a 'Q' staff appointment in the Headquarters.

In 1961 she came back to the North of England as Schools Liaison Officer before being posted as Deputy Assistant Adjutant General (DAAG) responsible for officers' postings. From there she became OC Cadet Wing at the WRAC College in 1965. Following promotion to Lieutenant Colonel in 1967 and a short tour in Scotland, she moved to Singapore as Senior WRAC Officer and 'Q' Staff Officer with particular responsibility for Quartering in Malaysia.

Returning, on promotion to Colonel, in 1970, she was appointed as Colonel Assistant Adjutant General and in May 1973, she was promoted to Brigadier and became Director WRAC, an appointment she held until June 1977. She was appointed CB on retirement and served on as Deputy Controller Commandant until 1984.

During her career, Brigadier Nolan experienced several significant changes to the employment of women in the Army and, indeed, to the structure and very existence of the WRAC itself. In

Libya, she had to balance the strict Muslim rules about the behaviour of women in public with the gregarious way of life which servicewomen wanted to follow, At Camberley, she was involved in broadening the field training of the WRAC cadets in line with those of their male counterparts at Sandhurst and in MOD, both as Colonel AAG and as Director, she was in constant negotiation and discussion about the future employment of women, whether or not they were combatant and the whole issue of the introduction of weapon training.

All of these issues were dealt with in her usual firm, diplomatic but determined manner. Brigadier Nolan was not one to sway or, indeed, be swayed, once she had made her decision - a decision based always on what she believed to be in the best interests of the servicewomen under her command.

Brigadier Nolan should also be remembered for the outstanding work she did for the WRAC in the international arena. She was instrumental in organising the Conference of the NATO Senior Women Officers in London and was the Chairman of that Conference between 1975 and 1977. She also had a long and close associations with the US Women's Army Corps and forged a lifelong friendship with her counterpart there, Brigadier General Mildred C. Bailey.

Lioness 2006 No.1

Barbara Gratton

Barbara was always a very private, self-contained young woman, but as for so many women of her generation, her life was to be transformed by the War. She was in a reserved occupation in an aircraft factory which she hated. Unbeknown to her parents, she joined the ATS in 1943 in Wolverhampton. Her mother never forgave her.

Barbara was not called for basic training at Pontefract until February 1944 but from then on things moved rapidly. She was posted on 6 April to No 1 MTTC Camberley, a small challenge as she could already drive. Postings to Kent and promotions soon followed.

In 1945 she passed her motorcycle trade test, qualified to drive solo and passed her driver mechanic trade test, coming top of the mixed course. In 1946 she was promoted to Sgt with a great reputation for exceptional organisational skills.

On 21 March 1949 she re-engaged into the WRAC and was posted to 14 Bn in Berlin. In 1949 she was promoted to SSgt. Berlin was in a sorry state at that time as it was just after the Berlin Airlift.

She avoided going into the Russian sector but found the two-day journey from Harwich to the Hook and then by train very trying.

Usually being the only WRAC senior rank on the military train she would be locked in a compartment on her own. Going through the Russian sector, chains were put around the door locks and blinds had to be securely closed. Armed Russian soldiers searched the train at stations and sidings, and everyone was much relieved when the train finally reached the British sector.

On her return to the UK in August 1951 she was promoted to W02 and posted to Chester, then in Sept 1953 to Huron Camp, Hindhead as an instructor in WO & NCO Wing. She was there until Oct 1954 when she went to TA Bns in Southampton and Taunton. By special request she had another period at Huron camp and while there was promoted in March 1956 to W01 and appointed as the youngest RSM at only 32 years and 3 months of age.

Postings followed to WRAC (TA) battalions in Liverpool then Leicester. (TA Bns had a regular RSM when there were over 100 women.).

Her final posting was to HQ 48 Div (TA) in Shrewsbury where she completed 22 years' service on 24 Feb 1966. The very next day, she was appointed to a TA Commission and posted as Capt PSO to 48 (S.M) Sig Regt (TA). Shortly afterwards following yet another TA reorganisation she was posted to 35 (S.M) Sig Regt(V) in Birmingham. During her time with this Regt, which had a BAOR role, she did return to Germany several times for annual camp and found the journey much improved: this time travelling by air some 25 yrs later.

Barbara was a mentor to all ranks of the WRAC and was a meticulous holder of various regimental accounts - a vital cog in the well being of the Regt. Throughout her varied service, she was always fair and looked after those under her command.

Barbara retired on 31 March 1984 very proud to have served her King, Queen and Country loyally and expertly for 40 years and 39 days. I am very proud to have known her for over fifty years. Anyone who knew her will recall that she loved her Jaguar cars which she had from 1953 until she passed away: she was driving until just three days before she died.

Obituary written by Doris White and published in Lioness 2010 No.1

Joan Huxtable - Join the ATS and see the World

In the October of 1939 I became 18 and old enough to volunteer to serve in the Auxiliary Territorial Service, the women's section of the Army. I left my job in the anticipation of an early call up but had to wait about 8 weeks for the papers to arrive. In the meantime, a weekly event for me was attendance at the local Unemployment Exchange to sign for 'dole' money, seven shillings and six pence.

Finally, the papers arrived, and I reported to the local recruiting centre in the Ocean Hotel, Saltdean, on the outskirts of Brighton. For many girls it was their first time away from home and as we were volunteers, we were given three days to settle in. Several asked for a railway pass back to their homes but I was very keen and thoroughly enjoyed the experience of kitting out, lectures, route marches and the food. Physical training on wet days was held in the ballroom which had a sprung floor. It took some pounding from about a hundred auxiliaries jumping up and down. Our pay was 5 shillings a week.

At that time there were only three types of jobs available, cooks, orderlies and clerks. I became a clerk and was posted to the Royal Artillery Records Office in Sidcup, Kent, to join the 25th City of London Company. We were billeted in private houses which meant that some of us had quite a walk to work. A short time after I arrived the British Expeditionary Force was driven out of France by the Germans and we had to work overtime sending our notices to the next of kin reporting the men who were wounded, missing or dead.

In September of 1940, the office was moved to Ibex House in the Minories, a short distance from the Tower of London. The Company was billeted in the Bourne and Hollingsworth Hostel in Gower Street, opposite the main University of London building.

The Blitz started soon after we had settled in. For a while we were able to travel by bus from the hostel to the office but gradually due to the bombing of buildings and roads we had to travel by underground railway. Finally, we had to walk to and from the office going different ways because the diversions due to unsafe buildings or bomb craters, some of which were huge, that had been caused by land mines.

There were basements in the hostel and when an air raid siren sounded at night we had to leave our beds, take a blanket and our gas mask and go down and lay or sit as best we could in the small spaces available which meant that nobody was able to get a good night's rest. After a few weeks we didn't go down but went out into the corridors so that if there was a bomb dropped near us, we wouldn't

135

get cut by the glass being blasted out of the windows. A few 78 more weeks of that and still not getting a proper sleep, we were given permission to sleep in our beds and risk getting hurt. One night a bomb landed just across the road from the hostel, it went straight down by the central tower of the University of London building. The blast shattered all our windows, so I got covered with broken glass as my bed was near the window. Fortunately, none hurt me, and I was able to shake all the pieces off. We were all evacuated from the building and spent the rest of the night in the basement of the School of Tropical Medicine which was next door. It was a bit strange trying to sleep surrounded by large bottles containing specimens of weird looking tropical spiders, snakes etc.

Due to the force of the blast the hostel wasn't safe to stay in so we moved to Gloucester Gate in Kensington which involved quite a long journey each day on the underground from Gloucester Road to Aldgate in the City. Each day we wondered if the office (Ibex House in the Minories) was still standing because so many buildings had been flattened round it and the Tower of London and Tower Bridge were prime targets a short distance away. The warehouse next to the office was hit one night. It was full of sugar which burned furiously to start with, then the sugar turned to syrup, so it took the firemen a long time to cool it, and the smell of burning sugar was awful.

In July 1941 I went on a Typists Training Course at Strathpeffer in Rossshire and stayed in the Ben Wyvis Hotel. It was my first visit to Scotland, and I enjoyed it very in the glen as the soldiers went on their route marches. The home of one of the girls I shared a bedroom with was a short distance away at Alness and she kindly took the other girl in the room and me there one day. Her home was a cottage in the grounds of the distillery, and we were shown the vats of whisky etc. The river nearby was in full spate, a wonderful sight.

During the time I was in Scotland the office had been moved from London to Rugby in Warwickshire. The hostel had belonged to Rugby Public School and contained study cubicles surrounding three sides of a quadrangle. The fourth side housed the toilets. There were cubicles with no doors which might have suited the boys but didn't please us, so blanket 'doors' were hastily put in place.

Civilian clerks began to take over our jobs, so I was posted to a Royal Engineers office at Stratford on Avon and was billeted in a private house. I spent a very uneventful day for my 21st birthday there.

In 1943 I went to the Deverrel Barracks at Ripon in Yorkshire to attend No. 2 Engineer Clerks Course (Advanced). It was January and very cold. The ablutions had a four-inch space at the top and bottom of the bathrooms. The wind seemed to come straight off the Yorkshire Moors, and it took courage to have a bath under those conditions.

After the course I went to Leamington Spa for a while and then was posted to a Royal Engineer office at Tettenhall in Staffordshire where I stayed in a private billet again. Mrs Duckworth was a good cook and I can still remember the lovely meals she gave me. During my stay there the 1000 bomber raids by the RAF were taking place. At dusk they would start flying over to Germany, wave after wave, the sky was full of them. The ominous drone of their engines made me at one moment feel safe that they were on our side and then I thought of the terror they would be causing in Germany.

Finally, my application to serve overseas came through and I was posted to London to prepare for embarkation. There were over a hundred girls in the company and we were given lectures on how to keep healthy in a hot country and had several injections, one being for yellow fever. That particular injection made several girls ill but I was alright. The issue of tropical kit caused a few laughs especially the bush hats, and we had to have several practice packings before we finally got all the kit stuffed into the one kit bag. We had to wait a few weeks and the time began to drag but finally the great moment arrived, and we set off in Troop Transports across London on the evening of 12 November 1943 to board the overnight train at St Pancras Station. All movement of troops were secret in those days, but the wise ones among us guessed we must be heading for Scotland.

In the morning we arrived at Gourock on the River Clyde and carried our kit bags from the station down to the quayside where we boarded a tug which took us out to the SS Arundel Castle lying offshore. Already aboard were a lot of RAF personnel and many officers of the various services. After we had been allocated our cabins, we trooped to the dining room for breakfast. The food was wonderful, plenty of it, well cooked and such a change from the restrictive rationing of war time Britain.

That night the ship sailed from the Clyde and we settled down to life aboard. The weather in the Bay of Biscay was very rough and many were seasick, but I wasn't, I ate my meals as usual. The only thing that worried me was the way the ship rolled. My life jacket hung on a doorknob when I was in the cabin and it swung from side to side with the roll of the ship. Once it seemed to stay at one side for longer than usual and I felt sure the ship would capsize but fortunately it righted itself. The ship was in a convoy of about 20 vessels and to keep our movements as secret as possible we waited until nighttime to pass through the Straits of Gibraltar. All the ships were in darkness,

large Italian house with a courtyard and a balcony on which were various large statues and pitchers. The room I slept in had an adjoining door to the private chapel in which were many religious relics. Little girls played outside this house and every day gave a different ATS girl a posy of flowers and a picture card.

The Royal Palace is a very grand place with wide marble staircases. One day one of the Italian staff let a few of us into a private room where we saw some of the presentation books that had been given to past Kings of Italy. They were magnificently bound, some in leather with gold tooling and some in silver with precious stones in typical Italian ornate designs. Leading off from one of the several inner courtyards was the entrance to the private Opera House and there I saw two operas, Cavaliera Rusticana and Paliarchi, sung by the members of the San Carlo Opera Company of Naples, a great experience. In the grounds of the palace, a straight mile away, was a large waterfall down a hillside, at the bottom of which were several fountains and many statues. The water was channelled into a wide stream edged with a stone wall on either side and had waterfalls at regular distances down the long straight path until it went underground near the palace. Along each side was a road which was a popular walk, where at night there were many fireflies to be seen and also many mosquitoes to bite us.

When the assault on Monte Cassino took place the noise of firing and convoys of troops going to and ambulances coming from was continuous. After the Germans were driven out of Rome, the Headquarters moved in and on our journey there it was very sad to see the ruins of that fine Abbey of Cassino and all the countryside devastated where the bitter fighting had taken place. From Naples to Rome there is a 40 odd kilometre straight road called the Appian Way, one of Mussolini's proud plans, but driving along such a long straight distance is very monotonous.

The billet in Rome was in a Catholic Girl Students Hostel of modern design, all white inside and out. In the entrance hall, in a niche in the circular staircase, was the figure of the Madonna wearing a royal blue cloak standing on a pedestal which stood in a pool of water, a very attractive sight. The office of the Italian Air Ministry had been commandeered as offices for the Headquarters. When we were off duty most of the interesting places to see were within walking distance of the hostel. I went to St Peters several times and a Private of our company was married there which was a great honour for the couple concerned. The catacombs where religious people were buried long ago interested some people, but I was terrified of the narrow sloping passages which always seemed to be going down. We carried lit candles and passing the recesses carved out of the rock it was eerie to see skeletons lying there. At one spot we went into a small cave and were asked to put out the candles and then just one was lit to show a holy relic of St Theresa. I was glad to get out of there. Another scary place was the cemetery of the Capuchin Fathers in a crypt below one of the many churches in Rome. Skeletons of some 4000 people had been arranged in various designs on walls, floors, ceilings and to come face to face with a whole wall covered with skulls can be a shattering experience.

One very pleasant sight was La Grotta, so difficult to describe, it was an amazing display of models beautifully arranged that one would need at least a week to study them all. I went twice to the Royal Opera House in Rome. The first time I was lucky enough to sit in one of the red plush boxes to see the opera La Tosca, the other time I sat in the circle to see the opera Manon.

I had a week's leave from duty which I spent at Salerno staying in a YWCA Hostel. Across the Bay of Naples was a wonderful view of Vesuvius. One day I went in a rowing boat with several others across the bay to Capri. After landing we went into a smaller rowing boat and were taken to the Blue Grotto, a sea water cave in the cliffs of Capri. It can only be entered by going through a tunnel at certain states of the tide and we had to lie flat in the boat as there was only just enough room for it to get through. The fluorescent blue water has to be seen to be believed, a real wonder of nature but I was glad to get back to dry land as I'm not keen on small boats. Later in the day I went on a car tour of the island and saw Grade Field's home and the house San Michele of book fame. Whilst in Rome I was among the ATS who were a Guard of Honour to General Mark Clark, the Commander of the US Fifth Army, when he presented a plaque to the American Women's Army Corps.

There was so much to see in Rome that our stay seemed short and as the armies were advancing rapidly after the retreating Germans we also had to move, this time to Sienna in Tuscany.

The billet was another students hostel but was so crowded that some of us were moved into a private billet with very nice people. When off duty for a day we were taken by Liberty truck to Florence where we saw more of Italy's splendours.

The Headquarter staff of the Allied Armies were gradually dispersed as their particular jobs finished and another girl and I were posted to the Army School of Education in Perugia. Our billet was with the Lady Secretary of the University for Foreigners, in a flat at the top of the building used by the school. There was a wonderful view across the valley terraced by vineyards to the town of Assissi on a distant hill. I worked at the library which had a large collection of books in English. In my off-duty time, I managed to get a lift to Assissi to visit the church and tomb of St Francis, and also to see the church of the Poor Clares, the Order of Nuns who were associated with St. Francis.

It was distressing on the journeys around the countryside to see the cemeteries that had been hastily created by some particularly tough battles. One would be all Canadian, Australian, New Zealand, Indian, Britlsh or American. War is so stupid.

I had a week's leave at Riccione on the Adriatic coast. It wasn't long after the armies had passed on and in the middle of a road junction was a surface grave of a British soldier, buried where he was killed. His steel helmet lay on top and a rough wooden cross stated his name and number. The grave was left there to remind the local people that he had given his life for them. Very early one morning about 4 am I heard a lorry stop and the sound of shovels. I looked out of the window to see soldiers putting the blanket shrouded corpse into a lorry with the steel helmet and cross, then they shovelled the soil away so that there was no evidence there. The dead soldier would be just another body put in one of the numerous military cemeteries.

In 1945 peace in Europe was declared and troops were being sent home for demobilization. When my turn came, I boarded a train at Rimini which stopped at Milan for the night. The next day the train continued its journey through the long tunnels of Switzerland but there were glimpses of the Alps and chalets in us to see. The journey across France was alarming in places when the train went around sharp corners at a perilous angle.

I left the train at Calais and stayed the night in a Transit Camp. I had lived by the English Channel for the first eighteen years of my life, but this was my first opportunity to sail across. After looking at dry and drab lands for over two years it was an exciting experience to see the White Cliffs of Dover and the countryside looKing so very green and fresh.

The demobilization depot for ATS returning from overseas was the place where I had waited so eagerly to go abroad. After passing through all the formalities of receiving the necessary forms to return to civilian life each girl was personally thanked for her service by the Commanding Officer of the unit. In my case she was Mary, daughter of Sir Winston Churchill.

Lioness 1994 No. 2

Phyllis Lowryhill

Phyllis was born on 17 February 1920 in Constantinople, (now Istanbul) Turkey where her father was in business. Soon after, the British had to leave Turkey and the family came back to England and settled in Greenwich. She was educated locally and then joined the Commercial Union Insurance Company in the City as a secretary.

In May 1943 she joined the ATS and trained at Guildford. Her first posting was to 487 Bty, 137 (M) HAA Regt RA located on North London gunsites until after D-Day. In December 1944 the unit relocated to Belgium as part of the air defences in Antwerp and she was there on VE Day before moving to an airfield near Hamburg.

She returned home in April 1945 having been selected for officer training at Windsor. Three tours in the UK followed and in 1949 she was posted to Singapore and I think that she enjoyed that tour as much as any. One of her duties was to be appointed Registrar for Births, Marriages and Deaths for the Far East Land Forces. This was at the time of the emergency in Malaya and required a good deal of travelling including to Hong Kong and up into Malaya.

After further UK tours she was posted to BAOR as Adjutant of 12 Bn WRAC in 1960 and then promotion to Major in 1964 took her to Aden as OC of the WRAC Coy, returning to the UK in 1966. That year she was married to Larry LowryHill, a former RAF officer whom she had met during her service in Aden. She was then on her last posting, at Donnington and in January 1967 she retired from the WRAC.

Lioness 2003 No.2

Vicky Tunbridge - Secretary to the C-in-C

I left school at 14, in 1938, and was working in an office in the West End of London when the war started. I left that job to work at Crown Agents for the Colonies at Millbank. At times when ships were sunk, we were asked to work overtime to get things to the Colonies and were able to stay overnight, sleeping in the basement. Sometimes getting to work was difficult because of the bombing, with bus timetables being interrupted. However, it was a lovely atmosphere – everyone helped everyone else.

I was anxious to join one of the services. My father wasn't keen on the idea, so I had to wait until I was 18½ to join without his consent. I tried the RAF but was twice refused as they hadn't any secretarial vacancies, and I wanted to keep up my shorthand and typing skills. I was therefore thrilled when accepted by the Army.

My posting came through in March 1943 and I was sent to Pontefract for initial training. After three weeks I was posted to HQ RA Training Establishments at Windsor. I was secretary to three officers, and sometimes the General who often had to go to the War Office – when he would take me with him, as he preferred the ATS to civilian girls.

We had some idea that things were moving when our drivers at Windsor were taken to help in delivering transport to coastal areas, and then we got news on the radio of the invasion. The only bubbly we had to celebrate was a tin of Andrew's [Liver Salts]!

When we knew that members were needed for overseas, one of my friends and I decided to put in our applications and got selected for the Allied Commission in Vienna, Austria. We were posted to Hammersmith; billeted in flats at Barons Court. It was quite exciting being in at the start of the formation of the Allied Commission. When our turn came to leave, we were sent to Liverpool to join the troopship SS Orontes. We were nearing the Bay of Naples when news came through that the war had ended. Listening to the news on the radio of the celebrations in London made me very homesick and a little tearful. On arrival at Naples we boarded open trucks for Rome, going via Cassino (so we were able to see some of the results of the fighting). It was very hot in May 1945 in Rome.

Within a few months we were off to Vienna. I was to be Personal Secretary to General McCreery, Commander of the 8th Army and at that time Commander-in-Chief BTA.

I was accompanied to the airport by two male officers and a male sergeant, where we boarded a small converted fighter. The male sergeant sat in the turret, the officers on the tail and I was on the step leading into the cockpit – this was my first flight; not exactly luxurious!

In Vienna we were given rather nice quarters next to Schonbrunn barracks. Vienna was badly bombed, and it was divided into zones – Russian, French, English and American – and we had special passes in all languages. We weren't allowed out unless in twos, and not in the evenings unless accompanied. Our place of work was in Schonbrunn Palace.

My friend and I were busy in the Secretariat, often having to carry on working into the evening typing minutes of the four-power meetings. As the electricity went off most evenings, this had to be done by the light of hurricane lamps, and as there was no heating, we made use of our greatcoats. It was quite eerie being in the dark in a large palace.

After leaving the ATS in 1947 I joined the Territorials with two of the girls I had been with in Vienna. We chose somewhere we could all get to without too much trouble – this was an HAA unit in Harrow, and we used to go to weekend and other camps.

Lioness 2018 No.2

Helen Morse - My Service History

In October 1945, I made a rash decision to join the Auxiliary Territorial Service (ATS). During a visit from my cousins who were on leave I informed Lex that I would be in the uniform next, but he informed me that I was Yellow (lacking courage and would not step outside of my comfort zone). On Monday morning, I visited the Recruitment Centre and completed the initial application form.

I was called for a medical in early December 1945 and I passed! I felt that I was now on my way to join the Auxiliary Territorial Service (ATS). On 4th January 1946, I travelled from Glasgow to Leicester to be based at Glen Parva Barracks for my basic training and the beginning of a most wonderful and life changing life.

On completion of my basic training, I was posted to RAPC Office in Kidderminster (Worcester, England). Where we were dealing with and paying the servicemen who had been demobbed for their final settlement. From there, I was transferred to the Royal Army Pay Corps (RAPC) Office in Glasgow, Scotland. Shortly after arriving, one evening I read a notice asking for volunteers to serve overseas. I was the first on the list and took this opportunity!

On the 6th May 1947, I was on embarkation leave. I had no idea where I would be going to. My only instructions informed me that I should travel from Glasgow to North Mymms in Hertfordshire, where transport would take us to the Holding and Drafting Unit. We went through the usual checking of health and ensuring we had received all necessary inoculations - for where we were going. We attended lots of meetings about different types of diseases, we may come across, then we were given the usual forwarding address card to send to our parents. That was when we realised, we were on our way to The Far East!

On a Friday morning, we left North Mymms Camp and travelled by road to Tilbury docks, where we joined the Troopship SS Toronto. What a journey, I remember sailing through the Bay of Biscay on Sunday morning. When there was quite high winds and the ship was rolling and rocking around. But it was so exciting, we loved every minute of the experience! Our first Port of call was Port Said, we were there and watching all the boats selling their goods. During the journey, I was employed when payday came along paying out the weekly pay to the troops. Our next port of call was Aden – we were allowed ashore for a few hours whilst the ship was in dock for supplies and refuelling. On the move again and waiting patiently for the next port, which was Colombo, that was where we were held up for 5 days as there was no berth available in Singapore. Our accommodation on arrival was the married quarters in Tanglin Barracks. My new life was now going to change from here!

Most of us on draft were about to change our trade. I was transferred to Royal Signals to be trained as a switchboard operator. It looked as though we would never be able to cope, but like all of us within weeks we were like old soldiers doing everything that was expected. We worked on shifts as we all knew soldiers were on duty 24 hours a day. During our time in Singapore, we were allowed leave, my first leave was to The Cameron Highlands in Malaya. The weather there was much colder than in Singapore, but it was nice to relax and enjoy the scenery. Our life in Singapore was good lots of places to see and lots of time spent near the beaches and picnics on the beach.

My next holiday was to Penang, the island at the other end of Singapore this was good most of the time we spent there on the beach or visiting The Temple, which was exciting, to see and hear about its origin.

The good life ended in November 1948, when we had to pack our bags and head home on the next Troopship to enjoy our disembarkation leave and spend some time with our family.

In January 1949, I was to join Northern Command Signal Regiment in York. Whilst there the demise of the ATS was forthcoming on 31st January 1949 we removed our ATS Cap Badge and inserted the Women's Royal Army Corps Badge (WRAC). So, the end of one and the start of another but none of us would forget our time as a member of the Auxiliary Territorial Service (ATS).

During my time at Northern Command I tried very hard to see if another opening would come for further travel overseas. I was later transferred to Scottish Command working at the Castle. This was also very interesting, as time went on I still wanted to travel overseas. I believed there was a chance of going back to the Far East, in 1952. But, when I arrived in Singapore, I was informed that I would be posted to Hong Kong.

When I arrived in Hong Kong, I really fell in love with the island. Shortly after, we arrived we found ourselves working on the switchboard where again it was shifts. Whilst on duty one morning the engineers told us to evacuate the switchboard as there was the beginning of a fire in the equipment room. All personnel were able to get out without accidents. True to good signals engineers we had a Field Fortress switchboard installed in 2 days. We were now located in the old Japanese underground headquarters for about 8 months while the new switchboard arrived.

The next big day we had was trying to arrange the first ever Double Wedding to be performed in Hong Kong, St. John's Cathedral, 1952. The wedding was for Miss Edna Hollyhead and Mr David Snashall. The second wedding was for Miss Irene Dyson and Mr John Jacques. The reverend for this wedding was W.G. Haig-Brown. The bridesmaids for the weddings were myself (Helen Black), Hazel Duff, Julie Ruffle and Julie Barber- we were all a part of the WRAC. The reception was held at the Taikoo Club, Quarry Bay, 20th September 1952. It certainly was a wonderful day for all of us and the thoughts we had about that day were the old saying we now have - *WRAC The Best*!

During this time of upheaval along with a colleague I was fortunate to be able to get a cruise to Japan on the British India Steam Navigation Company. This was the highlight of my stay in Hong Kong. For the sum of £22.00 we had a 3 weeks cruise of Japan visiting Kobe, then on to Yokohama. Our next port of call was Tokyo, where we visited the Emperor's palace, then on to Kyoto the site of Mount Fuji leaves one inspired by the beauty of Japan.

Once again, my time was drawing to a close where we were due to be sent back to the UK in 1953.

After disembarkation leave, I was posted to 2 Ack Ack Signal Regiment based in Aldershot. During this time, I had the job of working with the 'Z' Reservists who had been organised in case of further troubles.

Now that things seemed to be settling, I started to seek for openings in overseas areas. One came up and I was on embarkation leave again this time it was to Egypt. On arrival at Port Said, we disembarked and were taken by transport through the canal zone to Fayad. Our destination was Ladysmith Camp. I was attached to 3 LofC Signal Regiment. I had just settled but after 8 months I had to pack my bags and fly to Nicosia.

Upon arrival, I was met by a colleague who took me to Kykko Camp Nicosia this was approximately November 1954. I soon settled into the routine of work, for I was now attached to Royal Signals Middle East. I worked both in the Comms Centre and Switchboard. I found that the arrangement of the work made life quite interesting. On the switchboard, we had local employees working alongside us. The shift pattern was quite good, we were able to go out on picnics to the beaches at Famagusta. Indeed, we had lots of fun in Nicosia. Once the troubles increased on 30ᵗʰ November 1955, the Governor announced that we were now on a state of emergency. It was during this time that I met my future husband whilst working on the same shift. My life suddenly took on a different approach and we decided that we would get married on our return to the UK.

The rest may be history but fortunately for me, I still managed to travel overseas with my husband firstly to Germany in March 1957. This is where we stayed until our first daughter was born in March 1958. However, we only stayed there for another 7 months before we were posted to Singapore in September 1958. During our stay, we had our first son in February 1961. We then once again moved to Norway in 1962. During our time there, our last child was born in July 1962. Eventually we moved for the final time with our three children back to England in 1968.

Written by Helen Morse for this book.

Berry Abbott - My Career in The ATS & WRAC

I joined up in 1944 and celebrated my 18th birthday at Queens Camp, Guildford on 7th September. My mother sent me a birthday cake which we tried to cut into 25 pieces, the number in our hut. I particularly remember how hard it was to mark our kit with a pen and nib.

I was posted to Fleet, to be trained as a driver. I was billeted in the grounds of a large house called 'Denorben Court'. At first we lived in two Nissan huts which were in a field. It snowed quite a lot and we had to wade through it to go up to the house for orders and meals. When on fire piquet we peeled two fire buckets of potatoes. I remember being given a tin mug of cocoa made with water to keep us warm. Later we were moved up to the big house.

On one of my driving routes, when we stopped for a tea break, I lost my lovely yellow leather driving gloves. I was put on a charge and 2/6p was deducted from my 13 shilling pay each week until they were paid for. However, I was quite proud when, on our drill competition, I was the only one with new clean gloves. My best friend was Eileen Farrell. When we were posted I went to North West Common, London and Eileen went to Weymouth.

I then had various postings: 598 Coy Tavistock & Plymouth, 597 Coy Salisbury and 721 Car Coy Bad Oyenhausen, Germany.

When we went to Germany, we had to make a will in the back of our AB 64 and we were each issued with a burial blanket! We were billeted in houses and I drove all over Germany.

Leave was supposed to be every six months, but we were given short leave in Germany every three months. I went to Bad Hazburg, Winterburg and Nordeny and learned to ski and ride. I was so lucky. In 1947 I was demobbed but joined up again and stayed for 22 years. I was posted to Germany on three two-year stints. 721 Car Coy became 36 Car Coy and there was a lot for the drivers to do with the 'Berlin Airlift' and the 'Nuremberg Trials'.

In 1954, as my parents were getting older, I applied for a Type 'R' posting which was Exmouth. I was posted to Dartmouth as PSI with the TA in Devon.

Lioness 2002 No.2

Josie Renwick - Extract from her diary Summer 1949

12 Aug 49 - We were allotted a wooden hut - ramshackle from the outside but alright on the interior. Two of the eleven beds had already been claimed but there was no sign of the claimants. Wearily, we each chose a bed and - dumping out kit on our choice - followed the Corporal who had showed us to the hut, back past similar wood edifices to the cookhouse. The sun had cooled with the evening and the short walk with the prospect of a cup of tea and a meal was a pleasant one. The tallness of the trees and the faint rustle of the wind through their leaves was balm after the eternal hurry that we were used to.

The cookhouse was very similar to Guildford's, except for the amazing fact that sparrows quite unconcernedly fluttered around settling on the tables as though they had every right. We ate hungrily and our strength at once returned. Soon we were back in the hut unpacking with energy and dashing up to the huge house wherein we were told was the NAAFI.

Horsley Hall had once been the home of a wealthy family. I was enchanted with the secrets the walls so obviously held. What an intricate ceiling in this room here, how beautiful it was "Jo - what are you gazing at? Come on there's table tennis." Tony and I played until sour looks from numerous waiting couples suddenly became apparent and sadly we surrendered the table. "We ought to go back down soon," said Tony, "and find out where the bathroom is." So we had another cup of tea each and then walked slowly back through the blissful beauty of that quiet and mellowed place which had once been the well-kept grounds of Horsley Hall.

The bathhouse was opposite the hut and was the most eerie place I've ever seen. There were two baths and numerous showers, which dripped and creaked in alarming manner. The bottoms of the baths were streaked with rust and the rafters were covered in dust and cobwebs. The lights were very dim. "I don't think - " I said, "I'll be having many baths during the next eight weeks."

Five minutes later however I was in the bath. Soon Tony surprised me completely by stating that she'd finished and there was I not even out of the water! "D'you mind if I go?" she called, obviously not expecting me to say 'yes', so I said 'No' and she went. Keroonk, tk. Keroonk, tk ... The showers were at it again, or was it the showers? It was so much more like the creaking of chains heaved along slowly by a tortured spirit. "This has been a garden shed," I thought. "And the gardener murdered some girl in here." I was sweating now and not from the heat of the water. Keroonk, tk. Keroonk, tk ... The noise went on with terrible regularity. I was petrified. "You're a fool" I said to myself but remained unconvinced. I took a frightened leap from the bath which wobbled violently adding to my terror and frantically I tugged my towel about my body. I flung on my pyjamas and dashed from that bathhouse across the path, up the steps into the hut where I collapsed breathless onto my bed. "Oh Tony," I said, "Don't ever leave me in there again!".

Lioness 2005 No.1

Janet Cox - Happy Band of Girls

In the summer of 1949, I saw an advertisement in the national press for ladies who could play any kind of instrument or had knowledge of music, to form the new WRAC Band. I decided to pop down to the recruitment office and sign up unbeknown to my father who had very Victorian views and would have disapproved.

I sat the examinations, had a medical and they found that I couldn't hear properly. After having my ear syringed a bead fell out which must have been there for years. I was then told that I was too young to join up as I wouldn't be 17 and a half years old until the following November. I went home with my hearing so clear and I was dying to tell my parents about the bead but decided against it in case I got a clip around the ear from my Dad.

One day during October I came home from work and Dad was sitting by the fire with a look of thunder on his face and in his hand was a very official looking letter. I had forgotten my visit to the recruiting office and wasn't really bothered about joining up, but Dad said "I have signed it. Go and don't bother to come home you will only get pregnant." What a start to my life in the WRAC.

At the beginning of November, I travelled down to Guildford and after being kitted out with uniform, D.Ks, large bra, woollen stockings, brown lace up shoes and enough STs to last me until I did get pregnant!

After basic training I duly joined the Band. What a welcome. I believe that I was only the fourteenth girl to join. The other members came from all over the country, one was a Salvation Army girl, a couple from colleges, another couple from the Dagenham Girl Pipers and one or two who had transferred over from the ATS Band. Our Bandmaster was WO1 Fred Goddard who was so kind to the girls. We could talk to him about most things and "cry on his shoulder". I was enlisted as a cornet player and our instructor was Sgt Ted Stevens, the Band Sgt Major, who taught us all he knew about brass instruments. He was very strict but had an understanding manner.

On 22nd April 1950 the Band was asked to take part in a concert with the Kneller Hall Band for HM King George VI. By that time, we had 25 playing members and had been kitted out in our very smart No 1 Dress with gold braid. This was our first public appearance and it went down so well that we took off with a bang playing at such places as Eastbourne, Brighton, Worthing and Edinburgh. We also made a broadcast for the BBC on Music While You Work. In addition, we played at the Lord Mayor's Show, the Tattoo at White City and Edinburgh and played for the Queen's Coronation River Pageant.

Despite my father's prediction, I did not get pregnant whilst in the band but did have a bit of a scare when the band was playing in Catterick. A colleague in the band and I developed terrible stomach pains and reported sick thinking it might be food poisoning by coincidence both of us were suffering from appendicitis. When the hospital spoke to my father on the telephone the following day the nurse said to him, "Mr Skellon, your daughter is in the Royal Infirmary. This is just to let you know that they are both doing well." Dad put the 'phone down and said to himself "I knew she would get pregnant". Anyway, he decided that he ought to find out more and rang the hospital the next day to ask whether his daughter had a boy or a girl and was informed that I had had my appendix removed and that my friend was also at the same hospital having undergone the same operation.

From that day on my father trusted me. I left to get married at the end of 1953 but have very fond recollections of my time with the band and have not forgotten any of the musicianship that I acquired there and still play with various other bands. The original girls who joined the Band in 1949 formed a group called the 49ers and we meet once a year to reminisce and catch up on all our news. We all have wonderful memories of our time in The Band.

Lioness 2005 No.2
See images in centre pages

Pauline Hawker - The WRAC Band

It was 1951 and the world was still in a bit of a mess. For several years teenagers had given up dreams of what they wanted to be and I found my musical opportunity in the staff band of the Women's Royal Army Corps, with a reasonable knowledge of musical theory, and became a B/flat clarinettist with tenor saxophone as a second string.

The next few years were really exciting, playing anywhere in Britain where troops were on parade and the occasion required a band. Coronation year was especially good, though for itself disappointing since all bands were allocated to the various Royal parks, and most of the crowds stayed in the Mall with the rainy mist. It was much better in Edinburgh at the tattoo that year, bands were there in force, including the Canadian Mounties from Canada with their gorgeous horses. Each night we played to packed crowds, and every morning off duty we were allowed into theatres to hear some of the world's best orchestras at practice.

Of course, there were 'bread and butter' jobs as well, mostly at seaside bandstands, some better than others. Music could be blown into the sea on a windy day, while one person remaining to listen contracts demanded we continue the programme until our time was up!

In 1953, before foreign holidays were the norm, we were sent to Berlin where many troops were situated to help keep the peace. It was explained we would travel through Holland and the Russian Zone. This was one of the powers occupying parts of the areas affected by the war. Special trains were used at night with blinds closed during the journey. I could not sleep not sleep and walked about in the corridor, seeing a young soldier in our corridor I asked him if he would use his rifle if Russians stopped the train, to which he replied "Dunno miss because the officers got the ammunition and he's asleep in first class".

Berlin and a sense of shame. Shame because I had not realised, we had bombed their churches and schools too. There was a rehearsal almost immediately at the Tiergarten, a few hours rest, then back to our evening concert.

I had never seen Germany before and in spite of childhood experiences thought they looked much like people anywhere, and gradually we relaxed. Of course, they are music lovers and we appreciated the way they sang to us at the end of the concert, all prepared and yet spontaneous too. Next morning there was time for coffee in the broad, busy Friedrichstrasse whilst watching the town go about their business. Later there was an opportunity to visit in the Russion Sector, by coach of course and with an official guide, only stopping at pre-arranged places.

I shall never forget that ride, it was both fascinating and horrible and we all suffered agonies of unappeased curiosity. The chief memory is of ruins, ruins everywhere. People were living in them, coming up out of cellars to go shopping. Many of the women and children were barefoot in October. Two great shop-fronted streets named for Stalin and Lenin were full of goods nobody seemed able to afford and everything else was falling to bits. Women were on demolition work, bricklaying and street sweeping, old women with oined and heples faces, younger ones with resigned faces. They stared at us as our coach passed by, especially the 'People's' police at street corners, armed and with dogs.

It was all the strangest sensation, like being disembodied yet participating in a scene with strangers. We all felt it, the security of the coach with BRITISH stuck on a label up front seeming a frail fortress in an alien land. I found myself wondering how I would have reacted if geography and history had not been on my side. Fifteen minutes later, back in the American sector, there was relief at finding ourselves back in friendly territory, passing Tempelhof Airport.

Then on back to Holland, this time to stay in the Hague, give two more concerts and a little sightseeing. Among other places the Royal Palace was worth seeing if only to compare the difference between it and our own Royal Family's residence. It looked rather like a town hall, just off a busy road with no railings or guards about.

The last concert of our tour was memorable. We played one of the standard mixtures, overture, march, solo, selection etc and had decided to close the evening with my little find - the Windmill's Turning. I had thought someone might know it but none of us were prepared for the reception the audience gave to the tune. They sang it, rocking to and fro in time to it, and insisted in many encores. It must have been as well-known as their National Anthem.

The camp was in Penicuik and our feet didn't touch the ground from the Saturday we arrived till the Thursday evening of the first week. Life was so hectic that the Major (Hon V V Kitson) decided to give us all a rest day on the Friday my 21st Birthday. The unit spent the day on the beach at, if I remember correctly, Portobello. The day was glorious, and I have the fondest memories of sun, sand and sea, two Scots dolls, and a travelling alarm clock which has only recently come to the end of its days, having been used constantly from that August. A really delicious birthday cake was made by the cooks (two of whom are unfortunately no longer with us).

Many happy years followed in the company of girls who I will remember forever. True friendships were established as were many acquaintances. Greetings are still exchanged at Birthdays and Christmas. Two sergeants and one officer in particular I have to thank they will know who they are when/if they read this epistle.

My 12 years in the Service were varied, being a trainee driver, driver and then driving instructor and many tales could be told of the hilarious times, if I had the space.

One 'night rally' in particular during a fortnight's "holiday" (as my day job employer called it) is well remembered. We had to leave Barnard Castle late one evening. We had scrimmed up the vehicles during the day an exercise I would rather forget and when the 'wagons roll' call was heard we jumped into our vehicles and away we went. My three tonner had the scrim netting rolled up underneath and as I drove away the netting caught in the propshaft. Many hands to the 'sump' as I reversed as slowly as I could and the girls lying beneath the lorry unhooked the netting as I went. Not an easy job as they would tell. Unleashed we went forward, completed the rally and our unit came away with all but one of the trophies. We were ribbed for the rest of the week, but we did not care because we were on cloud nine.

Our battalion formed a Saddle Club and went horse riding on Sundays at Gracedieu Stables in Shepshed. One of the highlights of this was being in the company of Lady Isobel Barnett who was our Commander in Chief and a great storyteller. I remember volunteering to do kitchen duty at an Officers' Mess function she attended. I was very impressed that a Lady of her standing would come to thank us for the work we had put in; sitting on the kitchen table and eating chicken legs with us (no plates or napkins to hand). I was a Private then as I recall but still felt that I belonged.

I eventually reached the giddy height of full corporal never achieving my ambition to become a sergeant like my grandfather, still never mind, I enjoyed what I did.

The battalion disbanded in 1966 and I was given the choice of Signals (too much like my day job) and Nursing (not for me) so I reluctantly took my discharge after 12 years of agony and ecstasy. I received my Long Service Medal by post having moved to the Northampton Branch of same unit.

I have moved away now from Leicester/Northampton and live in Skegness, still a life member of the Association but unable mostly to attend the monthly meetings. Semiretirement found me doing bed and breakfast in an East Coast resort but again this was not for me so I found a job at the local hospital doing reception work. I found this especially rewarding for an oldie like me, as when I see the poor dears who attend it makes me feel good and young for my age. The adage "Grow up and you grow old" is certainly true. I still play 'tag' on the beach with an even older friend (when there is no one around to see the old fools). My friend and I have taken up dancing ballroom, sequence, Latin American, formation and line.

Having reached Gold Medal standard in most of these we are having a bit of a rest until we find something else to do or progress further on the dance floor. I say to all members, old and new, ancient and modern, if you want anything in this life GO FOR IT you never know what you can do if you never try. Why I'm saying this to you I do not know. I have never met so many "achievers" in my life as the resolute members of the now disbanded Women's Royal Army Corps.

Lioness 2000 No.2

Moira Applegate

My initial posting was to Queen Elizabeth Barracks in Guildford and then on to Yeovil for trade training. I was already a shorthand typist in civilian life though I did not join up until I was the grand old age of 22 years!

I was sent to work in London to the Ministry of Defence, which was then housed in Great George Street/Storey's Gate, overlooking St James' Park. I was told initially that I would be working for a Brigadier so would have to watch my Ps and Qs. However, we had only been there a few weeks when we were told that we were to work for Lord Mountbatten who was coming as the first Chief of the Defence Staff (CDS). Wow were my parents impressed, as they were not happy about me joining up in the first place. Why did I not choose the Senior Service instead of the Army!

We were a 3-man (woman) team, acting as shorthand writers to CDS and his staff. There was one girl from each Service as this was a Joint Service appointment. I was always disappointed that I never had a flash to wear on my uniform so always looked like a rookie.

I also remember having to type the Queen's Speech for Parliament and in those days, we had manual typewriters. We were not allowed to make any errors and you could bet your life we would get down to the last line and make a mistake!

We travelled up to London by coach, or underground depending on shifts, and had to wear civilian clothing. This was because there were so many officers around the Whitehall area and we would be forever saluting. We only wore uniform one day a week when we had to attend Pay Parade at, I think, the Civil Service Club in Great Scotland Yard. To get there, we would have to walk past the Cenotaph and would have to salute and 'eyes right' every time, so we used to take a shortcut through the Foreign Office and then through the gardens of 10 Downing Street where we would come out on to Horse Guards Parade. Most of the time this was OK but I remember one occasion when we suddenly came upon a parade already in position. We tried to beat a hasty retreat but were spotted by a Sergeant who immediately marched us across the Square and we had to salute the officer on parade, then go through Horse Guards' archway where the officers were ready for changing the guard! Were our faces red with all the tourists watching us?

Life at that time in London was quite exciting and we would go to the Nuffield Club and get free tickets for a West End show. We were also called on to carry out ceremonial duties and I remember being at the Royal Albert Hall for the Festival of Remembrance Service. We practised all day under the watchful eye of Sir Ralph Reader who would shout at us until we could march down those awful steps, then across the centre to arrive on stage and take our place without getting out of step. I don't think there was a dry eye in the house when the Chelsea Pensions came on!

I was with Lord Mountbatten for over 12 months and it was during that time that Lady Louis died, and we had the awful task of receiving, sorting and replying to over 6,000 letters of condolence. It was a very sad time and we also had to help with the arrangements for the Memorial Service at Westminster Abbey.

I was subsequently posted to Cyprus where I worked for the headquarters of the Near East Land Forces. I was there for 18 months and enjoyed every minute of it. Cyprus then was not a tourist area and we had access to the whole of the island. A lot of my friends there were in the Royal Military Police and I went with them for lots of trips out to Famagusta, Kyronia etc.

After my demob, I married the brother of one of my army friends, but this did not work out and I returned to my parental home where I am to this day. I am glad that at the ripe old age of 22 I joined up and, although there were a few times when I would cry into my pillow at night, most of my 3 years were just great. I was a very shy person with little or no confidence in myself, but the Army gave me that team spirit and confidence and the knowledge that I was as good as anyone else.

Lioness 2003 No.1

Helen Guild Meechie - Director WRAC 1982 - 1986

Helen, born in Dundee in 1938 and with a degree of Modern Languages from St Andrew's University, reported to the Women's Royal Army Corps School of Instruction in August 1960. This establishment was always known as Liphook because in those days of fewer motor cars (and particularly not for students!) the detraining station was Liphook. As a University entrant, Helen lived in the Officer Cadet Mess but was required to attend only a short Commissioning Course which, for her, was completed in December of that year.

Postings as a Subaltern Officer followed. It soon became apparent to her contemporaries, amongst others, that Helen was a 'flyer' and that she warranted 'career postings'. These were not of her choice but were those of senior officers of the day who wished her Army experience and background to be broadened. Of these postings one was to Cyprus as a Staff Captain 'A': (for those not conversant with Army abbreviations of those days, 'A' Branch dealt with all matters affecting the soldier as an individual; not operational matters nor supplying the Army with its material needs). She was, in fact, later posted to Hong Kong where she did deal with these other staff subjects.

Whilst in Dhekelia, Helen was tasked with the revision of a Families Guide Book. This book received universal acclaim, fuelled as it was by the outpourings of the ubiquitous coffee pot of a fellow WRAC officer on the staff there at the time. It is also now known that whilst in Cyprus a performance of "Noyes Fludde" was arranged. Helen played the cello in the orchestra. An informant states "I do not think that many people know that she was a cellist". The informant was undoubtedly right!

Helen's career was not that of a "blue stocking" and it would therefore not do her justice simply to provide a detailed list of postings. She represented the Army at InterService level in both tennis and hockey; and her introduction to golf is now known to have occurred long before she was stationed in Aldershot. With friends, she was camping under canvas somewhere in UK and at nightfall had pitched tent on an apparently suitable stretch of greensward. At dawn, unaccountable objects were falling on the tent, and investigation caused equally unrecognised shouts of "fore". History does not relate on which fairway of which golf course this happened, but undoubtedly it did.

Before her posting to Germany, on promotion to Lieutenant Colonel, Helen attended a course at the National Defence College at Latimer. She felt at home in Rheindahlen, the "Home of the British Army of the Rhine," with another Queen's Avenue as its main thoroughfare; a road which led not only to Holland in minutes but passport free travel to all other surrounding countries. She enjoyed this facility to the full with the freedom that fast roads gave her. Other long journeys by road were taken, mainly after retirement, to visit friends in Scotland for whom she was always a welcome guest.

Some will remember Helen for her own generous hospitality at her flat in Frimley whilst she was stationed in Aldershot a flat owned by a retired officer of the Corps, which was to be occupied by others as postings permitted. Helen's progress to becoming Director can perhaps best be described in modern parlance as "seamless".

One of her achievements in this appointment was to instigate the publication of "The Corps Today", complete sets of which are held in the Public Record Office and the National Army Museum. A Retired Officer on Helen's staff at that time has said of her "I found Helen a very understanding boss". Another officer, very much her junior, says of Helen "what a demanding employer she could be but it was always done with humour and was always for my benefit". Helen might have concurred happily had she known of that 'assessment' of her at the time!

Helen's successor as Director Women's Royal Army Corps writes: "During her tenure as DWRAC Helen was elected to hold the Chairmanship of the NATO Committee on Women. The Committee met each year at NATO Headquarters. Its membership consisted of the most senior serving women from all the services from each NATO country; its remit, to study and make recommendations on the employment of women in the armed services of NATO. In many ways she came to carry the hopes not only of women in this country but also of the senior serving women throughout NATO".

Expectations and hopes were high and there was genuine rejoicing when after her tour as Director (at a particularly early age) she was selected to attend the course at the Royal College of Defence Studies; another "career posting" for only the most promising of senior officers and in Helen's case, a 'first' for a female officer of any service. She was posted on completion of the course to the appointment of Deputy Director General Personnel Services (Army) in the Ministry of Defence.

Sadly, her undoubted talents were not rewarded by the great prize of the next step up the promotion ladder. However, her qualities were to be acknowledged in other spheres. She was appointed Honorary Colonel of Tayforth Officers' Training Corps another 'first' for a female officer. She received an Honorary Doctorate of Laws from Dundee University and she had become a Freeman of the City of London.

In 1993 she was appointed, and completed, a five-year tenure as a Deputy Colonel Commandant of the Adjutant General's Corps; in recognition of the fact that the WRAC on disbandment had been one of the antecedent Corps from which the AG Corps had been formed. In 1997 Helen became Vice President and Chairman of the WRAC Association, but retired with grace at what she judged to be an appropriate time after the onset of her illness.

In retirement, Helen had moved to Wiltshire and continued her passion for golf. Typically, when it became obvious to her that she would never play golf again, she gave her Hill Billy electric golf trolley away. This apparently simple act of generosity must have been a heart-rending step for Helen. The wife of the recipient says now "whenever I see the batteries being charged, I shall remember seeing Helen playing a tee shot which seemed nearly to reach the green 343 yards distant".

Perhaps Helen's character and qualities have already been summed up appropriately by the author of a book entitled "On Laffans Plain" (a history of Army Golf Club and its courses 1883 2000). He, a retired senior Army Officer and a golfer, has written an enduring epithet. His words read: "Reference to Service Ladies would not be complete without mention of Brigadier Helen Meechie. This remarkable person was Director of her Corps and formed the WRAC Golfing Society. She was Chairman (none of this 'Madam Chair', 'Chair Lady' or 'Chairperson' nonsense for Helen) of the society which made Army Golf Club its home."

The style and spirit that Helen helped to create were remarkable and the WRAC were always among the most competitive of service teams. The happy, sporting atmosphere that pervaded the WRAC Golfing Society continued after the demise of the WRAC and translated easily into the formation of the Army Golfing Association, Ladies Section.

The AGA Ladies Championships were played at Army Golf Club in June of Helen's final year. The serving competitors played the 36-hole scratch competition for the "Meechie Shield". Helen attended although she was very unwell. But, characteristically and bravely, she attended to support an event that her drive and enthusiasm had generated at a club with which she had a long association. We can hope that Helen's bravery, above all, will be remembered.

Lioness 2001 No.1

Valerie Odell – "Have you been to London?"

In the early 1960's, I was a medic at Larkhill. One duty I had to perform was to accompany a patient from Tidworth Hospital to Woolwich Hospital by ambulance. We completed our journey there without trouble.

As we were leaving to return to Tidworth, a young captain asked if he could cadge a list, which we agreed to. London was at a standstill, so the driver decided to move things on i.e. Blue Lights! The traffic parted and we made good progress. On the outskirts of London, the driver was very worried, we'd picked up a police escort. Eventually we were stopped, by this time I had the captain on a stretcher, head bandaged and drip in situ. He was a very good patient! The police officer put his head in the cap and asked if all was well. I just said, "He's not too bad, head injury, going to Tidworth". Our escort took us right out of London, sent us on our way and wished us luck. Great relief was felt by all, especially the captain.

I knew this was against the rules and it was never mentioned on camp, but we enjoyed it. I did meet the captain sometime later, he just asked me "have you been to London?"

Written by Valerie Odell in 2018

Margaret Grant MBE - Courier and Postal

In October 1953 I completed my basic training at Guildford and was posted to 12 battalion WRAC at Kingston Gate Camp in Richmond Park, Surrey. I then attended my B3 course at Inglis Barracks, Mill Hill.

The group of us travelled in old coaches to and fro, stopping sometimes at Ace cafe on the North Circular Road for a snack, which was good if you'd missed breakfast!

One day as we were going to the classroom, we saluted an officer coming towards us but he did not salute back. All of a sudden there was an almighty shout for us to halt and he returned to us and boy did we get a telling off for saluting him as he was not an officer, he was the RSM. We apologised but as he had a peak cap and raincoat on we could not see his badge or rank. He explained about the canes so we would know in the future.

After passing the B3 course we then travelled daily to and from the Postal Depot at Knightsbridge, just up the road from Harrods. There was no heating most of the time or any modern equipment so on the shifts we wore slacks and leather jerkins or greatcoats if the weather was really cold.

In 1956 we moved to the Postal Depot at North Acton which was a bit more modernised. We still had to travel to and from Richmond Park. We had our meals at Gunsite Camp where the Royal Engineers were stationed.

In 1958 I reached the rank of Sergeant and was pleased to become the first WRAC Senior rank in Postal. It was then that the CO asked me if I would do a spell in the Pay Office, until they got someone from the Pay Corps. So, I agreed and when the campm was moved to Mill Hill I went to the pay Office for a while, I had some good National Service lads in the office with me and they were good workers. I had my lunch in the RE Sgts Mess, and even though I was the only woman, they made me very welcome.

In October 1962 the WRAC had a big parade on the square at Inglis Barracks and the Princess Royal - Princess Mary laid a foundation stone as 12 Battalion WRAC became 12 Company WRAC. We eventually moved from Richmond Park to our new unit at Inglis Barracks.

I was promoted to WO2 and since I had done nearly every job in the Postal Depot also worked on sections 1 to 6, I found myself back in the Mails Branch and also dealt with Couriers and Long Range Couriers for a while.

I caused quite a stir as I was wearing the badge of rank with the crown and laurel wreath around it. Some REs informed me that I was wearing the wrong badge of rank, alas they were in the wrong by only wearing the crown, so they had to get the correct ones from the Q stores and have them sown on straight away.

For many years we represented the WRAC at the Festival of Remembrance at the Royal Albert Hall and at the Cenotaph. I was also on parade as St Pauls for Sir Winston Churchill's funeral. I was awarded the MBE in the New Year's Honours in 1967 and was proud to go to Buckingham Palace for the investiture with my parents. I felt honoured to receive this award for doing the jobs that I loved. In 1971 I was presented with my Long Service and Good Conduct medal by Major General James Bowes-Lyon.

Later I was asked to take a Commission but it would have meant leaving Postal so I declined. Many tried to get a EWRAC Officer appointment in Postal but at that time they could not, but I feel that I opened up the past, for this as eventually it did happen after I was demobbed. So sadly, in 1975 I left the WRAC after completing my 22 years and I started my civilian life in my local Post Office.

Written by Margaret Grant for this book.

Janice Robinson

Janice was just 18 years of age when she was commissioned into the Women's Royal Army Corps in 1960, thus beginning over 40 years of dedicated service to the Corps.

Her first posting was to the Central Ammunition Depot at Kineton in Warwickshire as a platoon officer responsible for the welfare of all the WRAC servicewomen who were employed there. A fellow WRAC officer who was serving at Kineton at this time remembers Janice's exuberance "she was full of life and always out to parties!"

From Kineton, Janice moved to HQ Eastern Command at Hounslow as the MT Officer and it was here, in 1964, that she first met Desmond, a serving Royal Naval Officer.

Her third and final appointment was as staff captain "Quartering" in HQ Cyprus, which is where her natural flair for staff work really came to the fore. Her marriage to Desmond in 1965 meant that although she had to leave the Army, she continued "to follow the flag" (or perhaps I should say "the White Ensign") with Desmond.

Fortunately for the WRAC Association, Janice kept her ties with the WRAC after her marriage becoming a life member of the Association in 1965 and a founder member of the Greater London Branch in 1971. She was a staunch member of this Branch as well as being both Secretary and Chairman. Subsequent Chairmen and Secretaries all said that Janice was an extremely hard act to follow!

In January 2003, Janice was elected as one of the Vice Presidents of the WRAC Association Council an appointment which she was thrilled to accept. During this period, Janice was the linchpin between the National Army Museum and the curator of the new AGC Museum ensuring that important ATS and WRAC artefacts and archives were correctly and accurately presented.

But is was for her nine years in the WRAC Directorate, where she served as a Retired Officer from 1983 to 1992, that she will be best remembered. She played a pivotal role in that organisation, loyally serving 3 Directors and making a significant contribution to the Corps.

Janice was a born researcher and historian with a keen analytical mind; she was widely read, extremely knowledgeable on a variety of subjects and a real expert on the ATS and WRAC. If anyone wanted to know anything about the history of Women in the Army, it was always the same reply "Ask Janice".

One of her significant achievements in this appointment was to produce and edit "The Corps Today", a publication with news and policy issues about life in the WRAC. Complete sets are now held in the Public Records Office and the National Army Museum, thanks to Janice's foresight when the Corps disbanded.

Janice was the mainstay of the WRAC Directorate throughout those nine years and was highly respected, painstaking in her duties, always fluent and measured in her responses whether written or spoken with the unique ability of being able to communicate at all levels.

Extracted from the obituary written by Sue Westlake MBE in Lioness 2004 No.2

Sue Hirst - Those smashing girls I used to know

My Mum cried and bribed me with all sorts to change my mind. My Dad muttered and said, "You'll not stick it, you'll be back home within 2 weeks!".

I travelled on the train from Blandford down to Hobbs Barracks at Lingfield in Surrey on 7th October. I was seventeen & a quarter years old. I never felt so alone in all my life and wondered if I was doing the right thing. On the train out of London, I was sat in a compartment opposite a long lanky girl in a white mohair coat. We sized each other up, not saying anything. That girl became my first friend, her name was Dot Wilson and she came from Liverpool. We found ourselves in the same barrack room and we both went on to be Comcen Operators with the Royal Signals.

I was in 2 Company; 5 Platoon and we all wore green flashes. Sgt Williams was our drill instructor and Cpl Gibson our room NCO. It was quite a culture shock to be in a barrack room with 11 other noisy girls all with different accents. There was no privacy. Most of us in our room were all destined for the Signals, so we all got pretty friendly. My first night there I decided to go for a bath. Lying there in a very basic bathroom, I espied a pretty floral container at the side of the bath. "Great, they even supply talc!" I thought and so I dried myself off and covered myself in Vim!! Where did I think I was? The Hilton?

Next day we were issued with our kit. Dot and I were the only size 7s and were issued with BROWN shoes. They were obviously ex ATS shoes left over from the 40s! I thought they were ghastly, but over the weeks I began to form quite an affectionate relationship with my "Beetle Crushers" and have never forgotten how to "bull" them.

The weeks flew quickly by with drill, PT, classroom lessons and endless jabs! Before we realised it, our passing out parade came, and we were on our way to Catterick Camp for our Signals training. Basic Training was something I didn't really enjoy. I suffered terribly from homesickness, but Dad was going to eat his words. I was going to stick it out, no way was I going home I would not give him the satisfaction of being right!

24 Signal Regiment, Catterick Camp was the coldest place I have ever been, but what a social life! The winter of '63 was quite a bad one and I can remember it snowing quite hard. I was at Hooge Lines, Spider 1 Room 1. My NCO was Cpl Angie Fish. My roommates were Joan McCourt and Roz Deakin. I remember the weekly room inspections, standing there with bated breath awaiting the dreaded arrival of SSgt Botham!! I am sure many signals girls will remember her.

She once entered the room on inspection and saw, through a tilted dressing table mirror, that I was smirking. To this day I had no idea why I was smirking, probably to take my mind off my knocking knees. She made me stand outside in the corridor like a naughty schoolgirl!

Trade training was interesting. We trained on old teleprinters in draughty prewar barrack rooms which had black stoves, and which had been changed into classrooms. We began our typing training on old black typewriters with shields so we couldn't see the keys. "Wheels Cha Cha" was one of the favourite pieces of music we typed to. Everyone's bell was supposed to ring together, but there were always a few whose bell rang first or miles behind everyone else! Mine used to do it often, which brought me out in hot sweats of embarrassment, I blushed very easily in those days. Then we were put onto teleprinters, The Beatles', "Roll over Beethoven" always brings back memories. We were in mixed classes. We all got on well.

Many romances occurred at Catterick. I had my moments, but nothing serious, I had far too much living to do. I had some good nights in the Roundabout Club, it even had a small bowling alley! In fact, I had such a good time at Catterick, that one day I was hauled in front of the CSM for not writing home. Mum got fed up with waiting for a letter and when she didn't receive any, she wrote to the CSM asking after my welfare and had she ever heard of me? Oh, the embarrassment, I was mortified. The CSM was so nice and "mumsy" I almost burst into tears. Oh, I meant well, I wrote many letters to Mum with all my news, but! just forgot to post them so much for homesickness, it had soon worn off!

After that incident, I never forgot to buy stamps again. I didn't know what Mum would do next; she was capable of anything! In the end she actually sent me some stamps! I remember my first weekend home on leave from Catterick. I walked in the door expecting a huge fuss and there was Mum in tears. "President Kennedy has been shot poor man" was all she could say to me. We all remember what we were doing on that day.

After my trade training, I was posted to 251 WRAC Signal Squadron at Fugglestone Camp in Wilton near Salisbury. In April '64 I arrived there on a sunny Spring day only to be told not to unpack, I was to spend the night there and then travel next day on detachment to Aldershot "just for two weeks". I ended up staying there for the rest of my UK posting.

What can I say about Aldershot? You either love it or hate it and I loved it. We were billeted at Mandora Hutments on Hope Grants Road. We shared with 10 Independent Coy WRAC. 'Hutments' was a proper description. We slept in wooden huts with a fire escape door at

167

one end. This fire escape door came in very handy on occasions. Many times, we used it to sneak out after bed check to go to parties because we knew where the hole in the fence was. One-time disaster struck. One of the girls unwittingly locked the door and we couldn't get back in. We had to sneak around looking for an open window. That's when we ended up in the OC's office!

I worked in Aldershot Signal Centre. The telephone exchange was upstairs. I began working days and then went on to shifts. I worked with Maxine Turner. We worked days, evenings and night shifts. We used to take hair bleach with us when we worked nights. After all the work was done, we used to colour our hair to change our image. More than once I have gone to work at midnight with brown hair and come off duty at 8 the following morning a blonde!!! No one used to bother us when we worked nights, but if the work was there it was done.

I remember calling a whole battalion of the Parachute Regiment off Christmas block leave to go to Borneo. I had to send a telegram to each one. I had obviously been noticed for promotion and the OC, Major Ross, sent me on an NCO Cadre Course for 2 weeks in Bicester. Not being a 'regimental' sort of lass, I didn't really want to go. Reluctantly I went, but failed miserably after a catalogue of disasters, which included taking drill. I stopped everyone on the wrong foot and in the end lost them in the early morning fog and found them all marking time in a ditch at the other end of the square!

Needless to say, the OC lost faith, my tape went out of the window and I blew it good and proper. However, not being a person to brood about things, I eventually decided that I had outgrown Aldershot and fancied a change. I approached my OC for an overseas posting. She couldn't get rid of me fast enough and I was posted to 235 Signal Squadron (Comcan) in Malta.

Now Malta was a different kettle of fish, I could not believe my luck. We were based at St David's Barracks in Mtarfa and I had my own room. We either worked a morning or an afternoon at the tape relay station, Fort Bingemma. We all went up there in the back of an army truck, it was a 20-minute drive in the warm sunshine with the top down. We never worked a full day or weekends, it was paradise. Later I managed to secure the job as PRI clerk on the camp. I just worked mornings and used to be driven around the outstations on pay day, collecting money from everyone for their Sunday papers etc.

Occasionally I was asked to go and do some classified typing for the OC. I enjoyed Malta and the friends I made there. I am still in touch with some of them. Now I am 50 years old plus VAT I often sit and think about my happy days in the WRAC and all those smashing girls I used to know. I am a Gran now and when my little granddaughter is old enough, I will tell her about my life. I was demobbed in May 1967 with an exemplary discharge (surprisingly enough!) and married John Hirst in August 1967. We carried on in the army until 1976, and we were in Berlin for quite a long time. But that's another story!!!! I've a lot to thank my Dad for. If he hadn't have said "you'll be back home in 2 weeks" I would have gone back home and missed out on a lot of life!!!!

Isobel Gordon - Segregation of the Sexes

In 1965 my CO, Lt Col The Lady Martha Bruce, dispatched me to Denmark as part of a detachment of the WRAC of the 51st (Highland) Division TA. The group included CSM Lily Bell and was led by Major Hazel Russell WRAC, the CO's Training Major. It was Hazel Russell, incidentally, who taught me an invaluable lesson. "Always remember, Isobel," she said, "the rule books and regulations only tell you what you can't do they don't tell you what you CAN do!".

We travelled from Perth to London by overnight sleeper, then made our way to Harwich to embark on the ferry for Eskbjerg. It was a relatively calm crossing, although I felt uneasy when I put in my front collar stud. When I visited the juniors in an eight berth cabin, however, I was met by some very pallid, not to say green, young ladies. They struggled on nobly, and by the time we berthed they were ready to meet our two liaison officers from the Danish Lottekorps, the Danish equivalent of the WRAC (TA).

We were whisked up the coast to Jutland to the Lottekorps' summer camp, and it was there we were made aware of a very strict rule none of the women was allowed to speak to a male soldier, on pain of being sent home instantly! The liaison officers pulled my leg constantly, always finding a reason for me to take messages to a tall, blonde, male officer who, from my height of 5' 2", seemed to be about 6' 6" tall. Not that we could talk to each other, my only words of Danish being, "Toosan tak," (a thousand thanks) while his English was just as poor.

We soon fell into the ways of the Lottekorps. At mealtimes, which were taken with all ranks together, if there was anything unusual on the menu, the girls would watch while I tried to discover how to eat it and then passed on the information to them.

One night, we went out on an undercover (!) operation. As an officer, I was given a torch to hang round my neck. Boy, did my party come to regret that! Not only did I kick a tin which had been placed as a boobytrap, I got such a shock my hand slammed down on top of my torch to illuminate us to any watching enemy. Let's just say I wasn't cut out for covert operations.

One evening, the Danish Second in Command and her officers invited the Scots to visit them in their quarters. They were most hospitable, offering coffee, cakes, biscuits etc. The exception was their PRO, a professional journalist who could have been invented by Hollywood. As I was PRO for our party, this lady took me under her wing. Waving a cigarette in one hand and offering me a strong G & T with the other, she growled, "You see these fools, Lootenent Gordon? When they come to camp, they bring extra coffee. Me? I just bring another bottle of gin!".

Hazel and I were very proud of our little gang. Keeping their eyes on CSM Bell, they didn't put a foot wrong, and charmed the Danish officers next day by having beautiful flowers delivered to them as a thank you. Very soon, our busy but enjoyable week came to an end after a special dinner on the last night. Busy? Suffice it to say that after I reached home, I discovered I'd lost half a stone in that memorable week!

Lioness 2003 No.2

Anne Workman & Catherine Corley - Memories of HQ MEC Steamer Point, Aden

In late 1965 or early 1966, the girls of 28 Coy WRAC were asked to give up one half day a week to help the soldiers on the checkpoints to search Arab women who worked on the base, or who went through the various checkpoints in Aden. This was to see if they were carrying small arms and bits and pieces concealed on their persons underneath the layers of clothing, they wore which could be used to make small bombs etc. The girls always worked in pairs taking turns to search the women.

These photographs (see centre pages) were taken in 1966 and show us sitting at the entrance to RAF Steamer Point waiting for the Arab women who worked on the base to come through the checkpoint. It was a very hot day and little insects from the tree were annoying us, not very nice.

Catherine remembers having three unnerving incidents while on her searching duties. The first was a woman spitting on her and shouting insulting names in Arabic at her. The second time was when she went to search a woman who then went for Catherine and gave her a nasty scratch to her cheek and a bite to her arm Whilst searching her shopping, Catherine found a thermos flask and remembered in time not to unscrew the top. She gave the flask to one of the soldiers on guard duty! The third incident was seeing a book with the middle cut out containing explosives. Such devices were designed to explode when opened but this one obviously hadn't worked. My experiences were not so scary.

I remember going with Cpl Jean Whittaker and armed guards in an open Land Rover over the causeway. We were travelling at great speed to one of the checkpoints and I had to hold onto my beret and hold down my skirt at the same time there were no seat belts then!

The second time I was on duty with LCpl Pat France. Because there had been a security incident, we were flown to the checkpoint in a Sioux helicopter no doors and we had to wear men's trousers and shirts. It was an experience I will never forget, flying over white houses with their flat roofs (ideal for sunbathing) and ornate walling which surrounded their houses. Initially, the Arab women wouldn't let us search them because we were wearing trousers, but we finally managed to convince them that we were ladies. When we had finished, we were taken back to Steamer Point in a metal covered truck. They were very dark inside, and I cannot remember exactly what they were called but I was glad when we were dropped off at our compound.

My final searching duty was just before I came home after finishing an 18-month posting. Again, I was on duty with Cpl Jean Whittaker but this time the RSM came along as well. The soldiers stopped a small truck (I called them moving bedsteads because of the fancy metal work which covered them) and said, "You'll be alright ladies; there are only four women to search." In fact, there were seven he hadn't seen the other three who had been sitting on the floor an old lady and six younger women. We searched the first five then Jean checked a tall woman who said an Arabic word when she had finished searching her, but it was the way she said it which made us smile. Then it was my turn to search the old lady. When I had finished searching her, she said we were 'Very nice girls" and if we went with her, she would look after us very well. At that moment, the RSM appeared and we both said we worked for her and said we were sorry we couldn't take up her kind offer or words to that effect.

It was a very dangerous time, but I am glad that we helped albeit in a small way to keep people safe. But it wasn't all doom and gloom we had picnics and sunbathing on the many beaches, nights at the pictures, dancing at the Mermaid Club and the Two and One Club, plus R&R for two weeks at the Silver Sands Leave Centre in Mombasa to look forward to, but that is another story.

Lioness 2008 #2 No.2
See images in centre pages

Diana Henderson

Diana Henderson, who has died aged 72, was variously a soldier, a development director at a number of public schools and universities and an admired military historian.

Diana Mary Henderson was born in Guildford in Surrey on May 21, 1946 and educated at Hawick High School, where she became captain of games (for girls) before going to Strathclyde University to read Law.

She joined the university OTC and, having graduated in 1970, she was commissioned into the Women's Royal Army Corps. As a TA officer for the next 30 years, she had many short-term assignments in Europe and the Middle East.

Alongside her military service, she practised as a solicitor in Arbroath and Inverness and immersed herself in Highland culture and traditions. She mastered the complexities of the bagpipes but her comrades in arms had rather mixed feelings about being awakened by a lively jig on a cold morning after an exhausting night's exercise.

In 1976, Henderson took a military dancing team to America as part of the bicentennial celebrations of the Declaration of Independence. Four years later, after gaining a PhD in Military History at Edinburgh University, she travelled by herself to the North-West Frontier and throughout India to study old Army sites and records of her forebears going back to the 1780s. She was given a warm welcome by villagers accompanied, on occasion, by invitations to inspect the local militia.

Horses had always played a part in her life and, in 1986, she trained with the King's Troop, Royal Horse Artillery. In 1995, she assumed command of 162 Movement Control Regiment Royal Logistics Corps and took charge of almost 400 service men and women.

An advocate of rigorous self-discipline and physical fitness, she excelled in many competitive sports including shooting and boxing, swimming and hockey and, under her leadership, many young women succeeded in a whole range of exacting tasks and activities.

Henderson's full-time appointments included, variously, that of director of development at Hopetoun House, Edinburgh University, Fettes College and Queens' College, Cambridge. She was also a director of the Earl Haig Fund Scotland and, subsequently, of the Royal British Legion's Poppy Factory. She advised a number of trusts dedicated to improving animal welfare. A professional in everything she took on, she was a most successful fundraiser and her speech-day addresses and lectures on military history were great attractions.

An entertaining guest, she was in constant demand to attend regimental or university dinner parties. A friend recalls that her rendering of The Ode to the Haggis on Burns Night suppers was unsurpassed.

But old ways of thinking die hard and she was once refused entry to a banquet given by the Garde Républicaine in Paris. "We were expecting Major Henderson," she was told. "But I am Major Henderson," she replied. Profuse apologies followed and at the end of the evening she was escorted to her car by a guard of honour.

In 1995, under the patronage of the Duke of Edinburgh and the chairmanship of General Sir Michael Gow, she played a leading part in establishing the Scots at War Trust with the aim of conserving the archives of Scottish regiments that were disbanding. For more than a decade, she organised seminars to enable veterans, often for the first time, to share their recollections.

In 2011 she married Peter Jones, a widower. He was Emeritus Professor of Philosophy and Director of the Institute for Advanced Studies in the Humanities at the University of Edinburgh. After she retired in 2013 because of ill health, they moved to Norfolk where she created a beautiful garden and was able to practise her beloved bagpipes.

Pauline Milnes

I joined the army in 1970 at just 17 years old, after an encounter with army recruitment officers at my school in Gloucestershire when I was 15. This left me intrigued and excited about a career in the military. Prior to meeting the recruitment officers, I had been totally unaware that there were roles for women in the army that may suit me. Two years later, I joined the military as part of the Women's Royal Army Corps (WRAC) and served for four years.

I remember the day I took my oath of allegiance so well, after I walked out of the recruitment office I suddenly realised that my life was about to change and I would be stepping into the unknown, but I also walked with a spring in my step knowing from that day I was actually a soldier. My family were happy for me, but I'm certain they were wondering how I would cope with the discipline I would be subjected to as I was what you might call mischievous.

I don't recall too much of my arrival at Guildford, but I remember vividly the rest of my time there. I loved all aspects of my training, especially drill, there were many times when we practised with the band, I had to stop myself from dancing to the music. My passing out parade went by in a whirl, but I know that my family were so proud of the person I had become in just a short time.

After completing my basic training at the WRAC Centre, Guildford, I was posted to Blackdown Barracks, Deepcut, where I did my trade training as a supply controller, before being posted to Central Ordnance Depot (COD) Donnington in Shropshire.

My final posting was to 29 Company WRAC, Rheindahlen, NATO headquarters West Germany for the rest of my military career. Whilst serving there, we were subjected to an IRA terrorist attack; a bomb was planted in a dustbin behind the cinema. Fortunately, when it detonated most of the personnel had already vacated the building, but it brought home to all of us, although far away from the UK mainland, we had to be on constant alert for this type of incident. As it was the era of the cold war and Reindahlen was a Garrison we also had to look out for cars with Russian number plates as they would probably be spying on us.

Sport was my great passion, so was fortunate to have represented the British Army of the Rhine (BAOR) in their Netball Team and participate in various other sports throughout my service.

As told by Pauline Milnes for this book.

Jeannie Spence

Joannie was born on Wednesday 21 July 1954 in Gorebridge, south of Edinburgh. Her father, a very proud, hardworking milner, instilled a strong work ethic into his five children; "Save for what you need and always stand up for the underdog". As a young girl Jeannie was very close to "Goods", her Granny, who was the matriarch of the family and gave all her Grandchildren unconditional love.

Jeannie joined the Women's Royal Army Corps at 17, with her father's words ringing in her ears, "I'll give you three months and you'll be back home ". Of course, Jeannie was riddled with her Catholic PhD in guilt for leaving, and like most of us spent some very homesick nights, but the three months stretched to 22 years!

Jeannie loved Guildford, everything new and exciting, marching, bulling shoes, ironing, learning many new things and of course trying to understand all the new accents. Then it was on to Blackdown for her trade training.

Her first posting was Bicester and that is where I first met her in January 1973, little did I know she would be my greatest friend for over 40 years; loyal, loving, a quick wit and a wonderful sense of humour, but who could nag for NATO on a good day. Jeannie was posted to Germany from Bicester but became ill and was transferred to Westminster Hospital in London for a year, with throat cancer. She was devastated, not for herself, but for her family. No mobile phones, no internet etc, it was such a difficult time for her and of course her family. The consultant at Westminster gave her 6 months to live, but Jeannie wasn't having any of it and she got over her 'little blip' as she called it.

After retraining as a clerk, she was posted to London for 3 years and had a fantastic time; theatres, clubs, restaurants etc meeting people from around the globe. It was there that she met Ann (Galan) who, like me, was a friend for life. They got into some scrapes, but Jeannie loved every minute of her London posting.

Middle Wallop was another posting she loved because she would go on flying training to Scotland to see Goods and pop in for a cup of tea. Helicopters didn't register on Goods' radar; she would tell everyone that Jeannie came up on the train.

Into the 80's now and Jeannie was back in Germany. Galan and I were also posted there, along with Dolly May, Nerys, Jess, Marge, Babs Robinson, Jane Kelly, Lyn and Alison. We all had a ball, laughing hysterically at each other's misdemeanours.

Jeannie went on to Cyprus and her life changed forever. Sun, sea and love struck; she met the dashing Fusilier Mr Spence with his good looks. Jeannie soon realised it was his kindness and caring ways that she loved. Then it was onto Deepcut and Sandhurst for Tony. It was Jeannie who proposed to Mr Spence, she didn't want a big wedding, but Tony did. So, it was on 17 June 1989 that they married in Canterbury, with all their family and friends around them, fluffy white dress and all.

Tony was the best thing that ever happened to Jeannie, at times they were like two kids in a sweetie shop they were so happy. They had such adventures on holiday; from nearly getting jailed in Africa, mugged in Russia, car jacked in America, it could only happen to them.

When Jeannie left the army, she and Tony settled in Alum Waters, just outside Durham. She became a SSAFA caseworker and driver, ceramics teacher and PAT dog carer at St Cuthbert's the local Hospice. Jeannie said this was the most rewarding work she had ever done.

When Jeannie became ill there were so many flowers, texts, emails and humorous cards sent which really lifted her spirits and kept her strong. Jeannie's words now ring in my ears, " I have been truly blessed with a charmed life, I would have liked a little longer with my loved ones, but my greatest honour was to become Mrs Spence". For Ann and I we haven't lost our loyal, generous, loving friend, she has just gone into the next room and is waiting for us to join her (but not just yet though Hogis).

From her obituary written by Jenny Quirke in Lioness 2014 No.2

Terry Simpson - Call Sign "Coffee Pot"

It was in September 1972 whilst serving as a Sergeant in the WRAC Provost stationed with 160 Provost Company Royal Military Police in Aldershot when the call came through. There was a need for all military policewomen serving in NW Europe to go immediately to Northern Ireland.

We in the company were just getting over the bomb placed in the Officers' Mess in 16 Para Bde which had killed many civilian staff and the Padre. This was my first contact with the troubles in Northern Ireland. We were met by the then OC of 181 Pro Coy Captain Janet Lawson who travelled with us to Thiepval Barracks, Lisburn. What a shock. The whole of the barracks was a war zone. Armed soldiers everywhere, security in place, no one could enter or leave without being checked or searched.

The next shock was the accommodation. Thiepval Barracks was never designed to house so many people and their equipment. The JNCOs had double bunks and we seniors found ourselves in single rooms accommodating at least two.

On our first day we were issued with our protective kit: a tin helmet with visor, a flak jacket and a truncheon! The helmet was made for men so the girls having smaller heads found it difficult to get one to fit. Mine would move backwards and forwards covering my eyes and the visor would then snap forward covering my complete face! The flak jackets were no different. If you were lucky enough to find one small enough to fit, you guarded it with your life.

The reason for our posting to NI was made clear on the briefing. The whole of Belfast City centre would be sealed off. Every car, bus, lorry and person entering the City would be searched. And our job was to support the Infantry in this task for six days a week from 0800 hours until 1800 hours come rain, hail or shine. We travelled daily from Lisburn into Belfast on a military bus painted to look like a civilian vehicle. We stayed throughout the day in the Grand Central Hotel. It was not Grand, and it no longer looked like a hotel. Not a carpet in sight, chairs were at a premium and a table was something we dreamed of.

On the first Monday morning we were out to take up our appointed places to find the world's press watching our every move. Initially we were well received but this did not last very long. By October it was realised that there were not enough WRAC Provost to maintain the regime and the call went out worldwide for volunteers from all employments in the WRAC to go on a six-month tour of duty as a searcher in NI. After a course in Scotland they all sailed to the Province in November 1972 and the Company moved to Aldergrove Barracks. Newly built, it had a life expectancy of 12 years. It is still there!

With winter approaching our uniform of jackets and skirts was impractical so we were allowed to wear the green jumper, red cravat and to protect us from the rain, drivers' jackets. The footwear problem was solved by the bulk purchase of the infamous "Derry Boot", which was great for those with thin calves but impossible for those with thicker than average ones.

As I mentioned we were in support of the infantry and were on call every day. Our communication with the ops room was via a field telephone located in the sitting room. It would ring and the message relayed, "Coffee Pot required for deployment, to be at the helipad in ten minutes".

As I slowly made my way around to each square, I received mostly the same greeting but with anticipation for myself. I found I hid behind a couple of RSM's on route as at the second drop the guys almost pulled me into the square. That was a bit scary. There were comments at the gates with 'you're popular tonight'. RSM's were ready to escort me to the CO. As I moved from camp to camp the silence of the place for most turned to a party atmosphere.

There was only one regiment that was told to embark that night. I cannot remember who, but I think it may have been the Lancers. But they did it in silence and total professionalism. They were already moving out the gates before I even left. There was one regiment with a few grunts of disappointment that they did not get the call.

The whole experience and memories of that shift has stayed with me in vivid form. I will never forget it. I arrived back to HQ exhausted but on a high. It was a euphoric moment for me of which I knew history had been made that night and I, ME, had been the one who had delivered that message which sent most of our men back to bed. They had been 'Stood Down'.

The story however does not stop there. About 8yrs ago 2010, ish another chapter evolved. I used to work as an Instructor with BMF, British Military Fitness. All their staff is either serving or like myself veterans. I was attending a social evening for our customers and staff. I told a fellow colleague this story. As I was telling it he became very excited about it. To me I thought he was being a bit over the top about the whole thing. He could not wait to tell his Father. Obviously, I asked him why. He then explained that it was in fact his Uncle who had given that very 'Stand Down order' that I had that night delivered across the garrisons of Salisbury Plain.

Written by Mandy Jarvis for this book.

Herme Emary - The Turkish Invasion of Cyprus

Where were you when the Turks invaded Cyprus in July 1974? I was a Cpl WRAC/RAPC serving at the Command Pay Office in Dhekelia. It was all pretty much a low-key affair as far as I was concerned. Some of the chaps in the office went off to man the Ops Room at HQ Dhekelia Garrison, but I did not have an Operations role so had to help in the office.

Most of our civilian staff were unable to get to work. The Turks, because the Sovereign Base Area was in the middle of a

Greek area, and the Greeks, because most of whom lived in and around Nicosia, were cut off by the Turks landing at Nicosia airport.

I got back to the block one afternoon and was asked by an RMP friend if I minded helping out down at the Civilian Evacuation Centre that had been set up at the other end of the Sovereign Base Area. I got on my trusty Honda 90 and reported to Lt Col Bate RADC.

I was given the task of greeting the evacuees as they arrived and making sure they knew what was happening. It was all very well organised. All evacuees were sent to the field at the bottom of the hill where they formed into orderly queues (don't the British just love queuing!). They were then transported up the hill to be processed; we tried to look after every one of the evacuees including tourists as well as some locals, adults and children. The only people who tried to queue jump were the Press trying to get to the other end of the island with their film and stories. Needless to say, they were told to "go away"!

We felt a bit happier when HMS Bulwark arrived with its contingent from 41 Commando. They did a helicopter landing behind the Civilian Evacuation Centre and then were told to go back and do it all again because the Press wanted to film it and they had not been ready!

We had 2 marines based permanently at the Civilian Evacuation Centre, one who did the communications and a gopher (it was he who "liberated" the petrol for all our vehicles). All they had was in their packs and they did not rotate back to HMS Bulwark so after a couple of days I offered to wash their kit for them. Well it was Cyprus in midsummer.

It was all quite exciting really. One poor South African journalist (who had waited), collapsed in my arms with an epileptic fit. He recovered well and for some reason was very embarrassed. Edward Woodward, who was very prominent on the TV at the time, turned up. He had a home at Kyrenia and insisted on evacuating himself and his Greek staff by driving at great risk through Turkish occupied territory. When he did finally arrive, he insisted on waiting in line with the rest of the evacuees. He was a perfect gentleman.

In between working at the Civilian Evacuation Centre, I visited the office every day to see if I was needed there. Most places, including the banks, were closed. However, soldiers still needed cash, so the pay offices around the island were making cash payments - not a problem until we ran out and the Command Paymaster had to go in an armed convoy to Nicosia to get some from the Central Bank of Cyprus.

Lioness 2006 No.1

Anne Field - Director WRAC 1977 - 1982

Brigadier Anne Field was a forward thinking and extremely able staff officer, she believed in the employment of servicewomen in a wide variety of roles alongside, with, and on behalf of their male counterparts. She worked towards introducing changes which paved the way to the integration of women into the Corps and Regiments of the Regular Army. She was admired by her male counterparts for her overview, her grasp of staff matters, her tenacity, her dedication and her convivial company and common sense.

Anne Field became Director in 1977. She was aware that married women officers were leaving the service and wished to stem that loss. She championed the simple solution of co-locating postings with their husbands. She also encouraged the theme of integration by backing a trial of mixed platoons, one Infantry and one Royal Artillery. There were real and practical issues to overcome and as it turned out the experiment was not, at that time, continued.

However, as Director she successfully negotiated that the WRAC College at Camberley should become the 4th College of RMA Sandhurst. This was a significant step forward towards equality and integration.

Anne Field (nee Hodgson) was born on 4th April 1926, at Keswick, in Cumberland. Her father, Captain Harold Derwent Hodgson, who had served in the Royal Engineers, was a company director. Anne was brought up in a close family in Keswick and went to the local grammar school before moving to St Georges, Harpenden. She subsequently took a place at the London School of Economics but left to join the Auxiliary Territorial Service in September 1947.

She became a Lance Corporal Clerical Instructor until December 1948, when she was commissioned into the ATS, which became the WRAC in 1949. Her first postings were as a Platoon Commander in UK but, with the background of a communist

182

insurrection in Malaya, she travelled to Singapore to take up the post of Officer Commanding 4 Independent Company WRAC which had a company strength of 400!

In 1953 she returned to England to attend the WRAC Staff College at Frimley Park. Following this 6-month course, she had Staff and Regimental Duty appointments in the Old War Office, with the London University WRAC OTC, as Adjutant of 317 (Scottish) TA Battalion WRAC in Stirling and in Catterick.

In 1956 Anne married Captain Anthony Field; this marriage was dissolved in 1961. In 1961 she was promoted Major becoming Chief Instructor at the WRAC Centre, Guildford, under the Command of Colonel Lucy Davies, a wonderful character, with whom Anne shared a love of Horse Racing, style, and a sense of fun.

1963 found her in Aden, another hot spot, as DAAG Manning, with the added responsibility for the WRAC personnel, employed with Signals, RMP and as Clerks. Anne dealt with casualty notification and compassionate leave for the Command and ensured that she understood the terrain and the dangerous tasks with which her colleagues were involved.

It was back to the UK in 1965 to be Deputy Assistant Director WRAC at Lansdowne House, Berkeley Square. This was situated over the top of the Colony Club, of which George Raft, the famous American gangster, was Chairman and host until 1967. The Army Legal Corps and the Inspectorate of Physical Training were also installed in the building, so it was a most convivial and interesting time.

On promotion to Lieutenant Colonel in 1968, she assumed an MOD appointment working on redundancy and short term career planning until she was posted to BAOR as Assistant Director WRAC based in Rheindahlen, responsible for WRAC employed in BAOR and Berlin. This posting gave her the chance to travel extensively across Germany visiting units as well as being able to discuss policy, manning and other matters with her male colleagues.

Promoted Colonel in Dec 1971, Anne became Commandant of the WRAC College at Camberley, where she was responsible for Regular and TA Officer Cadet training as well as Warrant Officer and NCO training. It was here that she struck up close ties with RMA Sandhurst experiencing at first-hand what needed to be achieved to ensure the future integration of male and female Officer training.

She moved to Wilton in 1975 as Deputy Director WRAC at HQUKLF. This HQ was brimming with good minds and interesting companions both on and off duty. They included, FM Lord Bramall, Commander-in-Chief, UK Land Forces, and his wife Ami, who became long standing friends.

She achieved the pinnacle of her career in June 1977 when she was promoted Brigadier, Director WRAC and Hon ADC to Her Majesty the Queen. She was then able to put her experience into practice by encouraging and actively moving towards the integration of women into the Army Corps and Regiments.

She retired in April 1982 and was awarded a Military CB. Brigadier Field continued to be a staunch supporter of the WRAC after retirement and gave it and its members her considerable and lasting support. She served first as Deputy Controller Commandant from 1984 - 1992 and then as Deputy Colonel Commandant of the AG Corps until 1994.

She also held the following appointments: Chairman of the ATS & WRAC Benevolent Fund from 1984-97, Chairman of the WRAC Association Council 1991-97, Vice President of the WRAC Association 1984-97 and life Vice President from 1999. Her love of comradeship led her to be Chairman of the ATS Dinner Club from 1996 to 2011. She was also a long-term supporter of the Army Women's Lawn Tennis Association. In 1995 she received a Civil CBE for her services to the WRAC Association.

She made her home in West London and returned to her beloved Keswick for holidays. She was made a Freeman of the City of London in 1981. In 1982 she became a Director of London (West) Regional Board of Lloyds Bank pic until 1991, and her interest in the City was reflected in her membership of the London Guild of Spectacle Makers from 1990. She was appointed one of her Majesty's Commissioners at the Duke of York's Royal Military School, Dover from 1989-2004, to which she gave her accustomed 'all'. She did the same for the Army Benevolent Fund (now ABF - The Soldiers' Charity) and served for 23 years on its main grants committee. She was a Trustee and a supporter of a number of other ex-service organisations, including the National Army Museum, and the Royal Hospital Chelsea. She was thrilled to be remembered by the Aden Veterans who appointed her their first Patron in 2002.

Brigadier Field loved all sports but, in particular, Horse Racing, Tennis, Rugger and Cricket never missing annual trips to Ascot, Wimbledon, Twickenham and Lord's. She enjoyed a glass of good wine, entertaining companions, lively discussion, and was a generous friend and a formidable adversary. She was a loyal member of the Army and Navy Club (The Rag'), where she regularly invited friends and family; she was particularly pleased to be the first woman member of the Redsocks lunch group.

Family and heritage were most important to her, especially her younger brother, David, who predeceased her. In her last year her underlying and debilitating health problems sorely tested her. She dealt with failing sight and other frailties with her usual strength of character, and with a little help from her niece, neighbours, and friends, Anne Field was a bright, brave, feisty and fun lady. A legend to those who knew her.

Obituary by Sue Westlake MBE published in Lioness 2011 No'1

Marie (Sammy) Simon

Sam was born in London on 22 April 1959 and almost immediately went into a children's home at Romford in Essex. At school she was a popular pupil who was quite shy and not a great academic. However, at an early age her sporting talent shone through and at the age of 12 she was noticed as a potential Olympic athlete.

Sam left school at 16 and went to college to obtain the qualifications required to join the Army, following in the footsteps of her brother Michael who was serving in the Royal Anglian Regiment. Sam joined the Women's Royal Army Corps in April 1977 and completed her recruit training in No 1 Training Company which I was commanding.

Even in basic training she stood out as a mischievous person who lived life to the full. She then trained as a driver and served in a variety of units in the UK and Germany before gaining promotion to Sergeant in 1988. She then retrained as an Admin Assistant serving in Northern Ireland and then as CQMS at the Junior Leaders Regiment Royal Artillery at Bramcott, where her leadership qualities shone through and her suitability for employment in a training environment was quickly recognised.

Her next move was to the WRAC Centre at Guildford to the Warrant Officer and NCO Training Wing where she was an instructor in leadership. It was a time of great change at Guildford, with No 1 and No 2 Training Companies being merged to form Training Company. Sam was quickly transferred to Training Company. She was a great team member, always cheerful with a very lively sense of humour, a great motivator who would instil the highest standards in the recruits. At the same time, she would always gain their confidence and trust and encourage them to rise to heights that their parents would never have thought possible.

Although relatively small in stature she was a larger than life character, who was totally dependable, always hard working and willing to offer advice. On formation of the AGC, Sam was posted to help establish the School of Employment Training at Worthy Down. She was again instructing in leadership and man management in the rank of Warrant Officer Class One although not called RSM that was the role she fulfilled very ably.

Throughout her Army service, Sam maintained an incredible standard of fitness, excelling on the sports field and gaining both her Army Athletics and Hockey colours. One day she announced at Worthy Down that we would enter a team in the inter unit athletics championships. We were not allowed to use trainees and the pool from which we could select our team was quite limited. However, over the next few weeks a number of reluctant athletes went into training, but on the day of the event we still didn't quite have a full team.

Before the team set off for Aldershot, I was handed a sealed envelope and told to make sure I brought it with me as we might need 'the evidence'. Only at that point did I realise that Sam really did have a plan. When I arrived at the stadium the team were on top of the points board and subsequently went on to win the event. The evidence I had been handed in the sealed envelope showed that Kelly Holmes was on the strength of Worthy Down whilst training for the Olympics. Sam had known Kelly a long time and had been in touch with her! Kelly had appeared and rather than running on the track, which would hardly have been fair, she had won the Long Jump and the Shot Putt events for us.

Sam's final tour was as the RSM at the Defence School of Languages in Beaconsfield.

Lioness 2008 No.2
See images in centre pages

Mary Woollard MBE

On the 20th February 1978 I caught a train from Abergavenny to Guildford to join the Army leaving my friends and family a little surprised by my career choice, however I didn't think I had chosen a career just an adventure for a few years.

I became WO462146 Pte Woollard and after 6 weeks at Guildford I reported to Worthy Down to commence my trade training as a Pay Clerk, later re-titled Military Accountant, and become permanently employed by the Royal Army Pay Corps (RAPC).

My first posting to Regimental Pay Office Brighton followed. Uniforms only worn on a Tuesday, which was also sports afternoon, the beach a mere mile away, lots of night/social life and London a short train journey away – who would not want to join the Army.

After completing both WRAC and RAPC promotion courses for LCpl – Sgt (WRAC) & SSgt (RAPC) I enjoyed postings to16 Sig Regt in Krefeld, Germany, the WRAC College, The Royal Military Academy Sandhurst, COD Donnington and in July 1987 I became the first female SSgt instructor at The RAPC Training Centre, where I taught Paymasters and Soldier's promotion and All Arms Service Funds courses.

In 1989 I applied for an Over 30's Late Entry Commission (LE) in the RAPC. Prior to 1992 the only way to be commissioned as a LE Officer was by application to the WRAC as the process required all females in the Army to be commissioned by their parent Corps.

After successful completion of the RAPC 3-day selection process, based upon the Royal Commissions Board (RCB) that direct entrant officers completed prior to attending Sandhurst, I was selected for a commission and 12 years after walking through the gates of Guilford my adventure continued along a different path.

My small claim to fame is that I was the first female ever to be granted an LE Commissioned by following a permanently employed Corps process, in my case the RAPC, and not via the WRAC and the only female ever to be granted an RAPC LE Commission. I converted my SSC(LE) commission to an SRC(LE) in October 1998 and was one of the first AGC(SPS) LE officers to be granted a Regular Commission in 2000.

My officer career was thoroughly enjoyable and rewarding. I served in Belgium, Bosnia, Cyprus, Croatia, Kenya, Norway (as part of the AMF), two tours in the MoD, and in the Directorate (DSPS(A)) in many varied appointments. One of my proudest moments was when my parents accompanied me to Buckingham Palace in 2002 to witness me being awarded the MBE.

I was a very keen sportswoman and won many trophies at unit and district/Divisional level in all sports and at Army level at rounders, hockey, volleyball, table tennis and golf. I was the Army table tennis and golf Champion and represented the Army in both.

In December 2007 I completed my 'adventure' 6 weeks shy of 30 years' service – would I change anything? – Absolutely not.

Written by Mary Woollard for this book.
See images in centre pages

Vanessa Lang

I first met Vanessa on 02 January 1980 when she arrived at the WRAC College, Camberley, to start her officer training. I was an instructor on Officer Cadet Wing, and she was one of 19 cadets assigned to my platoon. She was a model officer cadet; lively and enthusiastic which clearly set the tone for her future years.

She was commissioned on 06 August 1980 and posted to 16 Air Defence Regt Royal Artillery. Having travelled widely with this regiment, Vanessa, always at the forefront of new adventures, was posted as Assistant Adjutant to the 13th/18th Hussars, only the second female to have served with them.

She was particularly thrilled with this posting because of her love of all things equestrian and being with this polo playing regiment was an excellent opportunity for her to pursue her much loved hobby. In addition, being so close to the Harz Mountains, Vanessa was able to indulge her love of skiing. She was an excellent skier and captained the Women's Services Ski team for several years.

When Vanessa left the 13th/18th, the following appeared in the Regimental Journal: "Benjamin joined the Regiment in December 1983 and quickly established himself as the most uncontrollable spaniel ever to be granted a dog license. He brought with him a well proportioned, flaxen haired WRAC girl called Vanessa. Her arrival had met with much curiosity from the subalterns, eager to see what the powers that be would produce next to continue the trend of 'A lady in the Mess'. They did not have to wait long to find out. Whereas she appeared to have absolutely no influence on the extraordinary antics of her dog, she very quickly made her presence felt in the Mess. She was quite able to take the constant leg pulling doled out to her by her brother officers and equally able to deliver a wellaimed retort."

It was while she was serving in Dortmund that she met her husband to be, Christopher; they married in 1989. Sadly, their marriage was cut short due to Chris's untimely death from cancer in 1994; Vanessa dedicated herself to nursing him throughout his illness. Tragically, five months later her brother David also died.

After this very difficult time, Vanessa, now in the Adjutant General's Corps, completed an operational tour in Northern Ireland, served as a Regimental Administrative Officer with the Household Cavalry Regiment and 22 Engineer Regiment.

This included another operational tour, this time in Bosnia. During this time, Vanessa made her home in Wiltshire with her horses and Oscar and Mugsley, (Mugbug as she called him), her border terriers. This 'entourage' moved with her to HQ 2 (SE) Bde in Dover, and I will always remember the dogs scuttling around her feet in the office there.

Dover meant that she and I were to meet again and, more importantly, we were going to work together. I was therefore able to see at first hand all those qualities I had see at the WRAC College eighteen years before. A consummate professional, Vanessa was highly protective of her troops and always at her best when faced with a challenge.

In her own CV she described herself as an enthusiastic but untalented Sky and Scuba diver who enjoys cooking and fine wines those of us who have dined with her know the latter to be true.

Vanessa had a wicked sense of humour, like the time she appeared before Magistrates for driving at 107 mph at night on the M6 she managed to persuade them that she thought she was being followed by IRA terrorists. She got away with a nominal fine and kept her license!

She was vivacious, charming and always looked fabulous, very chic, no matter what she was wearing whether it be the latest Armani suit or Combat 95. As well as having a lively and energetic personality, Vanessa was remarkable in her fortitude. During a difficult time when she personally had to endure significant pain and suffering with her back, she showed tremendous inner strength, determination, tenacity and courage qualities that she had displayed throughout her entire career and which were much admired by all with whom she served.

Vanessa packed more into her forty years than most other people manage to pack into twice that time. She was much loved and respected by her soldiers and fellow officers alike. We all remember her infectious laugh, her fondness for Champagne and gin & tonic, but above all her great love of life and of the Army.

Vanessa was always happiest when she was doing something exciting, out of the ordinary and where there was an element of danger; she had recently parachuted with the French Foreign Legion in Corsica.

Vanessa Lang was on a Reconnaissance flight in Sierra Leone in October 2001. Tragically the helicopter crashed, and Vanessa was killed.

Lioness 2002 No.1 - Taken from her obituary written by Sue Westlake MBE

and soldiers who worked tirelessly to improve and develop policy against the backdrop of the conflicts in Iraq and Afghanistan.

In 2010 I decided to take early retirement. The 27 years that I spent in the Army was never dull and was always a challenge, but I had been fortunate to serve in an era when the roles for women would change out of all recognition. I joined an Army where women were separate and constrained by deployment rules and separate Terms and Conditions of Service and I left an Army that was well on the way to equality of opportunity for all.

My current role as Vice President of the Women's Royal Army Corps Association gives me the opportunity to celebrate all women who have served and are still serving in the Army. I want to ensure that these women are never forgotten and commemorate all women who have served their country from 1917 onwards.

Written by Ali Brown for this book.
See images in centre pages

Liz Kemp - Memories of Kosovo

Last year was an extremely busy time for the ACE Rapid Reaction Corps (ARRC). I came back from Christmas leave and we started working 7 days a week. I deployed to Skopje Macedonia last April. It was pretty typical, my husband had just returned from Komonova that Friday, and I flew out on Sunday. Still we had a weekend together!!

The flight out from Bruggen took almost 24 hours. Our Hercules almost blew up on takeoff and we had to make an emergency exit. I was shouted at by the load master for trying to save the box containing the General's teaspoons. A good start.

Our base in Macedonia was an old shoe factory in Skopje. When I arrived, it was still being turned into a workable headquarters. It was extremely dusty and hot. We lived in tents set up on the first floor of the factory, squashing people up as we arrived. Returning to your tent at night required a torch and excellent coordination and bearings as it was pitch black and there were about 30 large tents quite close together. As you were going to sleep, you could usually hear someone tripping over and cursing. We had no hot water for a while, but at least we had water and the food was excellent. The ablutions were scarce and shared, but you could sling your towel over the door to ensure that no one would walk in. A pair of flipflops were a must. Walking to the showers in your PJ's became the norm. We all worked extremely long hours; however, we could watch the General's TV when he was out and, most importantly, usually managed to get to the bar before last orders. The local beer was wickedly strong. I had a few headaches.

The one event I shall never forget was the plight of the refugees during the Easter Weekend. The Macedonian border became overwhelmed with refugees from Kosovo, women and children were stranded, exhausted with no food or water. The Army set up refugee camps and provided food. I visited one of these camps, it was huge. One child held my hand, and we handed out sweets. After about 4 weeks I returned to JHQ and deployed back out to Skopje in May, this time my husband came out too. It seemed as though we would be stuck in Skopje for a long time. Eventually on June the 9th the Military Technical Agreement (MTA) was signed. During this time, I was left to man the office, it was bedlam, all telephones ringing at once. Communication was quite difficult, and there were a few tense moments. As we were watching the General entering the tent on TV, a call came from the office of the Supreme Allied Command Europe (SACEUR) to say that the General must speak to SACEUR before the talks began! Needless to say, all means of communication were engaged. However, we succeeded in getting a message through to the Military Assistant (MA), and I aged about 10 years!!!

On June the 12th Kosovo Force (KFOR) entered Kosovo, it seemed as though all that waiting was now worthwhile and we could get on with our job. I flew out the following evening in a Chinook to the newly situated Tactical Headquarters (TAG) just outside Pristina. This was to ensure the General's communications and our offices (a loose term) were all set up. The flight was an experience, I had all my kit, plus a laptop, which I clung on to as we flew extremely fast in a zigzag pattern with the tail gate open into Kosovo. When we arrived, it was pitch black, one of the General's bodyguards directed the Chinook with his torch. For some unknown reason we had red tracer being fired at us as we anded.

My husband was already there, he had been part of the convoy which took almost 24 hours to arrive by road. He had no idea that I was on the flight until he saw me stagger off clutching all my kit. It was lovely to see him. TAG consisted of a large tented area, and the fresh air was marvellous after being cooped up in the shoe factory. That was however, until it rained a couple of days later, and everything and everybody got drenched and covered in mud. I have a picture of the ADC wringing out the General's smock which accidentally got left outside his wagon.

The females' tent floor had a river running through it, and although we had our GoreTex liners for our sleeping bags it was quite disconcerting to go to sleep with the rain dripping on you through the

193

canvas. This also made your kit damp in the morning, and uncomfortable to wear for the first few minutes. The incentive to get up was a big fat girl's breakfast. The field kitchen provided excellent rations, mostly consisting of boil in the bag burger and beans for the first couple of days, then followed by normal food like rhubarb crumble and custard excellent. We had no shower facilities apart from a segregated female washing area, where you filled up your bowl from the puffing billies, trying to avoid the men shaving, and washed everything from this bowl. I had the advantage of having small feet and being able to stand in the bowl, (unlike Penny, the Chief of Staff's PA), which caused great amusement. The portaloos were not particularly pleasant, and I found the trick was to light a cigarette before entering and closing the door. A few people started smoking for this reason!!! It is amazing how long you can hold your breath for. However, although we had electricity, this did not extend to the use of my hairdryer, so I just tied my hair back into a tiny pigtail (no time to be vain).

I had to take some documents back to the Shoe Factory. This was an ideal opportunity to have a shower and drop off everyone's washing. We flew by helicopter. We went via all the Brigade areas. It was a really interesting flight; Kosovo is a beautiful country. The pilot flew tactically with the side door open it was brilliant but what a disappointment later, when the pilots flew at a normal sedate pace.

We were at TAG for about 14 days, before moving to an old film studio in Pristina, which was nicknamed 'Film City'. The novelty of TAG had by this time worn off and it was great to work inside a building with air conditioning and, most importantly, plug sockets for my hairdryer. We still slept in tents but were given wooden floors which unfortunately attracted mice. It was a must to check your sleeping bag before going to sleep. Our tents were set amongst trees and it was quite picturesque, the cookhouse had tree stumps for seats. Portable shower units were set up and for the first time for over a week I had a hot shower, it was marvellous. Our office was pretty makeshift to begin with. We had a plasterboard wall, which separated the PA's office from the main KFOR conference Room, which was where all the important meetings were held. We usually had an officer banging on the wall to stop us from laughing too loudly, so had to shush everyone who came into our office. We found it impossible to keep quiet, as our small room was usually filled with the General's bodyguards, signallers and drivers. I went out with the General's driver on a couple of his recces into Pristina and the surrounding areas. At first Pristina appeared deserted, with some bomb damage, and PARA's patrolling the streets. Only a few shops were open but didn't appear to have any goods for sale. From our office we had full view of the city and watched as, gradually, more lights came on in the houses as people returned.

The picture shows the Front Office staff, and the view of the city from the roof top of Film City. I have been told to add here how good looking my Military Advisor (MA) is, he is the one standing to the right of General Jackson. We soon settled into a daily routine at Film City and we had many visitors to see the General during this time. I met Prince Charles, Tony Blair and George Robertson amongst others. Most importantly we had a date that we would be coming home. A laundry contract was set up (we had been washing our kit and smalls by hand), we had a tiny shop, (which sold melted chocolate), pay facilities, a decent gym, plus a bar which sold beer. We still worked long hours but set up our TAC TV and video in the office and swapped films with the Signals The ADC usually donated a bottle of wine most evenings, and I kept in touch with my friends via the internet. The days seemed to fly by work and meals broken up by Sunday routines which meant a lie in until 0900 hrs, what a luxury.

The downside to Film City was that the water was intermittent to say the least plus we had many power cuts, due to the damage caused by the bombing raids. I often used my Laptop in candlelight. You would walk to the showers in the morning to find the water off again and have to wash outside the tent with a bottle of water and some "wet wipes". Our office was filled with bottles of water, just in case, and most mornings Mick the driver and I would wash up the cups in a fire bucket as the water was off again. We didn't have the luxury of a hoover, so we would brush the offices with a broom and make it even more hot and dusty at the end of August John and I had 2 weeks Rest and Recuperation (R&R). On our return, KFOR started preparing for the handover to the next Headquarters LANDCENT. Soon I was making the brews in the morning and saying 10 days and a breakfast to go. The weather thankfully started getting cooler. On the last day, I went with the MA and ADC to the General's final press conference and then we took off by helicopter from Pristina Stadium to Pristina Airport, to fly back on the Queens Flight. I had two glasses of champagne and fell asleep, in fact nearly all of us did!!! It was, of course, brilliant to be going home.

We still reminisce in the office about me blow drying my hair each morning in the office at Film City, and being caught most mornings by the General, who would always make his own brew as he said "a lady should never be interrupted when doing her hair".

Lioness 2000 No.2

Frances Pennell - View from the Vitez Pocket

When I volunteered to join the 1st Battalion Coldstream Guards in Bosnia, way back in the mud of a wet Soltau exercise, I didn't think I would be given the opportunity. Luckily, Lt Col Peter Williams (Commanding Officer 1 Bn Coldstream Guards) called my bluff and I joined the Battalion in January. Employed as a primary watchkeeper, I worked mainly in the Operations Room but did stand in as Adjutant at times. The Coldstream Guards (BRITBAT 1) part of the United Nations Protection Force (UNPROFOR) have their base in what used to be the school in the small village of Stari Bila near Vitez. The playground is now a sea of mud, after hundreds of Aid trucks parked there during the winter. The engineers have made many modifications to the rest of the school to make it suitable for an operational base. The accommodation is simple; the soldiers live in ISO city and the SNCOs and officers in a series of houses rented from the local population. The rest of the school has been "hardened" to ensure minimum damage should any incoming rounds impact within the perimeter.

During my 4 months in Vitez there were remarkable changes. When I first arrived the war was ongoing, the Vitez Pocket was still in a stage of flux and there were a series of small offensives by both sides. The Battle of Santici (a small village to the east of Vitez) was just one example of the small localised offensives launched by both sides. It was watched from afar by several members of BRITBAT, as spectators in someone else's war. Signs of the war and ethnic cleansing are everywhere: bullet riddled houses, burntout houses, destruction and the devastation. The lack of normal civilian movement at the beginning of the tour was evident, but once the ceasefire was established, freedom of movement was introduced for civilians, though this was a gradual move as both combatants wanted to maintain control over the civilians and had fairly exCommunist approaches to many problems!

Our mission was to facilitate the delivery of aid to BosniaHercegovina: to that end, BRITBAT provided security on the Main Supply Routes and support to the United Nations High Commissioner for Refugees (UNHCR). The routes all have nicknames, hence reports of ROUTES DIAMOND, TRIANGLE, MONCK and PACMAN as well as countless others that run over the UNPROFOR area. During the winter the harsh conditions snow, ice and very cold temperatures meant the aid convoys and UNPROFOR resupply convoys took up to three days to move from the coast, north to Vitez or to the UNHCR warehouse in Zenica. During this time the war was ongoing and BRITBAT armoured vehicles were constantly in demand to secure the route and escort convoys through trouble spots. Perhaps the most famous of these trouble spots is "Bon Bon" corner. This is in the area of Lisac and Opara on ROUTE DIAMOND, where women and children regularly hold up convoys with improvised blockades and then raided them. At its worst, soldiers fired shots over the crowds and then the civilians stripped the vehicles of anything worth taking! At other points on the route UNPROFOR vehicles were sniped at from bunkers and there were some very near misses and two casualties, one shot through the shoulder and another through his boot. In the end BRITBAT fired 30mm HE into the bunkers which stopped it for a while!

As a watchkeeper my tasks were primarily to coordinate the flow of convoys north and south on the Routes and act as a point of contact for all the BRITBAT Liaison Officers. Additionally, I tasked callsigns to escort convoys through problem areas, and ensured convoys were able to pass on narrow parts of the route. At the same time the Operations room kept an eye on the military activity in the area and watched the military progress of both sides. The military tactics of the Croats and Muslims were fascinating, almost First World War tactics, but with a few modern weapons.

After the signing of the Peace Accord the efforts of BRITBAT I turned to setting up UN checkpoints on all major routes where they entered the Vitez Pocket; these were jointly manned by Muslims, Croats and UNPROFOR. Additionally, the Liaison Officers mapped the confrontation lines in conjunction with Officers from both sides, and confidence building patrols were sent out, to enforce both the separation of forces and search for weapons over 12.7mm. These weapons had to be removed to either a Weapon Collection Point and Active Site or moved out of the Exclusion Zone laid down by the Peace Accord. The Weapon Collection Points allowed weapons over 12.7mm to be rounded up and deactivated; the Active Sites were set up to allow Muslims or Croats to return fire against the Serbs (BSA) but not each other, to that end Artillery observers were located at each Active Site to ensure the accuracy of the fire possibly for the first time during the war! The ceasefire turned the emphasis onto the provision of civilian utilities and the reestablishment of the local infrastructure. In many cases the root of the problems lay on the other side of a confrontation line, caused by the opposing faction. In trying to aid negotiations a series of Joint Commission meetings were set up at all levels to coordinate the move from war to peace and military to civil authority. These meetings brought together both the Military leaders and their civilian counterparts to discuss the implementation of the Peace Plan.

She stayed in the pay and admin world to be SO2 SPS at UKSC(G) at Rheindahlen in Germany and then again at 143 (WM) Bde in Shrewsbury. She was involved in 2 separate tours doing IT projects, the first being Pay 2000 at Worthy Down and the second later at Gosport doing Discipline on JPA. She had her most rewarding tour as OC B Company at the Army Training Regiment in Winchester where her command was at times as many as 244 soldiers – she felt it was a real privilege to have such excellent staff and to train so many recruits for the Army. Staff jobs meant she served in various Headquarters: Brigade, Division, HQ Land and the MOD. Amongst all the work she still managed to run and orienteer and represented the Combined Services at orienteering.

It was when serving in HQ 20 Armd Bde and Paderborn Garrison that she was appointed to be the Chief of Staff Rear Ops Group for Op HERRICK 15 by Comd 20 Armd Bde. She was the first female to be appointed COS Rear Ops Group and the first AGC(SPS) Officer. This meant, in addition to her normal work, she was responsible for the Battle Casualty Replacements and the training programme for the following 2 years as well as organising the Bde support to the Queen's Diamond Jubilee celebrations, the Olympics and the Fuel Tanker Driver Strike and many other pieces of work. Her memories as COS Rear Ops Gp will live with her forever, 22 soldiers were killed and due to the deaths and injuries etc over 300 Battle Casualty Replacements had to be deployed to Afghanistan. The Rear Ops Gp held a 'Repatriation Service' in Sennelager at the same time the bodies were leaving Afghanistan and she was the officer who read out the poem For the Fallen (They shall not grow old) at every service and it was always emotional especially when she knew the soldier. It was hard work for over 10 months, and for this work she was awarded the MBE.

When her husband retired, she was keen to serve outside the UK, as co-location was no longer a factor, and was lucky enough to be appointed the DCOS British Gurkhas Nepal based in Kathmandu. She was responsible, as part of her job, for the payment of pensions to the Gurkha pensioners. Sometimes she was able to help the Gurkha Welfare Trust staff pay pensions, paid quarterly, some of the pensioners had walked for a number of days to reach the Area Welfare Offices and yet these wonderful old gentlemen always managed to stand up straight and salute when getting their pension even if they could hardly walk! She also was proud to be a part of the selection process for Gurkha recruits.

Her last posting in the Army was to NATO, the Joint Warfare Centre in Stavanger, where she was the Internal Review Officer. As a British Officer she attended a number of Battlefield tours in Norway, as the German occupation during World War 2 was still visible and emotive. She visited a number of gunnery positions, the Heavy Water factory at Ruhkan and even the remains of an aircraft but was also was able to pay her respects to those who fell on Operation Freshman and buried in the Commonwealth War Graves.

She retired as a Lieutenant Colonel in the AGC(SPS) in December 2018.

As told to the editor for this book.
See images in centre pages

Major Caroline Constantine – The Army's First Female Bandmaster

1993 saw major changes in the structure of the British Army under 'Options for Change' and with it the instigation of the Corps of Army Music (CAMUS). As the number of Army Bands reduced, members of the WRAC Band found themselves subsumed into a number of different Corps Bands and were consequently serving alongside their male counterparts. Newly recruited female musicians were technically able to be posted to any of the Army Bands, but it would be some time before all Army Bands had females serving within them. It was this setup that I found myself working in when I joined the Army in 1996 – little did I know what it held in store for me!

Growing up in Nottinghamshire, music had been a part of my life for as long as I could remember. Like many school children in the late 70's early 80's, I had started on the recorder, I soon progressed to the flute – apparently my mother having heard James Galway thought that it would be a nice instrument for me to play, although my older brother described my playing as 'wail, screech, honk', possibly not the greatest of starts then! I few years passed, and I started to learn the piano and music theory as well in order to improve my overall musicianship, however it was never my intention at the time to pursue a career in music.

Fast forward a few years, and 1991 found me at the University of East Anglia (UEA) starting a degree in Music (still not intending it to be a career though!). It was here that I started becoming interested in the administrative, organisational aspects of concerts etc. and ultimately took on roles such as UEA Music Society President, UEA Choir Secretary, Student Rep etc. Looking back now, I can see how all this activity ultimately linked into my military career. Following UEA, I moved to south for Postgraduate study at the London College of

Music, and whilst I was beginning to think that I might indeed finish up having a career in music, I actually started work for Oxford University Press in their Repertoire Promotion Department on Baker Street, London on finishing my studies.

My move from here to the Army was perhaps a little unusual. At the time I was also singing with the London Philharmonic Choir, and as a result of a chance meeting with the Grenadier Guards Band at a joint concert, realised that I did in fact miss performing. It was suggested that I consider joining the Army as a musician (on a three year contract), and within a week of making the initial phone call I had completed an audition at the Royal Military School of Music, Kneller Hall (RMSM), I was being interviewed at the recruitment office in Wembley.

Basic Training at Bassingbourn Camp in Cambridgeshire quickly followed. At the time, the Army was training males and females in mixed troops for Phase 1 Training. But rather than place myself and a fellow female musician Liz Bodin-Evans (then aged 23 and 28 respectfully) with a Signals Troop that was literally half-and-half male and female, we were placed as the only two females in an Infantry Platoon! Fortunately, this only lasted for a few days, not least because our accommodation lines were on the other side of camp to the males, and as a result we were literally late for everything! In the end we both passed out of Phase 1 Training 10 weeks later, with the Signals Troop.

Phase Two Training at the RMSM was definitely a better experience for me than Bassinbourn had been. My challenge here came with learning to march and play at the same time, having come from an orchestral background that very much involved sitting down. Once this was mastered, I was initially told that I would be going as the first female to the Guards Bands (due to age and experience), but at the time I knew that many of the men in the Guards Bands were vehemently against females joining. Not wanting to spend my three years of service in such an atmosphere I requested to be posted to a Corps Band, and in January 1997 I moved to the Royal Logistic Corps Band (RLC) in Deepcut.

This was possibly one of the best things that could have happened to me in the Army. The RLC Band had a number of previous WRAC Band members and as a result there was a highly supportive atmosphere for new females, in particular from WO2 Elaine Williams and Sgt Ann Barker. It was both my enjoyment of the job, and the way in which I was developed and supported that ultimately led me to stay beyond my initial three-year contract. Having stayed in the Army and experienced a lot of travel during those formative years – including meeting my husband at Episkopi in

Cyprus during a Band tour – when I was asked to consider applying to be a Bandmaster, it made absolute sense.

As I went through the process of selection for the Bandmaster Course, I wasn't particularly aware or phased by the idea of being potentially the first female into the role, because as far as I was concerned, I happened to have the required qualifications and experience, and just happened to be in the right place at the right time. It should be clarified here that the female Directors of Music for the WRAC Band had completed the three-year Bandmasters Course in the past, however they had been selected from the WRAC Band and commissioned as the WRAC Band Director of Music. The difference in my case was that I was competing against all male applicants from across the CAMUS on a level playing-field, and should I succeed, I would be the first female appointed as a Warrant Officer Class 1, Bandmaster.

Having been successful at selection, the 'Antonín Dvořák Class' (5 UK students and 2 from Singapore) formed up in September 2001 for the three-year Student Bandmaster Course which would see me go from LCpl to WO1 whilst also completing a degree in Music. It goes without saying that the course was tough, and we had to work as a team to get through. Particular memories range from 'Hell Week' – the first week of the course that involved a lot of late nights polishing every bit of brass on camp (think Phase 1 Training – but worse), to unending cabarets; the First Year Student Bandmasters being required to perform after-dinner entertainment for the Mess whenever requested – which was very often. Unfortunately, as a Class we were not good at this, and were mightily relieved when we moved into our second year and could hand this task over to the junior class! However, the opportunity to test our newfound conducting skills on audiences during the summer concert seasons more than made up for this, along with the multiple fancy-dress outfits that were worn in an attempt to entertain at children's concerts.

On graduation from the Bandmasters Course in the summer of 2004, as there was not a posting available initially, I spent a few months with the Light Division Band as their Assistant Bandmaster which included a short tour at the Royal Military Academy Sandhurst (RMAS). This was a great opportunity to get used to my new appointment, whilst also getting used to being viewed as something a bit unusual. The Light Division did not have females serving in the regiments, so when it came to the matter of my Mess Dress, nobody knew what to do with me, and I was just told to 'make something up' - which I did (with my old friend Liz Bodin-Evans helping with the design and sewing). I have to say though, that whilst I really enjoyed my time with the Light Division Band, I was somewhat relieved to move on as I really struggled with the faster marching speed. Because as a piccolo player in marching band I was always on the back row, and also because I'm short, I seemed to spend most of my time running to catch up the band!

In December 2004 I was posted to my first full appointment as the WO1 Bandmaster for the Army Air Corps Band (AAC) in Middle Wallop. Arriving just in time for the round of Christmas concerts, I quickly found myself deeply involved in both the musical and man-management aspects of Band life. This was further compounded by the Director of Music deciding to take early retirement a couple of months later, and leaving the Band and myself without an Officer Commanding for almost a year – not ideal, because as a Bandmaster you are on probation for the first year of your appointment and could be sacked at any time! Thus, with the help of the Band Sergeant Major running the day-to-day requirements, I settled into life as the training officer (musical and non-musical), recruiting officer, career and welfare officer as well as conducting the band on engagements and marching bands, and playing within the band or small-groups when necessary.

In 2008 I was posted as the Training and Development Team (TDT) Warrant Officer to HQ CAMUS back at Kneller Hall to undertake my first Staff Role. It was at this point my priorities began to change as it became more and more obvious that I enjoyed this kind of work but missed the developmental/teaching aspects of Band life. My role in TDT bought me frequently into contact with members of the Adjutant General's Corps (Educational and Training Services), and I became aware that if I moved to the ETS I would be both able to develop and teach soldiers, as well as utilise my administrative strengths in training development. So, I applied for commission into the AGC(ETS) and was surprised to be accepted, and thus became Capt Constantine in 2010. I am still serving with the ETS today.

Whilst it may seem odd that I moved away from CAMUS apparently having previously been seen as a trailblazer, I know I left legacy which has seen many highly capable females follow the same path. By the time I became a Bandmaster all CAMUS Bands had female musicians and recruiting had become about a 50/50 split for males and females. Two years after I graduated, Esther Hayes (nee Freeborn) became the first female Bandmaster of an Infantry Band (the PARAs) and later the Household Cavalry; more recently being appointed as School Bandmaster at the RMSM. Other females have become first female Bandmaster in the Guards Division and first to commission from WO1 Bandmaster to Director of Music. As the structure of CAMUS changed, the first individual to go from being an NCO to completing the commissioning course at RMAS was a female

(Lauren Evans), and the first female to undertake Direct Entry commissioning is also progressing through the Officer ranks.

So whilst I certainly got a few strange looks and odd questions during my time as a Bandmaster, I am pleased to say that whilst I might have been in the right place at the right time to push open the door fifteen years ago, many more have followed my through and will continue to do so.

Written by Caroline Constantine for this book.
See images in centre pages